Open Participatory Security

Open Participatory Security

Unifying Technology, Citizens, and the State

Jesse Paul Lehrke

ROWMAN & LITTLEFIELD
Lanham • Boulder • New York • London

Published by Rowman & Littlefield
A wholly owned subsidiary of The Rowman & Littlefield Publishing Group, Inc.
4501 Forbes Boulevard, Suite 200, Lanham, Maryland 20706
www.rowman.com

Unit A, Whitacre Mews, 26-34 Stannary Street, London SE11 4AB

British Library Cataloguing in Publication Information Available

Library of Congress Cataloging-in-Publication Data Is Available

ISBN 978-1-5381-0528-3 (cloth: alk. paper)
ISBN 978-1-5381-0529-0 (electronic)

Printed in the United States of America

Contents

Tables and Figures

Abbreviations

4GW	Fourth-generation warfare
AFRL	Air Force Research Laboratory
AI	Artificial intelligence
ARG(s)	Alternate reality game(s)
BiTS	Bureaucracy, (information) Technology, and Secrecy
CIA	Central Intelligence Agency
DARPA	Defense Advanced Research Projects Agency
DHS	Department of Homeland Security
DoD	Department of Defense
FB	Facebook
FOIA	Freedom of Information Act
HIP	Heroic Imagination Project
IARPA	Intelligence Advanced Research Projects Activity
ICBL	International Campaign to Ban Landmines
ICT	Information and communication technology
IED(s)	Improvised explosive device(s)
KGB	Committee for State Security
MMOWGLI	Massive Multiplayer Online Wargame Leveraging the Internet
MP	Minister of Parliament
NCW	Net-centric warfare
NGO	Non-governmental organization
OG	Open government
ONR	Office of Naval Research
OPS	Open participatory security
OPSEC	Operations security
PAM	Policy analysis market
PTSD	Post-traumatic stress disorder
RMA	Revolution in Military Affairs
SNS(s)	Social networking site(s)

Author's Note and Acknowledgements

Within academia it is important that one's work be original, and of course, if we claim authorship, that the work be our own. Here, I claim both, yet herein is a contradiction. This work was *too* original for me to do on my own. This may seem like I am humble-bragging about my own novelty, but it expresses a genuine concern I had: that my originality would make me an unheard voice in the wilderness. Much of this concern came down to the fact that this book is interdisciplinary, an approach which was necessary given that the solution it proposes to the problem of security is an interdisciplinary one both in theory and in practice. The book draws on everyone and is for everyone because security requires everyone.

However, instead of being seen as a positive, interdisciplinarity is often a strike against both book and scholar. Interdisciplinarity makes it hard for a publisher to identify an audience (market), for an institution's management (current or potential) to see how it fits into their strategic vision and thus how you fit into their institution, and for reviewers to deeply understand every aspect of the book and thus recommend it. Indeed, the author must be willing to learn a new subject and feel a bit like an undergraduate again, to not be the smartest person in the room and be willing to make mistakes, some of which may end up in print. Everyone, even its author, will find something they disagree with or do not fully understand in a book such as this one.

Thus, writing such a book requires courage and more than a bit of risk taking on the part of the author, university, and publisher. They require trust, patience, and support from each other and from their stakeholders. For the author this means from colleagues, friends, partners, and family. They need to be reminded the project has value, that it is important, and that they should not think about whether now is the right time professionally to write such a book and what future employers or tenure committees may think of it. Moreover, they need to be corrected and politely but insistently asked to explain themselves and clarify their ideas. I benefitted from all these forms of support; so in no particular order, and in no way comprehensively, let me thank a few of the people and organizations that have contributed to this book.

I would like to thank my employer, the German Research Institute for Public Administration (Speyer, Germany), and its director, Professor Dr. Jan Ziekow, for seeing the value in this project and in bringing it quickly to publication, thus giving me the freedom and time to devote to the book (while still collecting a salary). I would also like to recognize my colleague Kai Masser, with whom I first discussed integrating open government into Security Studies at the Transatlantic Policy Consortium (TPC) 2013 conference at Indiana University (Bloomington, Indiana, USA). This resulted in a joint paper presented in various formats at the TPC's 2014 conference at the National University of Public Service (Budapest, Hungary) and at the International Institute of Administrative Sciences 2015 congress in Rio de Janeiro, Brazil. While in the end this book was a solo project, the early discussions with Kai created a path dependency that greatly influenced its structure and approach.

I must also express my utmost appreciation to Rowman & Littlefield and all the people there who helped bring this book to print. In particular I want to recognize my acquisitions editor, Marie-Claire Antoine, whose positive attitude, engagement, competence, and support – from my initial email through to technical submission details – made the process the best in my publishing experience. As the manuscript progressed through the stages of publication I got acquainted with many other staff of Rowman & Littlefield and remain impressed with their competence and appreciative of their help.

As with all academic works, this book was in some sense a crowdsourced effort. I am grateful for the work of all those scholars, public intellectuals, and journalists whom I have referenced, as well as those whose work I read but for some reason did not make it into the final bibliography. In this era when plagiarism so often ends public careers, and is so easily identified with technology, I have erred on being inclusive in my referencing even if an author merely inspired an aspect of the sentence. I do apologize if it seems I have falsely attributed an idea to you, and of course also if I have excluded you in other parts or misunderstood your arguments. I encourage my readers to follow up their reading of this book by directly exploring some of the referenced literature.

Continuing with academics, I wish to express my thanks also to the three anonymous reviewers who supported this book and helped set it on a better track. Where I failed to follow your advice was only a reflection of time and space limitations, and I hope that I (or you, or others) can follow up this book with research on some more specific aspects of citizen participation in security.

In a less conventional expression of academic gratitude, I would like to extend my thanks to the regular participants in *Foreign Policy*'s E.R. (Editor's Roundtable) podcast. Unbeknownst to them, their weekly discussion provided an endless stream of ideas (and comic relief) and the occasional desperately needed citation from an expert (with my apologies for any taken out of context). *War on the Rocks* and *The Power Vertical* (a Russia wonk podcast) deserve honourable mentions in this regard as well.

Lastly, this book would not have been possible without the support of Yuki Hayashi, whose enthusiasm for the project surpassed even my own. Her encouragement and belief in the importance of the book's ideas kept me going even when my arguments were complicated by evidence or when words refused to flow forth. Moreover, she willingly subjected herself to reading through the draft manuscript, fixing not only technical errors but also providing invaluable advice to help ensure my academic argument was as accessible as possible to non-academics. I would also like to thank Valerie Ziegler for her excellent work to make my figures more professional. In this vein I recommend all academics without a hobby in InDesign seek such external assistance for artwork in their own publications.

Thank you lastly to the reader, and I hope you enjoy this book, or that it irritates you, preferably both, and that this reaction raises your interest and leads you to learn more and maybe even take action.

Chapter One

The Foundations of Open Participatory Security

Security is a dense and often depressing topic, so let us begin – as is appropriate for a book within which the Internet plays such a central role – by promising a story that ends with cats. After a particularly tragic month in November 2015, following the terrorist attack in Paris, which left 130 dead and many more injured, the hunt was on for suspects. When the investigation narrowed in on Brussels (Belgium) the city went into lockdown as police conducted their searches. With the citizens confined to their homes, they did what many of us would likely do in that situation – they got on their computers and mobile devices and started telling friends and the world what was happening. The police saw in this a problem, as terrorists have been known to use social media as a form of open source intelligence; by following the various posts and tweets there was the possibility that the suspects could learn of police movements and thus evade capture, or worse, launch a counter-attack. The authorities thus requested that citizens not share any information on the Web about police movements. The citizens, though, took this request one step further. They recognized that there may be defectors from the police request – whether motivated by ignorance, mischief, or sympathy with the terrorists – and thus they mounted an active defence to ensure so-called operations security (OPSEC). Using the hashtag #BrusselsLockdown they created enough signal noise to bury any reports on social media about police movements: in lay terms, they flooded social media with cat pictures.

While it would be several more months and another attack later before all the Paris suspects were finally killed or captured, for those few days in Brussels we saw the state and society working together using modern technology to preserve their security. Yet this was not the first such occurrence. In Paris only a week earlier citizens had used social media to organize places of refuge for those who could not make it home following the attacks there (#portesouvertes, meaning "open doors"). This act of social solidarity demonstrated and enhanced the resilience of society, its ability to persevere following attack. While we cannot know if the open doors prevented further loss of life by getting people off the streets, though it is certainly possible, it undoubtedly gave those far from home a feeling of security to know they had places to go. Even farther from Paris other anxious feelings were put at ease when Facebook rolled out its Safety Check feature, allowing those in Paris to easily let their entire social circle know that they were okay.

The Brussels and Paris solutions were ad hoc adaptations, the kind of rapid mobilization that the Internet excels at facilitating. Yet these initiatives represent only the beginning of the possibilities. Elsewhere in the world, governments have sought, or citizens have taken it upon themselves, to create more permanent technological platforms through which the state and society could work together to provide security. In Ukraine, citizens mobilize resources and provide intelligence; in Estonia they man cyberdefences. NGOs have mobilized citizens to help analyze satellite imagery, monitor ceasefires, and report human rights violations. In the United States the military has begun experimenting with how games can contribute to strategy and tactics, as well as how social media can help provide diffuse security by using citizens instead of having soldiers on every street corner. While these and other initiatives, to be discussed further in this book, are small and hesitant, they represent the cutting edge of military development, not only in how they bring together state and society in a way which seems a relic of the (perhaps idealized) past, but in integrating human and machine, people and technology, in a way which few of us even realize is possible, but which is indeed optimal or even necessary for many security tasks.

Yet these cases remain exceptions, for though the modern state embraces technology as a means for security, it holds just as tightly to the principles of secrecy and bureaucracy. Because of these principles most of the stories about security, how we were saved from imminent attack, will never be known. Yet in the modern world the state cannot keep the stories of insecurity from being almost instantaneously broadcast, shared, and discussed around the globe. Moreover, while the government's successes in providing security will never be known, in the modern world keeping an ongoing program secret is almost impossible in the medium term. When the government, for example, routinely spies on its citizens or practices extraordinary rendition, leaks (or hacks) revealing the program are inevitable, and the more controversial the program the more likely somebody will defect and report it. Ironically, we see only those policies our governments would most prefer to hide. Thus, when citizens have been made aware of the means of their security, the tools and tactics being used in their name for their defence, they often look at their governments with disgust, distrust, or even fear.

Yet the government alone is not to blame for these policies, nor are their security agents – the soldiers and spies – who in fulfilling their duties faithfully implement their orders (barring the most blatantly illegal ones). Citizens have been progressively withdrawing from security for decades for a myriad of reasons. As new communication technology transmitted images of war, ideas about war and even the nation-state changed. Subsequently, in the late– and post–Cold War period, security increasingly became taken for granted, a background condition invisible to most, ensured by technological systems hidden deep in bunkers or unseen high above us. With security seemingly assured by the threat of extinction, disinterest in security swept a population that was, justifiably and perhaps rightfully so, busy living life. Monopoly and secrecy were not simply seized by the government; they were also ceded by the people and enabled by technology. This situation persisted until the people's interest in security returned when events suddenly revealed that security was no longer there.

In many ways it is surprising that most of us, whether in government or private citizens, have rarely considered how technology could allow citizens to contribute to security. It would not be the first time technology has been used to spread information and mobilize people, or to find solutions to threatening problems. Even in this current decade we have seen the mobilizing power of the Internet, as people took to the streets in what were sometimes called WikiLeaks, Facebook, or Twitter Revolutions (the former in Tunisia, the latter two variously applied to Tunisia, Egypt, Iran, and Moldova). Yet these events also explain why the distributed power of the Net has only slowly been taken up in the West; while we may have admired their cause, people on the streets overthrowing regimes is not what we associate with security. The Occupy Wall Street movement, also (arguably) noble in its cause, did little to alleviate worries about the power of the Net to mobilize, and possibly destabilize. In a similar vein, while many abhorred or were outraged by what they saw on WikiLeaks, often these same people did not approve of Julian Assange's methods or of the whistle-blowers who brought the information to light.

Yet even these mobilizations were not seen to be the most severe problem. Technology has mobilized much greater threats. Internet forums were seen as having corrupted or radicalized our youth, turning them to Anonymous or driving them to ISIS (not to equate the two). Encryption hid terrorists' communications even while our open information – Google Earth and government transparency – helped them plan their attacks. Hackers or rogue states stole our data, confused us with viral stories containing half-truths and lies, and brought down websites, TV stations, and even power grids. Any American basement, Russian cafe, or Afghan cave has come to be seen as a source of dangers capable of reaching around or even encompassing the entire world at the speed of light. The Internet, originally designed as a tool for war but then spread to transform the worlds of commerce and citizens, has seemingly returned to its roots. It has morphed into an offensive operating system that when combined with the innumerable technologies embedded in our everyday lives – the Internet of things – creates a weapon capable – possibly, even if not probably – of threatening that very existence.

These things have conspired to leave many people with a bad image of the empowering role of technology. While somewhere in the back of our minds we recognize that our lives are dependent upon and greatly improved by technology, this fact is typically taken for granted, much like security. It is considered normal and natural, rather than amazing; we expect it to function flawlessly in the background and notice only when the system is down; we use it passively instead of in an enabling way. In fact, it often seems that only the disenfranchised or the angry use technology in an active and transformative manner. Moreover, increasingly, leaders and citizens alike are coming to recognize that the technology, the so-called "fourth industrial revolution" ushering in an information age, is creating more disenfranchised and angry people (Schwab 2016; World Economic Forum 2016; see also Cave 2000; Cookson 2016; Richard Clarke in Singer 2009, 293).

Given these developments, some have cast technology itself as a villain, a fear of technology reflected in both our fiction and reality. Yet our technologies, despite what we project upon them, are neither good nor bad; until the day when humanity invents an artificial intelligence (AI) with a consciousness, they lack the capacity for such human traits. Yet this does mean technology is neutral. Technologies, no matter how seemingly automated, are tools designed and put into service by humans, which together form a socio-technological system. Because of this human side, technology – when it analyzes our data and executes our orders – reflects the intentions and values of the individuals and social system which design and use it. Yet because technology facilitates action and enhances capabilities, it enhances the characteristics of the individuals and society, both the good and the bad. Thus, technology has not only a problem-solving or task-performing character, but a normative character inherited from its designers and users; its outcomes are not only functional, but social and political, affecting even our psychology and physiology (see respectively, Jasanoff 2004, 14; Carr 2015; Mindell 2015).

Yet despite their duality, and the fears that some have of technology, other actors, the state amongst them, have placed a tremendous amount of faith in technology (generally, see Morozov 2014). They take the human-technology duality to its opposite conclusion, wherein technology is not to blame for bad outcomes, but user error. The human side of the system is derided as biased, flawed, and the "weakest link" in security (DARPA official quoted in Singer 2009, 64; see also Hammes 2006, 7; Schneier 2003, 133, 145; Slayton 2013, 216). To resolve this problem, the human is to be replaced: algorithms can do our thinking, automation can take our actions. With this system directed by a faceless bureaucracy representing, in theory, the general good, it is free of human values and flaws and can be directed instrumentally toward solving our problems. Secrecy is required, though, because the state recognizes the nature of power and how modern technology has distributed it, empowering individuals. If any information is known about how the system works, that system can be defeated. Algorithms can be "gamed," as any online marketing ("optimization") professional can tell you, and automated actions can be predicted, as Hollywood has shown us when the clever criminal knows in advance every move of the police as dictated by bureaucratic routine (as seen in every *Die Hard* movie). When any individual is a possible threat, any information increases his or her capabilities, and any openness in our system, even amongst colleagues or comrades who don't "need to know," increases its vulnerability. Thus, even while being the object of security that the state seeks to defend, citizens have lost not only privacy but also their voice and agency, because they *might* just be the threat that the state seeks to defend against.

Yet while the dangers of openness and the need for secrecy and monopolized expertise may be valid, any such judgement needs to consider actual risks and benefits. The question is not about balancing security and liberty, as it is often framed. Rather the question is the balance between a closed security system, such as we now have, or an open security system. To determine what this balance should be we need to understand not only what we currently do well, which governments love to talk about, but also the weaknesses and risks of our current approaches. Then, we need to consider not only the risks of openness, but also what the promises of transparency and participation may be. If we are going to blame Edward Snowden for lives lost, as some have done,[1] we need to consider not what the system would look like without Snowden, but what it would look like if Snowden were not necessary because his actions were part of a normal process of openness in security, one in which citizens not only had the information he had, but in which they used this information to help provide the security that his government job entailed.

OPEN PARTICIPATORY SECURITY

This book argues that our current security system is no longer sufficient for a world in which technology has led traditional threats to be eclipsed by diffuse networked threats operating in a complex, and fragile, interconnected socio-economic system. Built for a different era, our security system has been buttressed by adding new technologies to old weapons platforms and doctrines even while the world, and people, have transformed radically. Given the ever increasing complexity of security, the current dominant security approach leveraging bureaucratized and monopolized technological solutions to solve security problems is insufficient, and even counterproductive for some types of security. The resulting gap that some have observed between the state's capabilities and the requirements needed to address current threats has, moreover, contributed to a gap between the state and society as older social contracts based on an exchange of security and loyalty, respectively, no longer seem valid.

Yet the answer to these problems arising out of technology is to be found neither in neo-Luddite anti-technology policies nor in reflexively continuing until the "technological singularity" saves us all.[2] In the technology that has created new challenges is the very solution to them if the human side of that technology can be reintroduced. The establishment of an open participatory security (OPS) system applying the appropriate tools for enabling participation, as determined by the nature of the task, would create a unified techno-socio-political system that leverages multiple network advantages to solve complex objective security problems and restore a subjective sense of security by creating trust amongst the citizens and institutions that emerge. Such a system would be *organizationally* centred on the idea of networks and swarms rather than hierarchical command and control; *technologically* focused on systems designed to enhance and complement human capabilities and to meet human needs, rather than designed to replace humans and meet the needs of pre-existing technology; and based on the *idea* of openness for empowering individuals to contribute to the fulfilment of their own needs while also releasing the emergent (that is, not merely additive or even logarithmic but totally new) properties of individuals working together. Such a security system would be consistent with the state of the art in scientific thinking, modern approaches to technological design and production, contemporary views of legitimate knowledge and authority, and the socio-political institutions and values of liberalism. Thus, OPS would be a unitary and thereby stable system.

Moreover, such innovative solutions are already emerging and have even been deployed for some state, social, scientific, and commercial purposes.

In the guise of open government, open innovation (and peer production), open science, and open source, numerous actors have combined humans and technology to develop solutions to problems, improve performance, and build communities. The concept of open government (OG) has recently become a mantra of politicians and policy makers across much of the world, especially in the West. Yet opening government to the citizens as a solution to state and social dilemmas is not a new idea. From the Magna Carta to the open bureaucracy of Louis XIV, through to the first freedom of information laws in the late eighteenth century and the growth of liberalism in the mid-nineteenth, governments have over time slowly been opened to an expanding citizenry as the state's needs expanded. Yet today's concept of OG goes beyond transparency and accountability. Openness is about more than having information; it is about being able to use that information for action. Modern OG calls for deeper and wider participation, deliberation, and co-production with citizens to improve efficiency and effectiveness (see, for example, United States, White House 2009). It is thus based not only on the historical (or natural) "rights of man" that are foundational to liberal democracy, but on "the wisdom of crowds" and decentralized action that can now be maximized through modern technology, on leveraging technology to drive human solutions to social problems and to build social relations.

Yet despite this new idea of openness, the realm of security is still typically held to be a "special domain, where the normal calculus of open government does not apply" (Roberts 2004, 69–70). The view that security can be attained only through secret expert knowledge implemented by equally secretive bureaucracies trumps trends in technologically enabled participation. Security and military modernization and reform, which a range of literature even calls a "revolution,"[3] remain confined to the margins. Only in the *march* (boundary) and revisionist states, where threat is high and innovation essential for survival, have some initial real-world programs using technology to get citizens to contribute to security been trialled, while in the West experiments, though existing, remain confined to laboratory settings. Here, entrenched security actors resist, understandably and even somewhat justifiably, a systemic opening that could threaten their professional status and which they view as unwelcome intrusion in matters too serious for laypersons. This situation is somewhat ironic, as participation in security is nothing new. Especially in times of complex (versus structured, i.e. state versus state) insecurity the wider release of enabling technologies and the inclusion of society in security making has often been critical not only for real security, but to make citizens feel secure so that normal life can continue.

As the state has increasingly turned its eye toward the individual, usually in the name of defending him or her, but sometimes to target him or her, it has implicitly recognized what many citizens have missed: that the people do hold latent power, even if they only occasionally exercise the capabilities they possess. The very success of the state, the economic system and technologies it played a role in creating, have distributed power, skills, and resources. This distribution has in turn made the state increasingly dependent upon their citizens. Technology makes the state and world transparent and gives the people new power, the means to their own survival. If the state's system of security does not match these new power structures, does not leverage transparency to capture capabilities, it will not be able to meet its citizens' security needs, who in turn will see no need for state institutions. This book demonstrates how modern diffuse empowering technologies can be matched with the diffuse specialization of modern society to create a unified system of open participatory security, one which takes the abilities unique to both human and machine, individual and organization, society and state, to produce outcomes better than any single one could attain alone.

By reintroducing the human element, this book highlights not only how technological solutions can fail in an objective sense, but how dependency on technological security alone deprives a given social order of the subjective sense of security that is essential for stable state-society relations and progress. Building on this observation the book examines how current tools of participation, co-production, and gamification – all predicated on transparency – fit the needs of complex contemporary security policy making, problem solving, and provision, and how, through feedback mechanisms, such an open security system can be successfully built and sustainable even in the face of contemporary citizen apathy and state austerity. Moreover, open security can be effective not only in security provision, but also for restoring (an upgraded version of) legitimacy to the state historically tasked with and held accountable for protecting society.

Throughout history, successful states (and other political units) under threat have matched technological innovation with social innovation, thereby restoring security and at the same time fundamentally altering state-society relations to attain a sustainable social contract (Hammes 2006, 12; Lipschutz 2000, 7 and passim; McNeill 1982; Morris 2014 passim; Polyani [1944] 2001). However, such action does not occur through the state alone, or rather we must understand the state as international relations defines it: consisting of government and people, as well as territory. For the state to innovate, not only must the government see a threat and thus be willing to learn and adopt new ideas; society must also have an interest in security innovation. Such interest is sparked also by threats, but can transform into something productive (rather than fear and withdrawal) only if information on how to meet those threats is provided. This information must be matched with an organizational approach that facilitates the participation necessary to create new technologies and ideas for security, ideas and tech that can only come from society given the current structure of knowledge (and even physical) production and of the threats that must be met.

Technology is a problem, but it is also a solution. It enables new vulnerabilities and threats, but it enables also the participation able to secure against these. Such participation in security provision not only creates security but enables trust – in one's self and others, in technology, and in the state – which in turn further reinforces security and the system providing it. A "perpetual beta" system of open participatory security offers the possibility of a sustainable, survivable, self-structuring, self-reinforcing, and self-improving system that can enhance security policy, problem solving, and provision while in the process also altering the individual citizen and social relations for the better. Yet before we can begin down the path to OPS we must do some conceptual ground clearing, clarifying exactly what security is and how it is attained. This discussion will also further foreshadow some of the deeper explorations to come, with the ideas introduced here being returned to and elaborated upon in later chapters.

DEFINING SECURITY: ASPECTS, MEANS, AND OBJECTS

Defining security is not a straightforward matter. Security is a contested concept because "the right to define security provides not just access to resources but also the authority to articulate new definitions and discourses of security, thereby directing the policy that leads to real, material outcomes" (Lipschutz 2000, 48). Definitions are thus not merely academic; they determine what is defended, and thus what (or who) is left vulnerable, based on what is important to whoever articulates the definition. Broadly speaking, the participants in the definitional debate can be divided into two camps: those advocating a narrow definition of security and those advocating a broader one.[4] While both camps agree (mostly, not universally) that "security is about survival," they diverge as to exactly what is "posing an existential threat" to what "designated reference object"; that is, exactly what must we defend from what (Buzan, Waever, and de Wilde 1998, 21). The narrow definition camp typically sees the state as the object of security and other states as the threat to that object; the wider definition sees many threats – economic, environmental, cultural, etc. – in addition to political-military ones, each affecting a corresponding critical area (or sector) of life. While herein we prefer the wider definition, both conceptualizations offer valuable insights into security and require further exploration.

The narrow definition is by nature most effective and efficient during periods when the security context is well defined, structured, and stable. The wider definition, conversely, is required for complex unstructured eras when threats, vectors of threats, objects threatened, and capabilities to meet threats are ill-defined and/or rapidly changing. The narrow definition is thus preferred, often even in the face of evidence that it is inappropriate, by status quo states (typically great powers and their allies), as their own authority and power rests on that definition. The wider definition is preferred by challengers, revisionist states and groups, and critical thinkers, which also can include certain specialized sub-organizations in status quo states (e.g. special forces).

While the wider definition may dilute the instrumental utility of the concept of security, as some contend (Walt 1991, 212–13), it can still be preferable to a narrow definition: there are times when the instruments and the purposes to which they can and should be put are unclear. There is a temptation at such time to equate familiarity with utility, but during periods of rapid change old instruments will increasingly be useless for attaining policy goals and security. Thus, though the wider definition makes it harder to address security, it does so because its greatest value is when security *is* the hardest to address, when we need to account for numerous unclear threats to numerous different actors and objects that we rely upon for our survival.

Sir David Omand, former director of the British Government Communications Headquarters (GCHQ) intelligence agency, offers a good first cut for a wide definition of security, calling it "a state of trust on the part of the citizen that the risks to everyday life, whether from man-made threats or impersonal hazards, are being adequately managed to the extent that there is confidence that normal life can continue" (Omand 2010, 9). The key concepts herein are trust, managed, and normal life, with the idea of continuity running through each of these. The idea of "normal life" draws from resilience studies, which identifies "vital life systems" as the object that needs to be secured (for example, see Lakoff 2007; Ries 2012). This is somewhat wider than mere survival, physically understood, of a person, government, or state; it is about ensuring all those conditions and subsystems that provide survival needs and that also fill that survival with meaning and allow for progress. This idea recognizes that the state is dependent upon citizens leading their normal lives for the state also to continue its existence. Security is "managed," though, because security is about trade-offs and negotiating between these (Schneier 2003, 279). Not everything can be secured, and what can be secured cannot always be secured within acceptable costs or with acceptable sacrifices. Thus, there will also be security failures. Because of the imperfect management of security, there must be a level of trust to fill in where security is lacking and allow the continuation of life even when security fails (Schneier 2012, 17).

Omand's definition, with its ideas of trust and management, highlights what has long been recognized, that "[s]ecurity is both a feeling and a reality" (Schneier 2003, 9). These two sides of security are often referred to as subjective ("felt") security and objective ("real") security (Buzan, Waever, and de Wilde 1998, 30; original idea attributed to Wolfers 1962, 151). Objective security is what most people associate with security. It is measurable in, for example, the number of terrorist attacks, while how it is attained is quantifiable, for example, in number of soldiers. However, objective security need not be narrowly military; diseases and climate change can also have objective security implications; even obesity has been called a national security threat (prominently, but not solely, by Major General Allen Batschelet; see Costello 2015). Subjective security is a less tangible internal mental state of feeling secure. However, it does still have physical manifestations, realized through the way people behave, in how they continue or alter their lives. While such behaviour is influenced by real, objective threats, it can also be totally independent of them: people can keep calm and carry on even as bombs fall, or they can be anxious even in the best of times. Providing subjective security (or manipulating subjective insecurity) entails information, persuasion, and elements of social engineering.

As the above description hints at, the two sides of security are not independent of each other; the feeling of security must be grounded in the reality of security, while the reality of security is real only to the extent that a threat is perceived and accepted to be real (making it "intersubjective"; see Buzan, Waever, and de Wilde 1998, 30).[5] Without one side of security, the other side cannot be maintained in the longer term. Overreliance on one form of security can even undermine the other. The tools of total objective security can be oppressive and constantly remind a person of all the threats out there, thus making them feel insecure. Total subjective security can lead to complacency, which can in turn lead people to withhold the resources (e.g. money) and support needed for objective security, thereby undermining the very objective security that made the subjective security possible in the first place.

Providing security is thus a balancing act of providing security "in the background" so it is not oppressive and yet keeping a population aware enough of security, and possible insecurity, so they have faith that security is being provided while also not taking it for granted. Because security itself is an imprecise concept as well as never fully attainable, while security failures are so clear and visible, the *means* to objective security – soldiers and police, walls and cameras – should be as transparent as possible for subjective security to exist. The means must be visible or at least understandable, preferably leaving some trace in the real world while also not altering that world so much that life must alter to "accommodate" security. Much of our Cold War propaganda served this purpose: to remind us that there was somebody standing on a wall and that we needed them on that wall because we did not want to be on that wall (to paraphrase the film *A Few Good Men*). This brings us to the importance of the narrow definition of security, which offers insights into how we attain security practically.

The narrow definition of security largely restricts security to issues involving the actual or threatened use of force, that is, to the military and strategy as, respectively, the means and way to security. Though there have been some shifts (see below), the state has traditionally been central to this idea of security, as the object of security (i.e. that which needs to be defended) and as the threat to security, though this threat, of course, comes from other states. As a state by standard definition constitutes a government, territory, and population, threats could be to any of these necessary elements; their relative importance varies based on the character of the threat but also across time, space, and type of political unit. Even narrow security advocates are sometimes open to including threats not only of physical destruction, but also those which threaten the character of the state's elements, for example, threatening to change the type of government or the identity of the nation. For this reason military institutions have had both external and internal roles at various times in history (Pereira 2003; specific example in Adams 1995).

This variation in external-internal orientation over time demonstrates that the view of security as purely a military-strategic matter is applicable only at certain times (Buzan, Waever, and de Wilde 1998, 2–3; see also Bousquet 2009; Ries 2012). The reason this perspective is now so dominant is that indeed it was applicable during the Cold War period, from which most of our thinking comes. The way we understand the world influences the way we design our tools and the way we apply them to solving our problems. Thus, we make our vision of the world true via our tools and their application, as these influence the structure (or lack of it) that the world has. The twentieth-century international system was a product of specific systems of thought, of a rationalizing instinct from the earlier era of scientific discovery that was progressively applied to the technical, political, and social worlds (for example, see Agar 2013). The Cold War was a time of highly structured, identifiable geopolitical-level threats which were met with equally structured tools and tactics focused on control and counter-force in the belief that certainty was possible even in the fog of war.

With the end of the Cold War this structure began to break down. The political ends policy should pursue became unclear while liberalism ran free, altering society, technology, and the economy with its individualizing force, typically at the expense of state power. With a lack of political (policy) guidance and no appetite for military spending or reforms (we won after all, so we must have the best military already), security institutions wandered in the desert for ten years. Only with the attacks of 9/11 did a new mission emerge. This event and those that followed led a significant set of actors to realize that the state was no longer the appropriate object of security, nor were other states the greatest threats; as highlighted above, power and threats now lay elsewhere, with individuals and the networks they join. While military and security organizations could not alter their means and ways overnight, they are more flexible than oft recognized and could redirect these, shifting tactics at the margins and adding new sustaining technologies to adapt old weapons platforms to new missions. While directly transferring means previously used for levelling cities to new forms of warfare was an imperfect process, decades of obsession with increasing precision – with the circular error probable (CEP) of their missiles (Leonhard 1998, 25–27) – had left security actors by the late 1990s with modern technologies that made the targeting of the individual possible. Moore's Law (on ever faster computer processing speeds) and its unremarked equivalent in data storage, as well as excess Internet bandwidth following the dot-com crash (1999–2001), ensured there was information to feed into selecting these targets. While the tools and tactics remained essentially the same, the mission changed; the whole apparatus once directed at the entire Soviet Bloc could at any given time be – and was for a time – directed at one person (on individual targeting, see Arkin 2015). Yet the uneven (or lack of) progress in this War on Terror demonstrated that the old military-strategic approach was no longer appropriate (Chapter 3 will cover this in more depth). The means not only did not match a clear policy end (winning against a vague idea of "terrorism"), but also the structure of the problem, which was not just an individual, but individuals networked together within numerous networked and embedded social, political, and economic levels.

The shift to individuals as the objects and targets of security, recognizing their centrality and power in the system, presaged a larger shift, one which is seeing individuals also become the means to security. If an individual is the means to a threat, that is to insecurity, then an individual can also be the means to security, especially if we get enough of them working from the same page. Russian Chief of Staff General Valery Gerasimov is perhaps the most prominent believer in this shift, stating that "the focus of applied methods of conflict has altered in the direction of the broad use of political, economic, informational, humanitarian, and other non-military measures – applied in coordination with the protest potential of the population" which often "have exceeded the power of force of weapons in their effectiveness" (quoted in Galeotti 2014b). The nature of security institutions, their mission and orientation, and their tools and tactics change over time. We are entering an era when other security actors may be more mission critical than the traditional armed forces when facing the most prevalent and serious security threats and crises. Before military officers reading this book sneer or despair, the new era does not mean all the old military traditions and institutions will or should disappear. However, they will come to look unlike what we currently think of as a modern military (for agreement, see Tom Ricks and Rosa Brooks in Foreign Policy 2015b; see also Arkin 2015, 283). The trajectory and implications of this transformation and its management are a central concern of this book.

Following from these considerations, while defining security is important, thereby identifying our ends, defining the means to security is also important. Means matter because they can shape the world, but because they do not determine the world they can also end up irrelevant in the world. Yet many people will remain devoted to outdated means for security. Such hesitance is even understandable; one must be careful with change: it is the source of our progress but as indicated above, it is also the source of many problems, and the faster that change, the more destabilizing it can be. Thus, herein we advocate an evolutionary approach over the revolution in military affairs that some like to speak of and pursue. In keeping with this preference, while this book takes a wide conception of security, it remains focused on our existing military and security institutions, as these are the means that must transform into our new security providers, or more accurately, partners.[6] The next section will examine these means in more depth, in the process clarifying the key concepts of technology and participation and how they progress.

THE MEANS TO SECURITY: TECHNOLOGY, ORGANIZATION, AND IDEAS

As the title of this volume and the discussion up to this point allude to, technology is important for security and, especially today, is seen by many as the determining element. Indeed, technology serves as the foundation for numerous models and theories of military development (e.g. McNeill 1982; Knox and Murray 2001; Krepinevich 1994; Slayton 2013), security studies (Lacy 2014), international relations (Horowitz 2010; Lieber 2005), and indeed the entire course of history (Hobsbawm 1997). However, while technology plays a key role in strategic and security thinking, it is not deterministic for security. Technology is part of a socio-technological system, one which may or may not be receptive to a new technology. Even once accepted into a system, technology is not deployed and used in isolation. It is dependent on its integration with supporting organizational and ideational systems. Together these components – technology, organization, and ideas – form a triumvirate that makes up the means and ways of security. These three factors are, importantly, not causal, but as Antoine Bousquet puts it, part of a machine (2009, 19; referring to Gilles Deleuze and Félix Guattari's concept of "machinic"). If this machine is to work as it is intended, to produce security, then the components must all work together, creating a balanced system. Not that each component's emphasis needs to be equal; having one gear in a machine that is bigger than the others is common, but the largest gear must still match up with the smaller gears. If the system is not balanced, then even vast superiority in one area cannot ensure victory and can even sow the long-term seeds of defeat (Gray 2002; Lieber 2005, 33 and [implied] passim; Leonhard 1998, 7; see also Hammes 2006, 26–27).

Yet as will be shown throughout this book, balance is not so easily attained, as these factors can be manipulated only to a certain extent. Moreover, the interaction effects produced by any given combination cannot be known with certainty. Thus, a given system configuration can lead to unexpected outcomes, perhaps not producing security after all but total war or revolution. On top of this, once a system has been created it produces feedback effects that alter the components of the system, and even the nature of the state and society using the system, thus requiring that system be constantly rebalanced. This complexity alone explains why many modern institutions are slow to change, have strong status quo biases, and prefer to use new technologies in a sustaining manner (e.g. see Horowitz 2010). There is a lot of risk in change, making incremental and iterative approaches to defence transformations a wise idea.

This complexity makes discussing the three interconnected components in a separate, linear fashion equally complex, but necessary given writing progresses in such a way. Below we will start by discussing technology, to further explain how technology, while not deterministic, is a tangible entry point into the study of social phenomenon like security. Subsequently, ideas and organization will be discussed in the context of technology. While the role of the people will be seen within this discussion, a final section will turn specifically to the concept of participation given the different perspectives on what exactly participation is, which in turn has a big influence on how participation is treated. Further specific ideas and theories on innovation and competition, technological adoption, and openness and participation will follow in the subsequent chapters directly before they are needed, thereby spreading out the theoretical burden into more manageable bits.

TECHNOLOGY: AN ENTRY POINT, NOT A DETERMINANT

Of security's components, technology seems to many actors to be the most malleable, able to be designed from above and directed with precision at a problem. This perception has led security and military thinking currently to be especially tech-centric in their solutions, though the security sector is by no means alone in their belief in "technological solutionism" (Morozov 2014). However, though likely easier (and more desirable) than engineering social reorganization and spreading new ideas, the belief in our ability to manipulate technology for our own ends is only half true. Technology tends to evolve of its own volition, accelerating the more units that are in a system and the more scarcity and need that exists, in other words, the more open competition there is. While putting resources toward developing a specific technology can and has worked, such command innovation is unlikely to be truly transformative. Firstly, organizations with enough resources to pursue command innovation are those most invested in existing technology and thus unlikely to want to see it replaced; thus, they will not invest in the transformative tech. Secondly, the more directed a technology is, the more specific its applications and thus the more limited its transformative nature. Command innovators find designing something flexible difficult; we are still waiting for successful modular naval ships and smartphones. Given these factors, most innovations today come from undirected processes of discovery, from exploring and tinkering for its own sake, not from directed research (Kennedy 2016).

Nonetheless, technological innovation is evolutionary and evolves in a more predictable way than biological or social evolution. Technological development is highly subject to path dependency, as science builds on itself, with certain technologies necessarily preceding and naturally leading to other technologies. Technology is also liable to suffer "lock-in," which closes off certain paths of development since new technology must build on decisions made regarding the development of older technology (Lanier 2010). Following somewhat from these phenomena, the research and development, even if relatively undirected experimentation, that goes into new "breakthroughs" proceeds deployment by years or even decades. The "surprise" around a new technology is simply an outcome of corporate secrecy[7] or the scientific practice of replication and peer review. In the military field, Colin Gray notes how each supposed Revolution in Military Affairs (RMA) "was waiting to happen" (Gray 2002, 271). The tech was often there in its rough form for years and could be developed further if so desired or once key subsystems were discovered/developed; drone technology, for instance, goes all the way back to WWII (Arkin 2015) and video games back to the 1950s (Ivory 2016). Because of this evolutionary nature, the future of technology can be seen with some accuracy even if not certainty.

While technological development is thus to some extent observable and foreseeable, technological adoption is less so because state, societal, and organizational receptiveness and responses to new technology are less predictable. The organizations and ideas that were designed to maximize the use of an older technology, and succeeded because of them, are often resistant to new technologies. Kodak resisted digital photography, and Lexmark missed the shift to the paperless office; the Japanese clung to the sword until Commodore Perry's visit, and crossbows were for a time outlawed across Christendom as a risk to the feudal order. Such rejection of new technology often involves foresight, a purposive resistance to a tech viewed as threatening, but can also result from blind spots in an institutional culture accustomed to one way of thinking; something "technically possible" may simply not be "bureaucratically imaginable" (Singer 2009, 46, theme passim; for case of drone development, see Arkin 2015). Yet resistance can also be rational and for the greater good. The state may reject a technology because they realize that the supporting technology, organization, and ideas that would allow it to be safely and effectively used are not in place. History is littered with examples of technologies that the time was not ripe for and which were thus not adopted (Diamond 1999, especially Chapter 13). Even the qualitatively best technology does not always win out, as other peripheral factors come into play; case in point is the triumph of VHS over Betamax.

Yet permanent purposive repression of a technology once it has emerged is possible only if that technology is both expensive and requires a lot of organizational change to use. These barriers must be high enough that there is no other actor to which innovators could transfer (see adoption-capacity theory in Horowitz 2010, 3–4, 9–10, 49). If these restrictive conditions are not met, any attempt to suppress an emerging technological innovation just moves the locus of innovation, in the process altering power configurations, which in turn ensures the non-adopting state becomes weaker. Thus, nuclear proliferation has been thankfully slow, the spread of chemical weapons somewhat less so, and the spread of cyberwarfare capabilities radically faster (for an example, see Runkle 2015).

Technology does not determine the future; the way we adopt technology does, whether we adopt it for and into our existing institutions and ideas, whether we adapt those institutions and ideas for the technology, or whether we do not adopt at all. Whether this then brings victory or defeat is based on whether the chosen configuration maximizes the technologies' potential in a way appropriate to the world context, the threats and vulnerabilities, and whether somebody else adopts it better. States have choices and social structures influence those choices, but if an actor does not adopt, then it had better adapt because if the technology truly is "revolutionary," then in a competitive and open world some actor – state or non-state – will adopt the technology and gain a strategic advantage.

HOW IDEAS ORGANIZE TECHNOLOGY TO SOLVE PROBLEMS

Ideas and organization are closely related; ideas tell organization how to act. Ideas express the legitimate and/or correct "ways" of doing things, which in turn influence the ideal social organization and military organization as the "means," setting who performs what actions. Ideas are needed firstly on a system level, to legitimate both access to resources and the means to security. These ideas establish systems of authority as embedded in political ideologies and policies. Ideas are needed also on an intra-military/security level, to appropriately direct the resources – technological and human – toward defending the object of security or attaining other political ends. These ideas take the form of military doctrines, strategy, and tactics. Without ideas translated down every level from policy and doctrine to tactics and tasks, a security system cannot act strategically to attain its objectives. In such situations the means to security are especially likely to direct security, such as happened in Vietnam and perhaps also in the ongoing War on Terror. With no clear idea on how to win, or what that would even look like, we focus on maximizing the use of our tools and measuring their effects: on drone strikes and body counts.

Ideas are perhaps the most difficult component to *purposely* change, at least in a controlled manner. For instance, in Napoleonic warfare, you could give a man a new musket and even force him to march in line and column within the new division-sized organizations, but getting him to believe in the revolution *cum* empire or to accept and use new skirmishing tactics, both which seem to invite death, was another matter. People, individually and within organizations, prefer the existing way of doing things, ones which become entrenched over time because those ways worked in previous contexts (or we would not have survived to have those preferences). Yet when these old ideas about processes continue to exist and are not adapted to new technologies and new organizational structures, disaster can result. In conservative military institutions the response to new technology is very often to simply try to integrate it into existing structures and strategy, when in reality new technology often requires fundamental doctrinal changes (Horowitz 2010, 216; Leonhard 1998, 6–7; Lieber 2005, 153). Old tactics and ideas of nationalism combined with modern technology and organizational capacity led to the trenches of WWI. The US Army has repeatedly learned, and then quickly forgotten, counter-insurgency warfare given organizing for such campaigns does not correspond to ideas about how they won wars in the past (or, if one is truly cynical, to procurement preferences) (Scales 2016). The implications of applying our Cold War–era ideas of hierarchical command

and control to new technologies incorporating flatly organized networks and swarms could be equally dangerous.

If ideas are not so easily created by states or people for instrumental purposes, where then do they come from? Simplifying greatly and remaining with our framework, ideas are born from the existing technology and the way it was organized in the recent past while also building on the ideas those older systems were built upon. In other words, ideas come from our experience of life. Change in ideas comes from what needs that life is failing to fulfil, whether basic survival needs or needs created by the existing system itself, ones we may not have even realized were necessary until they were made possible by human progress. In this way changes to ideas, from ideologies to operations, often come only after they are thoroughly discredited following trauma.

Changing ideas at the micro- and meso-levels, in individuals and organizations, often depends on changing ideas at the macro-system level, thereby allowing the formation of a unitary system of thought, a consistent world view. Antoine Bousquet (2009) makes an elaborate argument on how ideas of military organization and operations are rooted in overarching scientific paradigms that condition ways of knowing and thinking; these scientific ideas in turn may be rooted in even older monotheistic religious ideas (Gray 2003). The big ideas tell us what legitimate knowledge is and where it comes from, and thus where authority and power in a system lies or should lay, and from here, who may and should (or must) participate in a system and what their roles are. This then determines the small ideas, how knowledge, authority, and participation are applied to solve our problems, to lead our lives and realize progress.

Returning to the example of eighteenth-century France, guns – that is, technology – may have made the revolution possible (even inevitable), but their deployment and use were necessarily preceded by ideas: ideas by the state that guns could ensure their authority, which led them to allow guns to be manufactured; ideas in the military about how they could control the use of those guns and direct them to instrumental ends; and ideas in society, especially once armed, about what purpose those guns should legitimately be put to. The regime, of course, failed to account for the changes other technologies had wrought in society, how the economic innovations it had allowed to enhance government power had transformed the people. The government's plan to instrumentalize technology and its own people directly facilitated ideas in the people that opposed these plans, and without the people the state soon ceased to exist.

Yet the internal organization of a military, the means of security, does not always reflect larger social organizational patterns; drill sergeants love to point out they are defending democracy, not practicing it. While this can raise legitimacy issues, it need not necessarily do so since the military is (or at least should be) a means. Thus, it can attain functional legitimacy if it is successful at its task: providing security. How to organize the military to perform its function successfully is also based on macro-ideas, specifically conceptions of what the appropriate way to solve a problem is. Solving a problem is determined by the idea of who has valid information and legitimate knowledge, and thus can be endowed with authority to decide (in military, see Leonhard 1998, especially Chapter 11, specifically 204). Even older patriarchal organization was patterned on such ideas, albeit divine authority and royal blood were considered sufficient to endow knowledge and justify the hierarchical organization. Especially in the past hundred years, the science of military organization and motivation has come much further. Divine and royal authority to solve problems gave way to bureaucratic structures and managerial approaches. Yet today the dominant macro-idea is liberal individualism and possibly an emerging ideology of the network, ideas at odds in many ways with the older approaches to how technology should be organized to provide security. Thus, it may be time for a reorganization.

WHERE PARTICIPATION FITS IN

Participation is of central concern to this book, but does not appear in the usual means to security conceptualization. This is not because it is not critical in all security systems, but because technology, organization, and ideas – as well as the threats we face – all combine to determine the extent to which participation is required or demanded by the state or the people. How exactly these requirements and demands look today is the major theme of this book.

However, the question of the extent of participation in security that is desirable for a given security system is complicated due to disagreement over what even constitutes participation, something which often is determined in the mind of the participant and can change following the act of participation. The soldiers charging the Somme participated regardless of how they entered service (willingly or not) and their a priori feelings often differed from their ex post opinions. What some would call participation seems to others to be manipulation, a coerced contribution to a security that serves state or elite interests; others see the called-for future participation as opening the door to inappropriate interventions, a seizure of authority by the masses that undermines all the protections built into our democratic systems. If we take the basis of Omand's definition of security as the management of life's risk to ensure life's continuation, then in a way the citizen is always participating in security. We all go through our daily lives consciously and unconsciously accepting and managing risks or asking others to manage risks for us (family members, insurance companies, governments), usually offering something in return (love, money, taxes, and loyalty). Even just having trust in the government and getting on with life contributes to subjective security, which can then feed into objective security.

This disagreement arises in part due to the status of certain modes of participation as rights.[8] Yet from a historical perspective participation has not been determined by rights; rather rights have been driven by participation (concurring idea in Roberts 2004, 72). The amount of desired participation in turn, from the state's perspective, is determined by the extent and type of participation necessary to operate a given technology and whether mobilizing ideas to get citizens to support (even demand) this participation is possible, balanced against the risks of this upsetting the socio-political system (see Chapter 2). Revolutionary France gave rights because they needed manpower for their armies given external threats outweighed any domestic considerations (given it was already in chaos). As this example illustrates, the process is not always smooth. Ideas and technology often run ahead of socio-political organization, resulting in a new distribution of power not reflected in the organization of the state, a disequilibrium that raises the risk of revolution (following Karl Marx and certain later revolution theorists such as Chalmers Johnson).

The view of participation as a right, rather than a means to security which is a means to meeting human needs, has contributed to the "balancing test" fallacy, where rights are weighed against security and restriction on rights justified as necessary for security (Blanton 2003). Admittedly, some participatory acts have over time become rights, but this is not how they should be viewed when weighing them against security, against which they inevitably seem to lose since "survival" trumps every other human need and security somehow by extension offers this survival if we just eliminate rights. But risks and benefits do not co-vary negatively; cutting rights may reduce risks, but this reduction does not automatically transfer over into the benefits column (some ideas on this in Breakwell 2014, 125). Because risk is always a function of probability, there may be no actual security enhancement after restricting rights. If participation is instead seen for how it serves as a means to security, then the balancing test becomes less zero-sum and balances what is actually important to balance: risks and benefits. "What are the risks of participation?" then can be followed by the question "What are the benefits of participation?" (similar but less expansive idea in Roberts 2004, 78, drawing on ideas of Rena Steinzor).

The point here is not to downplay the importance of rights and reduce their emergence to purely instrumental factors; Immanuel Kant and Thomas

Paine may have called for democracy to restrain the wars of kings, but their arguments went deeper than this one aspect. Nonetheless, we can eliminate the confusion about participation when we focus on its instrumental nature in security institution design, rather than its natural, legal, or normative nature and whether it arises out of rights – presumably good – or responsibilities – often seen as bad or at least onerous. Instrumentally speaking, participation is about matching what a person can contribute to what the state needs to fill out its security capabilities, which are then used to ensure and promote the people's needs for not only security but also self-realization. Based on these needs and capabilities, an exchange can be made: land for service, taxes to delegate service to others, rights for total war mobilization. In political science these exchanges are called social contracts, and they ensure not only survival through security but progress through structuring social relations.

AN INITIAL MODEL OF SECURITY

Congratulations to the reader for making it through this quite heavy section of the book. With the above ideas and concepts now laid out, we can present in Figure 1.1 a first cut for a model of security. This model will help the readers organize their thoughts in the discussion to come and will in turn be

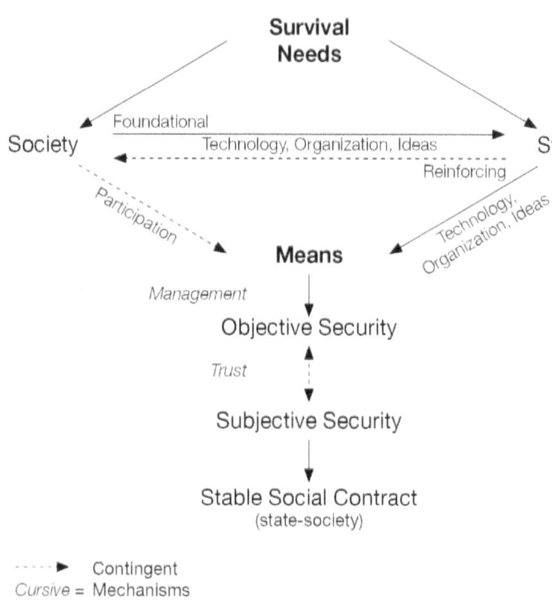

Figure 1.1. A First Cut of Security

developed throughout the book into a final model, presented in the conclusion, for how an OPS system would look. Turning to the present figure, to meet our needs and provide for survival humans have come together in state-societies. Societies provide foundational technology, organization, and ideas to the state, which then puts these together to create the means – a military – to provide security. However, the state is not passive; it promotes technology, organization, and ideas in society that can reinforce its preferred version of order and thus its power. In providing security, the state may also call upon the society to directly participate, depending on the requirements of the technology, organization, and ideas used. Through the resulting security system (means) the state seeks to provide objective and subjective security. Historically though, they usually focus on the former; by managing objective security they hope to facilitate subjective security. Thus, trust in a state-society is initially functional, and moreover it can help reinforce that function (that is, trust helps the state provide objective security). Successful security in both dimensions allows for the formation of stable social contracts that allow normal life and progress. The resulting system and social contract will persist until external changes again threaten survival needs, requiring reform or heralding extinction.[9]

"WAITING TO HAPPEN": A FRAMEWORK FOR DEFENCE TRANSFORMATION

The question now is whether knowing such a limited part of a complex process and system can offer any basis for prediction? In short, no, it cannot. As Peter Singer (2009, 14) points out in his bestselling book on the robotics revolution, "Social change can intervene and intertwine with technology, yielding not one definite future, but rather many possible futures." Nonetheless, while in strategic development "all things are possible, [. . .] they are not equally likely" (Gray 2002, 102). As shown above, technology evolves along foreseeable lines, and while the development of organizations and ideas is less certain, the social sciences have progressed far enough that we know a fair deal about human responses to change. Moreover, we know a great deal about the "initial conditions": the technology we will be examining herein already exists and is even quite mature in many regards, as are the organization and ideas underpinning the technologies' open use, even if neither are yet integrated into security thinking. We also know a great deal about system design, about how to put together technology, organization, and ideas while also buffering our design against unanticipated outcomes through agile and iterative development. Equally important, we know how socio-political units (whether states or not) and the agents of security behave in a competitive arena where survival is at stake. The number of winning scenarios in strategic competition are many, but they are limited.

If our goal then is to explore ongoing changes to security threats and capabilities to understand what means of security we need and how to manage the transition to a new system capable of providing a more holistic security, then we have existing frameworks for the analysis and policy of defence transformation upon which we can draw (Jasper 2009b). Defence transformation is "a continuous process" that entails "new combinations of emerging technologies, streamlined organizational structures, innovative processes, and adaptive personnel developments that exploit national advantages and protect against asymmetric vulnerabilities" (Jasper 2009a, 2–3). It is thus about finding the ideal combinations of technology managed through appropriate organization and maximized by the best ideas (processes, or doctrines) then put into practice by the necessary force structure (participation). Yet, as seen above, defence transformations cannot be confined to the traditional military-security institutions, and the more revolutionary the transformation, the more that supporting social, economic, and political structures will have to change as well. This means defence transformation is a larger political and social issue, and it means not only military planners but also citizens and their representatives need to be involved.

A defence transformation analysis requires first an examination of the context, the strategic environment. From this one can identify the capabilities required to deal with this environment. They help identify the "nature of the task," both the reform task and end task that these reforms must enable the fulfilment of (Omand 2010, 289). With this in mind one can conduct a capabilities gap analysis to figure out what the current security system lacks. By knowing current shortcomings one can then identify possible solutions available and examine how to bring these solutions – whether technology, people, or ideas – into existing military structures in a smooth and evolutionary manner (Omand 2010, 289–90; for an example, see NATO process in Jasper 2009a, 8). While this sounds like a very technical exercise, it has also a human component provided we bear in mind that the nature of the task is not just to provide objective security but also subjective security, that a technical solution that provides only physical security would not fill the entire capability gap since popular will is essential to any strategy.

The resulting framework from such analysis has both predictive and prescriptive outcomes. It first helps construct a theoretical model: by examining underlying human needs and human nature (initial conditions and our response patterns) and the structures (e.g. institutions) we therefore construct (what we call "history"), we can derive patterns of historical configurations and how these evolve and change. This model can then be used to understand the current world context and what implications open participatory security would have if applied to that world (for similar ideas to this approach, see Singer 2009, 9–10, 14; on approach to history, see Berlin 1998, 23–24). Moreover, this model can also serve as a map that can be used to nudge the future toward our preferred version by tweaking those factors amenable to manipulation using the knowledge we have accumulated on psychology, systems design, social engineering, and so on. No single factor determines our future, and while this means we cannot purposely and perfectly design the world as we like, it means we can influence the factors and events to shape the future we want to see.

PLAN OF THE BOOK

Turning now to what is to come, Chapter 2 examines how different combinations of technology, organization, and ideas have worked in the context of different historical human socio-political systems, and in turn how they have affected those systems and its components, down to the level of the individual's physiology and psychology. The primary purpose of the chapter is to discover how the character of technology and the threat environment influence the extent of participation in security, and how once realized, this alters the socio-political system. From this history we can then identify "established patterns in innovation" and their implications – psychological, social, and political – which can inform how the current transformation is unfolding and its likely trajectory given the character of current technology and the resulting strategic environment (Garstka 2009, 57). A secondary function of this chapter is to use history to communicate in an accessible manner some important theories about the way participation works.

Chapter 3 looks at the current (dominant) security system's capabilities and gaps in those capabilities given evolving threats – the strategic context – thereby also identifying our future tasks and the reforms needed if we are to fulfil these tasks. The core of the chapter analyzes the weakness of the three pillars of the current dominant approach to security – bureaucracy, (information) technology, and secrecy (what we will call BiTS) – which while offering advantages in the old way of war, are less suited for today's fast-moving threats and adaptive competitors. The chapter also discusses how the same technology that empowers threats has altered society, an often neglected yet traditional element of strategy, empowering individuals while simultaneously weakening social bonds and trust in traditional social groups, including the nation-state.

Chapter 4 introduces approaches to open government (OG), as primarily developed within the discipline of public administration, to security and strategic studies. Following a brief history highlighting the importance of linking information and action, the chapter turns to the limits of openness in the current system due to a paradox that leads transparency and accountability to result in inappropriate actions. It will also turn to the limits of transparency, to how total transparency is not a solution to current shortcomings in our transparency-accountability system. The last half of the chapter examines the mechanisms by which OG and related open approaches bring about technical solutions and social change before exploring specific approaches to OG, focusing on the broad categories of transparency, participation (what we call rights-based participation and participation 1.0), deliberation, open innovation and co-production, and gamification and serious games.

Chapter 5 discusses how the open participatory approaches introduced in Chapter 4 can be used to provide objective security, enhancing policy making, problem solving, and provision. The chapter draws on existing, experimental, and pilot initiatives that fall within the concept of open participatory security, but it considers also functionally equivalent private, academic, and corporate initiatives that demonstrate the extent to which participation can go. While information requirements are discussed throughout, a final concluding section brings this together, outlining especially how the amount of information and the specificity of that information co-vary negatively and how a broad transparency and information policy for OPS would look, drawing especially on ideas of targeted transparency.

Chapter 6 turns to how OPS increases feelings of self-efficacy, control, and intrinsic motivation, which directly increases feelings of security while also building trust in one's self, in others, and in the state and security system, thereby contributing to a social contract appropriate to the modern era. The chapter then discusses how by increasing self-efficacy OPS makes for a more resilient society that can both prevent and deter attacks, as well as help recover from them, thereby directly also creating objective security. The chapter concludes by exploring the possible danger that by altering risk behaviour OPS may promote risky, offensive state behaviour with wide popular support and a conviction that only victory will result, reflecting the worst excesses of earlier eras with open and participatory security systems.

With the reader then endowed with the necessary theory, context, and examples, Chapter 7 brings together the discussion in the form of a model of open participatory security that builds on the basic model presented here in Chapter 1. The conclusion also turns to discussing implementation, outlining an evolutionary approach that can gradually build effectiveness and support through applying the principles of gamification to the construction of the OPS system: a process of "levelling up" to ever more meaningful and effective forms of participation over time. Following implementation, we consider also other design issues, highlighting especially the importance of variation in tasks, platforms, levels, and participants, including the critical role of our current security experts. The discussion here also turns to the possible limits of participation, as well as exploring its expansion beyond the state, geographically but also to a post-state era.

CONCLUSION: SOME FINAL QUALIFICATIONS

The world is a complicated place; indeed, this complexity is part of our argument for open participatory security. Due to this complexity though, the argument constructed here cannot fully take into consideration every factor – economics and the market, demography, ideology, and so on – that shapes the evolution of the security environment and the world we now face. In this regard, this book represents a first cut at outlining OPS, one that will require further exploration.

On another academic note, the history, current context, and practical examples used in this book will draw mostly from what we generally call the West, almost as much but slightly less from the former Soviet Union, and more minimally from the Middle East and East Asia. Other areas will be mentioned only in passing (e.g. Latin America) or not at all. This slight Western bias is more due to the examination of successful security systems and innovation, which have clustered in the West for several (well-studied) reasons. However, a secondary argument of the book is that this may now be changing, as the locus of innovation shifts. Thus, the bias in examples does not mean the argument is not applicable to countries not covered.

Nonetheless, the world is also a diverse place, and the findings herein may not be universally relevant in every place simultaneously. However, the level of socio-economic development does not prevent the use of OPS; indeed, some approaches to OPS are even more called for in so-called transitioning states with weak economies and problematic social and political cleavages. Additionally, despite its normatively positive-sounding designation, there is nothing necessarily or exclusively democratic about OPS, just as there was not with the first newspapers and radio, which in some hands became tools for nationalism and propaganda for war (see Chapter 2). OPS may be most necessary and effective in democracies, but it can also be used in and reinforce more authoritarian regimes, even if the forms of openness and participation differ from what liberalism would call for.

Yet the possible dark side of OPS is no reason to not introduce it; indeed, the fact that somewhat more authoritarian regimes are already using variants of participatory security is even more reason for liberal democratic regimes to adopt OPS if they are to compete internationally. The controlled introduction of open participatory security in liberal democratic polities, who moreover would best be able to capture its benefits, offers the best guarantee for system stability both nationally and internationally. Yet essential to this stability is to keep in mind a refrain that will appear throughout this book: that OPS is and should be evolutionary in its development and not revolutionary. True revolutions in military affairs, rapid and radical, introduce instability to the world and moreover are rarely strategically successful for the introducing nation; that is, in the long run defeat results. Rather OPS should be developed and exist next to older forms of security provision in a hybrid security system, as each system may be appropriate for different tasks at different points in the fight.

Lastly, open participatory security can provide security and augment strategic capability, while also building a new, stronger social contract, bolstering especially subjective security in a way current security systems cannot. However, OPS is not a permanent solution; the argument herein does not claim that we have reached the end of history. Rather, the patterns of history will likely continue, and the proposed system will, like those before it, need to adapt as technology and threats alter. Yet OPS, through its ongoing integration of technology, citizens and their ideas, and state institutions, is ideally suited for ensuring that such adaptation and agile evolutionary development proceeds in a less disruptive manner than in previous eras.

NOTES

1. For example, the CIA director at the time, John Brennan, and former CIA Director James Woolsey blamed Edward Snowden for the 2015 Paris attacks.

2. *Technological singularity* is a term, popularized first by Vernor Vinge and subsequently Ray Kurzweil, referring to the point at which AI becomes capable of recursive self-improvement, leading to an autocatalytic process of ever faster technological development beyond human control and understanding.

3. The so-called Revolution in Military Affairs (RMA) starting in the 1980s (sometimes late-1970s).

4. Naturally, this debate is on a sliding, not dichotomous, scale.

5. While this book greatly appreciates the insights on the nature of security offered by critical security studies, and attempts to take these seriously in its consideration of security, it does not fully engage all the complex, philosophical intricacies of the field.

6. Barring revolutionary transformation, which as will be seen especially in Chapter 2, is not typically desirable and rarely leads to security.

7. The reasons for corporate secrecy differ from those for national security; it results less from fear of competitors than fear of undermining the product cycle if consumers wait for future products rather than buying the existing one (called the "Osborne effect").

8. For rights-based arguments for participation, see Fraenkel-Haeberle, Kropp, Palermo, and Sommermann 2015, especially the contribution by Gamper 2015.

9. External to the system, not necessarily external as in another state or environmental change.

Chapter Two

The Historical Evolution of Security, Technology, and Participation

Revolutionary and Napoleonic France and its mass armies already have made a couple of appearances in our introduction. Yet if we jump ahead just a little more than a century to a country westward, to Bletchley Park, the heart of the UK's cryptography efforts against the Nazis, we find "demure girls, obediently shuffling reams of gibberish through their machines, shift after shift, day after day, [who] have killed more men than Napoleon" (from *Cryptonomicon*, Stephenson 1999). Participation in security had changed. The technology of Bletchley would develop into some of the most important tools of our current security and threats to it. Yet tech alone would not determine what was to come. Their act of participation and contribution to security would change the Bletchley girls and their Rosie the Riveter counterparts. Their participation would not end on V Day (Victory Day, in Europe, 8 May 1945; over Japan, 2 September 1945) and would go on to alter the social and political worlds.[1]

Yet to understand these and even more recent events, we have to go back further. Participation in security is nothing new; a complex combination of cooperation and competition for survival against threats is built into our DNA and advanced through the evolutionary process of natural selection even before the development of society and social contracts. Since the first political units formed and recorded history began we have seen many different arrangements for participation in security provision, from militias to conscripts to professional forces, from whole peoples pitching in for the fight to mercenaries and pirates being tasked with the state's dirty work. Yet in recent years there has been talk of automation and drones – of technology – leading to the end of participation, an occurrence many see as both inevitable and desirable. Yet it is rarely so simple, as Chapter 1 discussed. Ideas and organization will affect technology even if technology's advocates seek to ignore them. Competitors will complicate the best-laid plans for the "perfect" security arrangements that technologists seek and occasionally promise. The technology itself could have unexpected negative implications, creating new problems even as it solves old ones. Moreover, participation in security could also have functions other than just objective security, so it may be necessary even if our security tech could in theory do the job alone. Thus, before accepting that technology will save us, we need to clearly understand what influences the actual and ideal extent, mode, and locus of participation in security. To do so, we need to turn to history.

However, it has become (disturbingly) popular to claim we have little to learn from history; our times are so revolutionary and current changes so rapid as to be without precedent. Yet while we like to speak of the revolutionary nature of our age, to marvel at the novelty of our newest creations and our progress over previous uncivilized eras, ours is not the only era of rapid change, and our level of "civilization" not indisputably higher than that of, for example, the Greek, Roman, Chinese, or Islamic states/empires at their height. Our own conviction in the superiority of our modern socio-political arrangements and our awe at our technological creations lead us to often miss that previous eras' innovations – both social and technological – were no less of breaks from even older eras and were held by contemporaries of those times in equally high regard (on this fallacy, see Domingos 2015, 287; Gat 2006, 445). Understanding these earlier processes of transformation and functional equivalents of previous eras can give us insights into the current transition to an information age and how it should be managed. Additionally, there is just as much and perhaps more to learn from when these eras came to their often violent and anarchical ends. We need to understand not just how security systems are ideally put together, but also why, when, and how they change or fail to change and the resulting implications.

Before commencing an exploration of history, how exactly can we learn from history? To do so we must naturally assume that history is not a sequence of accidents and, while not downplaying individual agency, recognize that it is constrained by the system within which people choose and act. Our understanding of history is thus built upon the assumption that it has vertical and horizontal order (Berlin 1998, 23–24). Horizontal order assumes an "interconnection between different aspects of the same stage" (Ibid.). This means the different human subsystems and structures – market, state, and society (for instance) – that we see in a given historical era are mutually constituting and supporting. They form part of a unified functional system that, if one were so inclined, one could give a name, such as, for example, feudalism, mercantilism, liberalism, and so on (called "social orders" by North, Wallis, and Weingast 2013). In Chapter

1 we saw examples of horizontal order in how a military system consists of technology, organization, and ideas that are embedded into supporting political, social, economic, and scientific systems.

Vertical order implies "succession in time," in other words, that what follows one era is dependent on what preceded it (Berlin 1998, 23–24). We also saw this in Chapter 1 when discussing how technology is subject to path dependency in its development. Such an evolutionary approach is increasingly favoured also in security and strategic studies (Gat 2006; Gray 2002; Hammes 2006). Many theories of historical change and development rest on how imbalances (often called "disequilibrium") in the components of our system – in our horizontal order – are corrected,[2] thereby causing disjuncture in the vertical order, that is, a transition to a new era or epoch. One can see these principles from Karl Marx's historical materialism to the socio-historical works of Barrington Moore's and Paul Kennedy's proposals on the rise and fall of great powers. In military affairs such disequilibrium occurs between technology, organization, and/or ideas, leading, as discussed in the introduction, to strategic setbacks or defeat. As will be shown, the resulting trauma in turn drives the learning and innovation that opens up a new era.

While the above sets a framework to understand history, history is long and complex. Just military/strategic history can and has filled volumes (see, for instance, Lawrence Freedman's [2014] 752-page tome *Strategy: A History*). Thus, especially if one is using history for comparative purposes or to derive patterns, one needs a lens through which to examine the specific phenomena of interest: here, the interaction of security, technology, and participation. Historians may object to how this approach simplifies too much by stripping the examples from the larger context, but it is nonetheless an accepted approach in many other academic disciplines.[3] To find our lens we need to pick an entry point into the interactive and iterative process by which security in a given social order is constructed before complicating this with more considerations.

As covered in the introduction, more than ideas and institutions, technology is a tangible entry point to examine history. Moreover, the character of the dominant weapons/security system – the technology – of a given era is a key determinate of participation in security making (McNeill 1982, 21; see also Moran 2009, 25, with references). To capture this character we do not look at the technical specifications or specific capabilities of the technology; attempting to compare a sword to a stealth bomber would tell us little about what we really want to know about participation and security. Rather, we look at the cost(s) of the dominant weapon system, an approach that draws from new institutional economics, which is especially interested in using costs to explain change (North 1990, 1995). Herein, cost is understood not only as material procurement costs in American dollars, German marks, or Roman denarii, but also cost in hours required for an individual to become proficient with the system and related implementation costs (often called transaction costs). It is not just about the financial resources required, but the organizational intensity required to adopt and then effectively use a given technology (Horowitz 2010).

Whether these costs are high (expensive) or low (cheap) determines the extent to which security provision and thus power is, or at least can be, monopolized by the few or instead is distributed in an egalitarian fashion across many societal actors. To illustrate (without stealing the thunder from the history section), chariots and knights are examples of expensive weapons that allowed for societies dominated by a narrow aristocratic class, with these same classes (and allies) also constraining state action and expansion. When weapons systems were cheaper and required less training – such as with later-era iron weapons, crossbows, or pikes – then violence and thus society had the potential to be more egalitarian. If political leaders were able and willing to mobilize the appropriate forces for the given technology, then they could attain superiority over external threats or competitors. If they could not, then they invited defeat, regime change, or anarchy. A key question in our study is to understand the sources and implications of both monopolized/oligopolistic security and egalitarian security provision – of what Douglas C. North, John Joseph Wallis, and Barry R. Weingast (2013) call closed and open systems – so we can understand the course and implications of emerging security systems once we identify their character. With this lens in mind as a starting point, we can now turn to seeing what history has to teach us.

EVOLUTION AND SECURITY: COOPERATION, COMPETITION, AND HUMAN (SOCIO-)PSYCHOLOGY

While it may seem superfluous to start our history lesson so far back, evolution has important things to teach us about progress, our needs as humans, and our responses to external situations. This information is in turn important for understanding participation and its implications, as the drivers of biological evolution exert influence also on processes and outcomes of social and thereby historical progress (and regression). Thus, they will play a role also in any transformation to come, especially in areas involving risk, uncertainty, and the need for human adaptation. While this review is necessarily cursory, the ideas here will reappear and be further developed in the chapters to come, culminating in the argument laid out in Chapter 6 and the model presented in the conclusion.

Security is, according to anthropological and socio-biological research, one of the oldest and most important tasks of any organism. Security is necessary for survival in a competitive environment filled with both internal group competitors and external threats. To attain this security even the earliest, smallest units of life – independent eukaryotic cells – came together in cooperative arrangements that allowed their genes to be passed on, gradually forming larger and more complex organisms (Dennett 2013, 5–6 and passim). This cooperation allowed for a process of evolution which selected and passed on those genetic makeups most fit for survival.

However, fitness is a relative concept (even if we set aside its socially relative side). Fitness is determined by external circumstances, the environment, which tends to change unpredictably without regard to any given species' comfort or survival. The key to surviving is thus adaptability, the ability to deal with change. Biology deals with this challenge by creating not the perfect genetic code resulting in the perfect species, but in creating a variety of imperfections. These mutations that make an individual different could, at the right time and place, make them the new measure of what was fit: children may tease the kid with webbed feet, but when the ice caps melt, that person will thrive and become a desirable mate. To ensure such imperfections exist in sufficient number that they can match the numerous possible changes in the environment, while also maintaining existing fitness for the current environment, the key is to maximize variation. Maximizing variation in turn required cooperation with others, that one breed beyond one's family for genetic diversity and group together with others that have traits and skills that complement one's own. Such cooperation ensures also that persons less fit for a given environment survive, ensuring their genes are available in the pool should the environment change.

As organisms evolved and expanded their habitable areas through cooperative arrangements, this entailed also the further development of the flip side, competition, as the social unit sought to secure more resources to ensure its survival and that of its progeny. Thus, in principle, as our species expanded, competition increased, which in turn increased the pace of evolution as the fittest survived. However, since such expansion entails risky competition, an evolutionary push was required to encourage expansion out of interest (even when things are good), not just desperation (when home life is unsustainable). Thus, we developed a physiological and psychological system that encourages individuals, to varying degrees, to not only accept but seek out competition, whether with nature or with other people. Instead of just adrenaline so we could run from the predators, we developed dopamine to give thrill to the hunt of prey. Competition with beasts and our fellow community members gave feelings of esteem – including its higher forms such as competence, mastery, self-confidence, independence – and self-actualization. These higher needs, thus, are intimately intertwined with the fundamental needs, those physiological requirements to sustain life (water, air, sleep, etc.) and the security to maintain these (Maslow 1943, 1954). They are not simply modern constructs; they are traits which we inherited because they were evolutionarily advantageous. The pursuit of security alone – historically often through violent competition – can help meet these higher needs, and if the pursuit is successful, ensure also the basic needs.

The chemical responses that our bodies evolved to promote survival do so also by promoting progress, in that they encourage learning and exploration, including the acceptance of the risks this entails. Specifically, we receive physiological rewards for wanting something, for seeking it, and for attaining it (Dignan 2011, 24–25, referring to the ideas and research of Kent Berridge; Panksepp 2004; Vanderschuren 2010; see also Eichenbaum, Bavelier, and Green 2014, 52). These rewards provide internal, intrinsic motivation to learn and engage in risky activities with uncertain and delayed extrinsic (external) rewards. Once we do attain something, further chemical rewards stimulate us to like it. However, the rewards are not permanent, and the chemical effect soon wears off. Such hedonistic adaptation causes us to experience further want and seek again; thus, it is sometimes also called a hedonistic treadmill (Brickman and Campbell 1971; McGonigal 2011, 45). It is through these processes that the act of participation changes people and, in turn, changes what they see as participation and what sort and extent of participation they seek or demand.

We are not designed to separate these biological needs and mechanisms for their fulfilment from other, seemingly less central (though often not) aspects of our lives. Thus, we do not design social or political institutions or build technologies and tools free of the influence of these factors. Subsequently, when we operate within these institutions or use our tools, the same needs and mechanisms will alter our experience of our human-made world. This inability to cordon off our different "worlds" was also a beneficial aspect for our survival. In particular, humans', and many other animals', physiological survival mechanisms allow us/them to experience "fun." In the pursuit of this fun a creature engages in play, especially during its formative years. Play is, despite our modern connotation of the word, not a useless activity, or evolution would never have allowed such a conspicuous waste of calories/energy. Rather, play allows the development of skills necessary later in life; "*fun is nature's reward for practicing survival skills*" (emphasis in original, Dignan 2011, 31, drawing on Karl Groos and Peter Gray). This practice (play) enables firstly and most obviously, the acquisition of directly transferable skills (e.g. fighting skills), but also allows for experimentation with a variety of survival strategies. Moreover, play is one of the few types of learning that promotes the development of transferable skills, which allow for "rapid adaptation to threats to survival that cannot be predicted" (Ellis 1998, 30; on general learning, Dale and Green 2016, 131–33 and 145; Eichenbaum, Bavelier, and Green 2014). In this process, the play itself also helps fulfil the higher psychological needs, giving the player not just the skill set but the psychological state of mind – feelings of control, autonomy, and relatedness – conducive to survival and progress (Eichenbaum, Bavelier, and Green 2014, 52; Henricks 2014, 197; Przybylski, Rigby, and Ryan 2010).

Because of the above, play has actually played a large role in human history, though its consideration and study began in earnest only following Johan Huizinga's 1949 book *Homo Ludens: A Study of the Play-Element in Culture*.[4] While Peter Gray (2009) has shown the importance of play for hunter-gatherer social structures and thus survival, one could argue that play's real benefits were realized only when social institutions and technology began to emerge, which induced human-driven change that progresses much faster than environmental change alone. This rapid human-driven change, in turn, required more human-driven variation, experimentation, learning, and adaptability since biological evolution could not keep up. Thus, the mechanisms in "play" have over time been used for other social engineering purposes. Militaries fine-tuned them not just for training but also to create bonds and esprit de corps; governments and public administrations did much the same to build communities; and eventually games became, as we shall see in later chapters, a major area of study contributing to human betterment. This transferability of our basic physiological and psychological means to survival to other areas which more indirectly affect survival is a key factor in history and essential for the proposed idea of participatory security.

The key lesson from genetics then is that in conditions of uncertainty and risk, "errors can have adaptive value" and the more errors, the better (Gilbert 2013, 63); put in popular terms "some bugs are features" and variety is the spice of life. Because of this variation, cooperation is called for; yet we need also to be able to compete – against nature and others – if we want our presumably successful internal variation to be passed on. These lessons have even led modern computer scientists to apply the principles of evolution, survival, and fitness to their own trade in the form of genetic algorithms and programming, while some have also begun exploring the use of biological engines (in computers) to solve our most difficult "hard" problems (Timmer 2016). The same ideas from evolution have been applied also to understanding various different social, political, and economic systems. Herein, the purportedly perfect system/society is defined by homeostasis, but there will always be conditions and variables external to the system that change. An internally perfect system will not learn, progress, or adapt and will thus not survive a changing context. The "noble savages" of an isolated Garden of Eden may have had the perfect social and ecological balance, but external conditions/competitors – a changing environment or explorers *cum* invaders – ensured they would not survive. Liberalism and the market on the other hand have terrible social and ecological imbalances, yet they persist and spread due to a basis in variation, competition, and survival of the fittest, an ability to advance even from failure and imperfection. With this in mind we must turn our attention to more historical tragedies, for while we are enabled and constrained by our biology, we have come far in developing organizations, ideas, and technologies which have enabled and constrained us in altogether new ways.

OPEN AND CLOSED SECURITY THROUGHOUT HISTORY

While the aforementioned internal drives to meet group survival needs through individual risk taking and skill learning spread our ancestors across the globe, it was only with the development of language, which allowed for better coordination, that they were able to compete, and eventually exterminate, our less adaptive ancient Neanderthal competitors (Diamond 1992, 44–48). This development, the *technology* of language, marks what one could consider the first era of openness, when exchange of information and *ideas* allowed for superior *organization* that ensured group survival and progress. This shows us that while the development of weapons technology matters, its effective mobilization requires something more. The primitive weapons of early man had not changed much; the technological edge of these weapons over the Neanderthal was (initially) not great, but being able to communicate opened up advanced cooperative actions that enabled these weapons, cheap and widely available, to be put to their most effective use. The interaction and proper arrangement of technology, organization, and ideas – facilitated here through information sharing – has been central to group survival and progress ever since.

Despite better communication, prehistoric hunter-gatherers could form groups of up to only 100 to 150 individuals (Dunbar 1992). While not as peaceful as was once supposed, these groups were "egalitarian, nonautocratic, intensely cooperative" (Gray 2009, 476; on non-peaceful nature, see Morris 2014, 58–59). It was only when new innovations in technology, organization, and ideas enabled a shift from homogeneous hunter-gather societies to differentiated agriculturally based societies that these smaller groups were able to coalesce into larger clans and then tribes. The food surpluses offered by settled agriculture allowed population growth, which in turn had internal and external effects. Internally, it spurred socio-economic differentiation, specialization by different persons in different skills. Externally it led to competition with other groups. In combination, they contributed to the emergence of a distinct warrior class, which while initially encompassing most males (by leaving farming to the women), gradually became smaller and more defined by special skills and tools (Gat 2006, 185).

Specialization allowed also for cultural innovation building on the original innovation of language. This included new organizational forms that enabled larger groups to remain stable through ideas (especially religion) and interdependence (via exchange, e.g. markets).[5] Combined, these traits enabled successful competition vis-à-vis other groups, an example of how social evolution mirrors processes of selection seen in biological evolution. Thus, this socio-economic pattern soon became the dominant form of cooperation wherever competition (with other groups) existed, leading to what we now call the Neolithic Revolution.

As most prominently (but not solely) noted by Charles Tilly (1975), the political unit and its monopoly on violence moved arm in arm with the Neolithic Revolution and the establishment of cities, and later (proto-)states. As needs were fulfilled, the aforementioned hedonistic treadmill led to the pursuit of higher needs, needs which we often associate with rights. This pursuit in turn gave impetus to the emerging political structures' – that is, the government's – pursuit of ever greater power to create conditions (especially security) in which those needs could be fulfilled. These interrelated pursuits of people and leaders created the conditions for new exchange relationships, for a social contract in which political units granted ever more rights and privileges in exchange for the resources needed to provide security to the community (Micklethwait and Woolridge 2014, 74, building on the work of T. H. Marshall). Over time the social contracts between ruler and ruled built less-personalized forms of trust, allowing complex social interaction, which together with advancing technology gradually made possible ever larger and more complex social structures (Gat 2006). This development became a pillar of modern political philosophy, elaborated upon first by Thomas Hobbes ([1651] 2010) in his *Leviathan*, wherein man must live under the security of the state or have life cut short under the state of nature. The likes of Locke and Rousseau reflected on these ideas later, modifying Hobbes for a more enlightened age, yet the fundamentals remained. Notions of citizenship (even if undeveloped) and security, rights and responsibilities, have thus always been linked in a social contract that ties together society and the state in a community of trust that not only ensures survival but allows for the progeny and progress that our genes and evolution demand.

With surplus (resources) and specialization (skills) in the emerging early cities, technology began to advance at a more rapid pace, driven further by competitive pressures to innovate or be swept away. The first Bronze Age cities consolidated into capital city–centred empires and city-states following the development of chariots and iron weapons. These weapons systems were expensive and difficult to master, and led to domination of the political units by a warrior class. However, this system also limited the extent to which these units could expand (Gat 2006, 326–27, 331, 336; Kissinger 2014, 37; Morris 2014). Local elites and interests predominated, often despite security threats that could not be met with local capabilities alone. To overcome these limitations, more participation was required. To enable this, in 744 B.C. in Assyria we find one of the first recorded exchanges of rights (in this case, the right to land) for conscription and taxes between a leader and the commoners (Morris 2014, 103).[6] Despite this great advance for the common person, the power that accrued to the executive (the king) was even greater, while the middle aristocracy saw their influence decline. Lands more protected from external threats and with excess resources (wealth) for buying off internal threats whether from peasants or elites, such as Egypt with its natural boundaries and Nile-centred agricultural system, could avoid such compromises for longer (Gat 2006, 88). Wealth and safety thus can in the longer term have perverse effects by inhibiting the openness needed for innovation, which is in turn needed for survival against competition in the longer term. Egypt was what today we would call a status quo power, a term we will see again in Chapter 3.

Over time new innovations in metallurgy led iron to become cheaper. Ian Morris (2014, 101) described the first cheap iron weapons as the "ancient equivalent of AK-47s [. . .] giving every angry young man the same killing power as the representatives of law and order." The result was the democratization of violence, leading to an era of instability in the ancient lands of the Fertile Crescent. Social innovation allowed some states to survive (or emerge from) this shift by opening the state. In cities like Athens, security making included direct democratic procedures and participation. The phalanx, tightly packed infantry (*hoplite*) formations, required egalitarianism for maximum tactical effectiveness. The military needs for egalitarianism leaked also into political structures of the Greek city-states: the "*hoplite* revolution" in the military contributed directly to the democratic structures of the seventh-century Greek *polis* (for the most recent scholarship, see Kagan and Viggiano 2015; original idea attributed to George Grote; see also Gat 2006, 291; Singer 2009, 6). Separation of the different sectors of a state-society – the military, political, social, and economic – is almost never possible even in the relative short term; events and developments in one will leak to another, altering the overall system, including its closed or open nature.

Yet more neglected is how these new arrangements of (distributed) power often eventually allowed the rise of populist tyrants by removing the need for the executive to accommodate security and social/economic elites (examples in Gat 2006, 301–303). This democratic-authoritarian Janus face of openness would reappear throughout history, especially when egalitarian weapons technology met with new communication technology that enabled direct appeals from the top to bottom of the social hierarchy. We may complain of the power of aristocrats and the military-industrial complex, but in many ways such middlemen serve a function that protects democracy.

The successor to Greece, the Roman Republic, also developed such participatory mechanisms even while making use of similar weapons and tactics, upgrading them in a gradually sustaining manner, thereby sustaining Roman power. Amongst the most notable innovations was the idea that conquered foreign peoples and lands could become citizens and provinces in the full sense. In doing so they were incorporated into a decentralized regional structure that allowed the empire to expand beyond what was possible under older systems (Ibid., 185, 315). Other political units unable to open their social and political structures, and thus unable to use the best new organizational-technological military means, were swept away by barbarians (meaning steppe tribes of central Asia), whose flat (participatory) social structure was generally better able to capitalize on the innovations of the preceding centuries. After first rewriting the demography and history of the old Fertile Crescent, these barbarians eventually swept Europe into the Dark Ages. During this time the Roman military force had become less participatory as society withdrew to enjoy the fruits of peace, and politics in Rome became less open (on society, see Gat 2016, 307, 365–66). Yet even while older weapons and tactics diffused to its enemies, no new innovative weapons emerged to buttress the legions' power, and no new lands or peoples filled their ranks as a path to citizenship (though money still attracted some foreign peoples as mercenaries). Thus, weapons with participatory potential are not necessarily positive if participation cannot be mobilized, and late Rome had neither the will nor ideas on how to open the system further.

While Europe fell into anarchy, with no actor able to give structure to the widely distributed means of violence, across the Mediterranean Sea the early Islamic movement could use its "in some respects radically egalitarian" structure to expand into an empire and become a centre of innovation (Kissinger 2014, 99). Reconsolidation of violence in Europe did not occur until innovative technology (e.g. the stirrup) was combined with new social structures (organization) that gave rise to feudalism in response to the Islamic threat, though once contained, the knights' concern with local interests prevented rollback of Islam for some time. While not egalitarian, security in this era truly was co-produced by all the Estates, from serfs to lords to the king, each with certain responsibilities and corresponding guarantees and/or rights (Morris 2014, 135). This new organization enabled the gradual consolidation of divine-right monarchies, but as with the old empires the dominance of one group in the use of violence, situated in the middle of the hierarchy, also limited the extent to which the political units could expand, with 500 plus such entities spread across Europe by 1500 (Tilly 1975). The oligopolistic structure did, however, allow the elites to pry some rights from the nascent "states," exemplified in the Magna Carta. This limited-scope openness put in writing for the first time in the West that control of violence, and participation in violence, entitled one to other rights, but that these entailed corresponding responsibilities, including to a higher political authority.

Larger, more complex political units came only with a new rise of the infantry as a dominant force, starting with the Swiss pikemen of the twelfth century following the Battle of Legnano (1176). This trend toward weapons that levelled the playing field between experts and novices was furthered with the addition of projectile weapons, such as the longbow and the easier to use crossbow, a weapon so threatening to status quo social powers it was even banned in many circumstances. These developments led to the emergence of a pre-modern form of combined arms battle, requiring more cooperation (or at least more sustainable exploitation) across the Estates than had previously existed. Yet both the use of infantry and combined arms required social innovation of the nature discussed above. Just like in ancient Greece, the maximum tactical effectiveness of the new infantry required egalitarianism; the Swiss of the Middle Ages had the most dis-unified command structure in Europe, yet often prevailed on the battlefield (Leonhard 1998, 195). Subsequently, just like before, this military necessity on the field was gradually reflected in social and political ideas, and eventually more democratic state structures.

Yet while the Swiss, and later the Dutch and even monarchical Sweden, could offer forms of democracy in exchange for military service, and excelled militarily as a result, status quo powers unwilling to alter their domestic institutions had to search for more creative methods to spark participation. The first solution was the establishment of divine-right monarchy coalitions, bringing together especially the conservative peasants and nobles. In these arrangements the divine acted as the open element, allowing access to the more important heavenly kingdom while keeping the earthly kingdom closed to most people. These coalitions were made scalable by the printing press and the resulting spread of new information from the 1450s onward, leading to the Protestant Reformation and then religious wars around which larger states were constructed. Openness in information – what we now call transparency – can thus be subverted in a manner that allows the overall system to remain closed. In such contexts information is mere propaganda for totalizing, exclusive ideas (i.e. ideologies), which means it lacks and suppresses variation. As such, the ideas prevented effective mobilization and use of the diffuse weapons available at that time. Yet because they viewed the end as an issue of survival – here even of the soul – the wars dragged on with no winner.

The return of peace to Europe in 1648 saw the emergence of a new system of absolutism and idea of what constituted a community. Rulers of the new political, rather than religious, units attempted to centralize control in their own hands. This included new restrictions on information and attempts to capture the open innovation in warfare seen with private military entrepreneurs during the Thirty Years' War (1618–1648). The use of mercenary armies, where cost and control was always an issue, gradually receded. Instead, states adopted the organizational psychology techniques developed in the Netherlands and refined in Prussia, methods which could turn the "scum of the earth," the poor and disenfranchised, into the "last argument of kings" (*ultimo ratio regum*) (former from Duke of Wellington quoted in Stanhope 1886, 14). While these practices led most of the population to be free of military service, contributing to security only through a "passive, taxpaying role" (McNeill 1982, 161), military development meant this cost rose beyond what peasants could pay, while turning to the lords would see a return of unwanted influence over the monarch. Thus, many rulers gradually, though inconsistently, opened the system to burgeoning market forces, allowing entrepreneurship and a new class to emerge. For some states these new organizational forms became extensions of the administration itself, especially in colonial areas, a pre-modern form of outsourcing, or what are called public-private partnerships. The (British) East India Company and its Dutch competitor, equipped even with their own instruments of violence (i.e. armies), exemplify such arrangements. This distributed mandate to use violence was even more open on the high seas given the difficulty in controlling such common spaces, a problem we face today in cyberspace. Here, state capability gaps were supplemented with privateers – pirates given a visage of respectability through legal means (so-called Letters of Marque and Reprisal). In time there were further openings to the lesser nobility and even different classes, not only of certain military occupations – especially the more technical, such as artillery – but also government ones, seen first in the open bureaucracy of Louis XIV (reign 1638–1715), which recruited personnel from beyond the traditional elite classes. Thus, absolutism became less absolute over time. While there was wide variation and relapses, those rulers who became most successful did so primarily by opening the system, diffusing power throughout it and finding creative ways to capture this power through contracts (social or market), thereby weakening the relative power of any challengers to the crown. Granting power to others can increase one's own power.

Thus, the birth of the state in the Peace of Westphalia, its triumph over the church, allowed innovation and enlightenment to flourish even within a centralized state and mostly monopolized security system. Yet this delicate balancing act was difficult to maintain, with any setback threatening social unrest by newly empowered, or disempowered yet still important, actors. As technological change began to build on itself and accelerate, so did social change, both designed by the state to increase its power and as an unintended implication of technology, war, and new state policies. With the mass production of cheap guns the old powers faced a new threat of democratized violence leading to actual political democracy. This technology (guns) was then joined by new ideas of how society and politics should be organized, ideas of right and openness, of taxation and representation. On these principles thirteen British colonies in the Americas revolted in 1776, and in 1791 the close linking of rights – especially openness – and arms – egalitarianly distributed – was expressed in constitutional form by the American First and Second Amendments, respectively. Only five years later, guns and rights would sweep away the old social contracts of Europe.

The French Revolution (1796 onward), with its *levée en masse* that armed and organized the people through the latest innovations and ideas – guns, cartography, and the rights of man – was the breakthrough moment of what we now consider the modern nation-state. As we saw in the introduction, though, this process was not easy, as attested to by the chaos of those decades. The chaos allowed also the second face of popular empowerment to show itself, in the tyranny of the Jacobins and ultimately Napoleon. While the latter did not serve the cause of the revolution, the Empire finally allowed the elements to be put together into a highly capable military means, even if the final ends were to serve the ego of one man. Old conservative monarchies that did not adopt the new technology, organization, and social mobilization were catastrophically defeated, exemplified by the disintegration of the Prussian army at Jena-Auerstadt in 1806. Prussia then came to exemplify how threat and crisis inspire innovation, and by 1813 it had cast aside its hesitance and mobilized its people in so-called insurrection warfare (full history in Clark 2007).

Yet fear of the forces unleashed by the events of 1796–1815 led to reaction and conservatism thereafter. Elite contracts defended the status quo, domestically and internationally, allowing it to persist in many ways until WWI despite the increasing internal contradictions. Old social structures and old doctrines were combined in the 1850s with new and deadlier technologies. Yet simultaneously modern economic development and its needs (for labour and consumers) contributed also to a new openness – facilitated by cheap paper, photography, telegraphy, and even education policies (and thus literacy) – that led information and new ideas to be more rapidly and widely disseminated (related short comment in Leonhard 1998, 16). Some states, especially those who suffered most in recent decades like Prussia, learned how to manipulate these new tools and shifted their tactics and doctrine early to ensure wars were short enough not to become blood baths (e.g. the Wars of German Unification). Other states instead saw tragedy, from the Crimean War to the US Civil War. Yet tragedy and trauma drove states that were open to learning, no matter the source and vested interests, to pursue reforms that enabled their longer-term competitive advantage. This is best shown in the case of the United Kingdom (UK), where uncensored media coverage of the Crimea campaign brought down the government and sounded the death knell of the British system of aristocratic management and the rise of middle-class civilian management in many new areas of government. This allowed for increased openness under Prime Minister William Ewart Gladstone and his interregnum and final successors, permitting the UK to maintain its smooth self-reinforcing and self-correcting exchange between technology, politics, demographics, citizenry, taxes, and the market (McNeill 1982, especially 269–70, 277). Openness facilitated an adaptability that was more consistent (than closed authoritarianism) with the rapidly changing world and the contemporary needs of technology and innovation. In turn the UK was able to maintain an internally consistent system and better align its military means with legitimate, and attainable, political ends.

In military technology, the so-called Cabinet Wars of the nineteenth century saw the start of the slow rise of indirect fire, first artillery to be followed later by missiles, as the dominant weapon. Yet there was little doctrinal/tactical innovation; thus, massed forces became even more necessary if they were to survive the massed firepower of the new weapons (Moran 2009, 32). Development in communication and transport technology obliged this need, naturally with governments' support, making control of larger military formations possible. Yet there were still limitations to this control. Unfortunately for the generals, for the possibilities of mass mobilization and new small arms to be fully realized, tactical changes were required which placed more independence and trust on small groups and even individuals (Horowitz 2010,

214). Such trust from the state was possible only by giving soldiers a reason to fight (beyond fear of execution for desertion), a reason for them to trust the state's sending them off to die.[7] To mobilize such mass participation typically would require an opening of the socio-political structures, but many states were unwilling to do so. Thus, nationalism was stoked via the new media as the only method of engaging participation, and channelling the discontent of the socially dislocated, while keeping the power structures closed. Nonetheless, the experiences of egalitarianism during military service, which to the contemporary citizen may seem meagre but at the time were revolutionary, slowly fed back into civilian political life. Even in one of the most absolutist of states, Prussia, veterans' associations became a "vehicle of participation" that were "plebeian and egalitarian" (Clark 2007, 602). States struggled constantly to contain these forces and channel them externally through little wars, colonialism, migration, and so on.

As WWI loomed, even innovation started to close off as militaries fearful that technology would spread to their enemies opted for their own, typically inferior, solutions and technologies (McNeill 1982, passim, for an example 297–98). The UK even sought to quash certain naval innovations they saw as threatening to the Royal Navy, which was the basis of their power. Yet with the first era of globalization under way these efforts simply drove innovation elsewhere. In other states, exemplified by post–Dreyfus Affair France, it was not only the security elite that closed themselves off to the outside, but also a society that withdrew from security due to their exclusion and mistrust. Without popular support, the military was starved of resources and could not deploy the means needed to keep the French military internationally competitive (Colaresi 2014; May 2000; Posen 1984). With innovation stagnating and closed societies with no economic or political outlets increasingly frustrated, once the colonial frontier closed it was only a matter of time before the people of Europe were unleashed to break the competitive stasis in the Great War (WWI).

Yet with the end of the "war to end all wars," peace may have returned for a time internationally, but not domestically. Distrust of governments, officers, and even neighbours led militaries to disintegrate, revolutions to burn, and *Freikorps* to roam the streets. Participation had been opened to the people, but the ideas and organization to structure their roles only slowly reconsolidated. The political experiments of the inter-war period that sought to channel the people's will led directly to totalitarianism, which in turn harnessed the people's new technologically enhanced ability for total war. Simultaneously, democratic states entered a period of doubt compared to their "triumph of the will" adversaries. Yet this self-doubt allowed (temporary) failure to lead to learning, adaptation, and eventual victory (RFE/RL 2015c; see also Roberts

2017 [not released as of this writing]). The victory was not without implications though; the required mobilizations were so extensive that military influence would be pervasive in the decades to come. The end of WWII, using atomic bombs on Hiroshima and Nagasaki, solidified the dominance of a qualitatively new form of elite-controlled indirect fire.

INTO THE MODERN AGE: CLOSED SECURITY IN AN OPEN WORLD

The success of the Manhattan Project in developing atomic weapons led it in many ways to become the new model for innovation (Colaresi 2014, 58–62; McNeill 1982, 359; Lipschutz 2000 22–23; also Micklethwait and Woolridge 2014, 192–93). Compared to the more free-wheeling, open innovation of the mid-1800s, solutions to security problems were increasingly developed from the top down through the creation of massive rationalized bureaucracies.[8] Secrecy and hierarchy were core principles of this model, required to develop and deploy the technological ends for security (on secrecy in the Manhattan Project, see Colaresi 2014, 35). While the monopoly the state once sought (circa 1900 onward) over military technology became less viable after 1945, the so-called "G.I./Greatest Generation" carried the military organizational model into the business world following their post-WWII demobilization, giving rise to an oligopolistic military-industrial complex, a structure later seen also in an intelligence-industrial complex (Bean 2011, 8; Mark Phythian in Johnson 2014, 807; Oreskes and Krige 2014, 432).

While many now like to criticize this model, and we will do the same in the next chapter, one must also consider that this model of security innovation and provision came about in a particular context. This structure had developed in an era of structured inter-state competition that saw global wars and then a long Cold War. Massive inputs were needed for weapons development and their global deployment. Because of the scale of inputs and the scale of (potential) war, efficiency mattered, in use of resources for production and, as a result, in targeting (to waste less resources on a given target), resulting in an almost obsessive search for increased precision (Leonhard 1998, 25–27). Likewise, the increased scale and scope of (potential) war and the fog this entailed meant a need for centralized control to direct these resources. To ensure this before the advent of modern communications, we developed fractal bureaucratic structures and procedures, a uniformity of elements that ensured continuity in conditions of uncertainty even if communications broke down. The system designed was meant to give war a measure of predictability, and everything from weapons procured to organizational structures and tactics adopted were chosen to ensure this. Thus, the system became self-perpetuating; technological development over time began to increasingly reflect the command principles inherent in contemporary militaries because this was the product demanded by the buyer (the military).

While mass conscription and the era of nationalism introduced a social contract predicated on participation in security, the new weapons of the Cold War required fewer soldiers and benefited from training and retaining these soldiers. These new weapons eventually put previously unimaginable firepower in the hands of what contemporary observers have called the "strategic corporal," the low-ranked soldier with capabilities that could have global implications (on early trend, see McNeill 1982, 381). Thus, once the mass mobilization of the World Wars and early Cold War gave way, we witnessed the gradual re-professionalization of security forces, their withdrawal into a more distinct group or class (Huntington 1957; Zirker, Danopoulos, and Simpson 2008; on this also in the intelligence sector, see Omand 2010, 252). Militaries become isolated from society, and the participation of society was reduced again to a taxpaying role; when cannon fodder was needed it was, as in the Duke of Wellington's day (1769–1852), the "scum" – the "Colored" or the Kazakh – that was sent to the jungles or mountains (Duke of Wellington in Stanhope 1886, 14). While most established democracies (unlike their less established counterparts) thus far have not become controlled by the new militaries, their domination of certain policy domains was re-enforced. The citizen is not expected to buy war bonds, plant victory gardens, or ultimately sign up for military service, but the experts and officers insist upon free rein in their trade.

Society was happy to oblige, for while new technology had transformed the military, it transformed society to an equal or greater extent. Individualism, long a part of Western philosophies, rose as the excess/reserve industrial capacity following WWII demobilization was diverted to consumerism (Berggruen and Gardels 2013). As social bonds to older institutions broke down (a phenomena of complex origins), self-efficacy and self-actualization was sought less as civil servant or soldier, but by accrual of wealth through structured competition in the market. There was a peculiar period of extended security at home and images of insecurity abroad delivered through the new medium of television, primarily showing national interventions in foreign lands. Thus, there was a feeling that participation in security was neither needed, on a community-national level, nor desirable on a personal survival level. While some of the "Greatest generation" derided the young at this time as a narcissistic "Me generation," the trends in self-help/improvement, self-made individuals, and pride in individuality had positive aspects. Everything from computers to punk rock emerged from private garages. These innovations spread to transform even more persons into individuals and empower them, playing a role even in undermining authoritarianism.

Yet as the 1970s turned to the 1980s both sides of the Iron Curtain recognized that a Revolution in Military Affairs (RMA) was under way, one that would see "the triumph of silicon over steel" (John Pike in Slayton 2013, 202).[9] This RMA led to a situation where the security sector, indeed government as a whole, needed the expertise of society again. The newest technologies of war and security necessitate the "interpenetration" of the security sector by "the technically proficient elites of civil society" (McNeill 1982: 379; for underlying convergence theory, see Janowitz 1960). As time has progressed the skill shortage in the security sector has only worsened, directly affecting both the industrial side and the military-security side of the complex. Volunteer militaries face increasing difficulty attracting individuals qualified for modern technological warfare when more lucrative private sector opportunities exist, while the intelligence agencies' culture (and indeed that of the entire government) is diametrically opposed to the libertarian hacktivist culture held by much of the current technological elite (Singer and Friedman 2014, 237, also 240 on corporate culture). The big technology firms meanwhile eschew defence contracts and cooperation as "not a market that's worth it to them," leaving many defence contracts to be one-bidder affairs amongst established firms (Ben FitzGerald in Brannen 2015).

The most recent wave of technological development, the information age that evolved out of computers of the RMA, has, we contend, begun to usher in a new era, one in which even "interpenetration" of the military-industrial complex is no longer enough but which requires full integration of civilian-military-industrial capabilities if it is to maximize the technological potential available and be able to address contemporary threats. The individual so reified by the liberal market and state as a consumer, a taxpayer, and the key object of security has been empowered by technology, for better or worse (Cronin 2006, 81, 86; Hammes 2006, 190–206; Horowitz 2010, 214). On the one hand, it has empowered individuals with capabilities previously only states possessed; the suicide bomber, the "anonymous" hacker, or the lone gunman really can change the world (idea derived from Lacy 2014, 137; closely related, see Gat 2006, 644, and Hammes 2006, 196). As individuals become technologically empowered, interacting with (perhaps even further driving) the social dislocation inherent in the economy's transition to a new epoch, threats multiply until they number all seven or eight billion "others" populating the world (Lipschutz 2000; Tinder 1964). On the other hand, an innovative state could capture this egalitarian weapon system, the participatory potential of the Net, to derive integrative and selective solutions to modern security challenges. This modern context will be examined in more depth in Chapter 3, while what our response to this context should be will form the remainder of this book.

PATTERNS IN OPENNESS AND PARTICIPATION

Over history, the competition of genes, individuals, families, and tribes was transferred to the larger social structures that were constructed as the benefits of cooperation accrued and became almost autocatalytic. As cooperation enabled differentiation and specialization, innovation became increasingly possible and rapid, enabling new and complex forms of competition that further drove groups to innovate. Yet new innovations entail risk: they may hold the promise of greater security against competitors or nature, but they can also spark domestic and international instability. Adoption of a new technology, and progress in general, entails change: change of socio-political structures and organizations, of ideas and ways of doing things, all which must support or at least be compatible with the innovation (specifically Bousquet 2009, 19; Slayton 2013, 216; less directly, Leonhard 1998, 6–7; Lieber 2005, 153). States must thus balance the risks of change and the benefits of progress. History shows us these risks and benefits and can help guide how to structure them to ensure domestic peace and international security.

ADAPTATION AND ADOPTION: INNOVATION IN OPEN AND CLOSED SECURITY

Each era responds to the environment and threats created by the technologies, and associated structures and ideas, of the previous era. Yet history is not linear, structures do not go from less to more organized forms, from militias to mercenaries to conscripts to professional forces in an endless march of some objectively measurable "progress." Rather, structures shift between different means and ways of security based on the technology, threats, and needs at a given time and changes in these as innovation (technology, organizational, or ideational) alters the available possibilities. The nature of this shifting means that over the longer term we see eras that alternate between those in which violence is monopolized and those in which it is more distributed. This is illustrated broadly in Figure 2.1: empire gives way to anarchy, conservatism to revolution, intensive production to extensive production (e.g. Morris 2014, 93 and 130–34). This pattern results from the nature of strategic competition and innovation, as challengers purposively

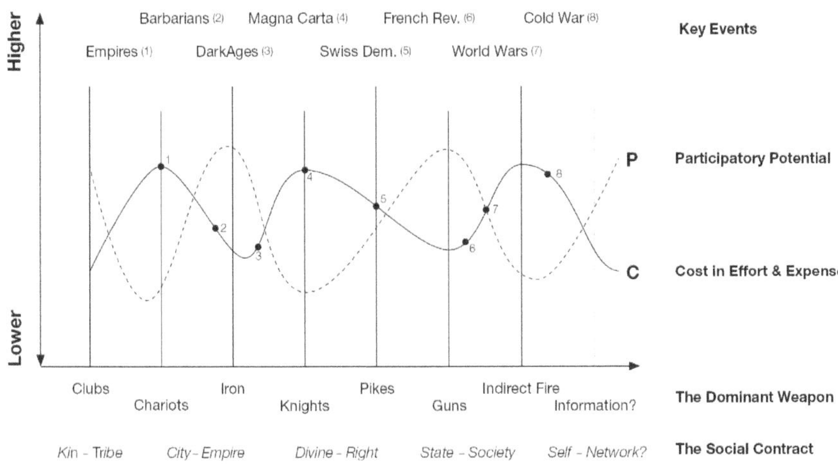

Figure 2.1. Illustrative Timeline of Historical Patterns of Security Innovation

seeking to shift to the opposite source of power as that which the dominant powers possess and in which they cannot hope to compete (on such "countervailing" shifts, see Robert H. Scales Jr. in Gray 2002, 272; also Hammes 2006, 12, with reference to Toffler and Toffler 1993). As status quo powers tend over time to turn to monopolized security,[10] freeing their populations to enjoy the fruits of the peace that the status quo state's hegemonic power enforces, these late periods of hegemonic stability tend to produce population growth and innovation, which diffuses power more broadly. Challengers are thus empowered, eventually becoming status quo powers themselves, and thus the pattern repeats.

However, while simplification is an important step in understanding, we must not oversimplify. There were also significant even if less epoch-changing shifts within these grand movements: loosely controlled roving wars of attrition (seventeenth century) gave way to limited force-on-force clashes of small professional forces (eighteenth-century *Kabinettskriege*, or Cabinet Wars), which then gave way to the mass revolutionary war of the Napoleonic era, then to limited wars of the nineteenth century, then to total war again in the twentieth century, which was followed by the re-emergence of professional, highly controlled, forces.[11] These interspersed reversals typically represent the status quo's fight back, fear of some newly unleashed innovation and an attempt to control the character of war. They purposely choose not to adopt the most powerful security system, counter to some theories' assumption that states (or older political units, whether clans or caliphates) are security-maximizing actors. This is because security has other concerns than international competitors; it must consider domestic cooperation. Embracing a new technology requires, and further creates, social and political innovation and even transformation, up to the rewriting of the social contracts. Not all states are equally able, or willing, to embrace such change. Adoption entails costs beyond those for procurement and implementation, costs to existing power structures and vested interests.

For instance, the use of the massed forces to mobilize the diffuse power our current era is begetting requires social innovation to get people to participate. Firstly, making any new weapon system requires socio-economic reordering, not only to make the product but to free the labour to be conscripted (or otherwise recruited into service) and create the ideas that limit evasion, whether due to more lucrative options or for personal safety. Secondly, maximizing the potential of emancipatory weapons tends to require loosening spans of control to allow greater tactical independence for individuals and small groups in combat. To enable such loosened control, internal military organizational and doctrinal innovation are needed, but such reforms not only encounter resistance by existing security actors but have implications in society afterwards that contribute to demands for new forms of political participation. Thus, domestic power issues, the need to ensure cooperation within the in-group (elites) by keeping relations within the state stable, can trump concerns about power vis-à-vis external competitors if the threat is judged, accurately or not, to be low enough.

Nonetheless, given the highly competitive international environment, a new security/weapon system that is perceived to offer a competitive advantage will be adopted by some actor in the international system. Subsequently, other actors must either adopt (the innovation), adapt (by developing a counter-innovation), or face a possible power transition in favour of their competitors and/or enemies. Because of these challenges to adoption, true paradigm-shifting innovation is often seen in *march* states (on the border of a regional state system/"security complex"), revisionist powers, or states that have experienced a crisis that discredited old ways and left them with little to lose (Omand 2010, 310; McNeill 1982; Lipschutz 2000, 54). In the first two cases threat drives adoption of innovative solutions; in the latter case failure induces a willingness to learn and innovate. In both cases risks are accepted given the undesirable nature of the way things are. On the other end of the spectrum, status quo states and actors – the rich and powerful – have high loss aversion and low risk tolerance. They thus innovate at the margins in a way that sustains the basis of their current power. However, while they may be able to close off their security sectors, they cannot shield their entire socio-economic sector from the changes technological innovation brings, and this will in turn filter into the military ranks, leading to discord between the old guard and "Young Turks." The resulting imbalances between social, political, and military ideas; organization; and technology can lead in time to revolution and/or military weakness and defeat. However, they can also be the condition that sparks reforms if society is allowed to influence the means of security, if the state opens up and soldiers are allowed to listen and innovate.

ENABLING PARTICIPATION: TECHNOLOGY AND ITS LIMITS

As we have seen, the character of technology, especially of the dominant weapons system, of a given era has a significant influence on the extent to which society can participate in security. Some technologies enable mass participation because they are cheap, relatively easy to learn and use, and empower individuals. These technologies diffuse power, and if a state wants to remain powerful, it must accept diffuse control of the means to security. Other technologies are expensive, difficult to organize, and hard to use. They require experts to both develop and deploy, and thus enable the emergence of security-military elites and military-industrial oligarchies. Moreover, as these technologies inevitably diffuse, albeit at variable rates, the problems and threats we face come to reflect the structure of the technology: empowering technology enables unstructured, diffuse, and networked threats; expert technologies enable structured threats, such as states. Thus, while technology is a solution to security problems, it also creates the problems and threats we face.

Yet history raises other red flags about technological solutionism as a way to address security threats. While a state must keep up in the technology race, the competition is in many ways subject to the so-called and (too) often cited Red Queen Effect: no matter how fast they run, they stay in the same place. As states compete and technology diffuses, any innovation that gives a temporary edge quickly disappears as other states either match the innovation or develop technological countermeasures: missiles giving birth to anti-missile systems, leading to evasive missiles to avoid these, and so on. With globalization spreading technology and competition, this process seems even to be accelerating. Thus, while many accuse the military and state of preparing and planning for the last war, the technological race may in the end negate many or even all our technological advances. Thus, the next war may indeed resemble the last one, or following our cyclical logic, the one before last.

Rather, what seems to give a state an edge is organizational solutions that enable humans to use technology to its greatest potential, even if that technology is a generation behind competitors, or that use the enemy's technology against them (for direct agreement, see Horowitz 2010, 2, 5–8). Prussia did not become the dominant land power in Europe because it had a technological edge. Even when for the briefest of moments it had a tech lead, only proper organization allowed them to realize the advantage that edge offered before it inevitably, often rapidly disappeared. Nor did the Third Reich conquer so much of Europe because of its often vaunted, but less often deployed, super weapons; indeed it was technologically behind in many critical areas for much of the war. Rather, victory was attained on the basis of organizational innovation, often extending from the tactical to the strategic to even the re-organization of social institutions. Their strategic failure in the medium term was rooted in not allowing innovation to extend to political institutions (Gray 2002, 276). Other, more liberal states were more successful at sustainable and internally consistent organizational solutions, solutions derived by ideas and information.

MOBILIZING PARTICIPATION: INFORMATION AND IDEAS

We saw in the above review of history also the appearance of the openness much sought after today (similar, albeit briefer, histories in Arquilla 2007; Leonhard 1998, 15–17 [with same emphasis of importance]). Yet when it appears, we see also the purpose openness historically serves: to mobilize – or demobilize – the action and participation which is ultimately necessary for security. The security/weapons technology available may *enable* participation by given groups, but it is not a sufficient condition to realize it. The state has to *mobilize* that participation, which it does through the release of information, spreading ideas and facilitating the creation of new organizations. New tools and techniques were used to spread not only mass information, but also to enable the accumulation and storage of information over time, facilitating the creation of knowledge that feeds into technological innovation and policy formulation. Conversely, states could instead seek to demobilize participation by restricting information, though also the well-timed repeated release of fear-inducing information – which does not contribute to knowledge, wisdom, or foresight – can demobilize and contribute to increased reliance on the government and security experts (Breakwell 2014, 137–38; see Chapter 6).

While one could specify them further, the first major such openness technologies were the development of language in pre-history, writing in early history, and then papyrus and other portable mediums. In the beginning of history the state's information release revolved around repeating and interpreting founding myths (religion) and then engaging in its own myth creation. These myths formed the basis of the primary non-familial bonding mechanisms, the source of trust which allowed the group to function and survive, early forms of what eventually would become social contracts. While one may then see a gap of several millennia until the next technology, this period saw the development and spread of intangible technologies, the knowledge of communication processes, management of expectations (i.e. law), rhetoric, and debate. These served to stabilize internal elite cooperation and control the population.

In modern history we saw the printing press (associated with the Reformation and religious war fought with new muskets), the pamphlet (French Revolution), the broadsheets (yellow journalism and "splendid little wars"), the radio (WWI and WWII), and television (Cold War) – and most recently the Internet. Such tools of openness allowed mobilization to maximize the dominant weapons system's potential, while minimizing the revolutionary risk as long as alternative information was not available (especially information that better matched experienced reality). Over time the tools of information and openness were increasingly used to enable the social reorganization that innovation, and resulting new military doctrines and tactics, required. These military ideas could not be kept out of the social and political realms though, and the feedback often introduced new ideas into society that complicated the state's plans.

Yet information technologies also led more open democratic countries to allow unprecedented civilian penetration of the military and security sector and policy. Often, such openness followed military fiascos, with its purpose being not out of principle but to spark innovation and mobilization by proving information and opportunities for participation. What the state sacrificed in terms of power over its citizens was compensated for by increased overall power over external circumstances, whether natural or other states. However, over time the state was increasingly less able to control these technologies, and sources of information began to multiply (Borer 2007, 238; also Robinson 2007 on how this began even before the Internet with cassettes, printers, etc.). As we will see in Chapter 3, information technologies have come so far that they are no longer just a tool of war mobilization and propaganda, or a part of security and military organization enabling their operations, but an entire front in itself that equals and occasionally exceeds traditional fronts in importance.

ORGANIZING PARTICIPATION: THE SOCIAL CONTRACT

Another important observation emerging from the discussion is that the social contract is not just a concept of interest only to political theorists, but a structure that has important implications for the actual ability to provide security.

Early institutions for promoting social-state trust and the more elaborate social contracts that emerged determined where legitimate knowledge and thus authority lay, and thus the necessary flow of information. Information in turn determined the exchange and flow of resources and the extent and forms of participation, the actions to be taken and who had to take them. All of this was designed, in theory, to reinforce the power and trust in the main governmental institution and social contract, creating a circular feedback cycle. Also, in practice, this would typically work, providing stability and security, but only so long as where information and knowledge truly lay did not change. If it did, then reality and expectations would diverge and the state-society would enter crisis until it reformed or disappeared.

The social contract calling for loyalty in exchange for security has varied over time, as has the social structure and political relations that resulted. We can even give these names, as one can see in Figure 2.1. While in pre-history small group dynamics and full participation dominated, in early history goods in-kind or taxes sufficed, with these enabling the provisioning of specialists in violence to provide security. Over time though, as new technologies made security increasingly complex, the state required more participation, from basic military service to total war effort by all of society. In exchange the state was forced to grant more rights, such as property, the franchise, and other liberties. When the state did not grant new rights, but changes in where power and knowledge lay had altered where authority properly should be, then the people forcibly demanded new rights. Thus, we progressed through reform or revolution to ever more complex exchanges that built shared communities of fate: modern nation-states.

Though it simplifies, in a way the rise of the mass infantry and its technological and tactical needs brought about democracy, but that era is now over. In recent decades, technology has become for soldiers the "dead labour" of Marx's proletariat. Smaller teams with the aid of expensive advanced machines can now bring more firepower to bear than ever before. The resulting specialization resulted in a withdrawal of the citizen to the traditional limited participatory role: taxes. While democracy in principle could mitigate this disconnect, the needs were so technical and the secrets so sensitive that the public and often even their elected representatives were mostly removed from the debate and even oversight (Colaresi 2014, 33–34). Yet blame falls not only on the state and military; it was not only the purposive exclusion of citizens, but also their voluntary withdrawal, the reappearance of a popular apathy that often emerges during eras of affluence and when (monopolized) security is seemingly taken care of "in the background." Just as participation changes people, so does lack of participation (more in Chapter 3).

CONCLUSION

These observations and lessons highlight several important aspects of innovation in security. Specifically, security requires actively understanding threats and how they relate to our own existing security arrangements, and how they can be met by learning through information, failure, and diversity, which will give us the foresight to change when needed, to become adaptable in meeting our needs. An understanding of the actual security environment, both the threats that exist and the capabilities that we have as well as their distribution, is critical to successful transformations to new systems. While trying new things – change and transformation – entails risk, this risk must be considered in light of the external changes in the world. Sometimes risk taking is essential for progress, sometimes for survival. The key to knowing whether we need to take a risk and try something new is to first consider the nature of the change we are seeing: where is power shifting and to what extent; is the change linear, logarithmic, or a radical disjunction? The key to recognizing change, and then changing yourself, as well as learning and understanding the world and our problems, is to maximize sources of information, the number of contributors to knowledge, and the number of participants in providing solutions, whether directly or in supporting roles. Yet in doing all this, in perfecting our means to security, one should never lose sight of the ends; the way we make our security will determine the kind of state and society we live in – whether it is sustainable in the longer term, and tolerable in the near term.

The technologies we developed, the way they transformed our armies and ways of war, and the new forms of emancipation they engendered with new state-society social contracts have culminated today in "the replacement of the sovereign state by the sovereign individuals as the subject of world politics" (Lipschutz 2000, 3; related shift in Omand 2010, 309; see also Félix Guattari in Lacy 2014, 45). Simultaneously, they have engendered new forms of diffuse, unstructured threats that match and maximize the technology we created, leading to a world in which "the future might just belong to the raiders" rather than nation-states (Pomerantsev 2014). How the state can recapture the individualist society it both intentionally and inadvertently fostered, mobilize it to counter the threats that the government and its security apparatuses cannot tackle alone, is a central dilemma facing the state today (Cronin 2006, 86–87). Chapter 3 will turn to an examination of the reasons for the contemporary state's (real and perceived) inability to protect itself and its subjects, or to pursue reforms that could enable security. This will ensure that the solution developed in later chapters properly uses historical lessons to leverage current capabilities in a way that matches the characteristics of the contemporary context and problems.

NOTES

1. We have taken some poetic licence here; the process of women's liberation began before WWII. The fact it goes back further does not undermine our argument and in fact supports our evolutionary approach.

2. How they are corrected varies based on what is being examined and, naturally, the theory being proposed.

3. North, Wallis, and Weingast (2013, xviii–xix) take a similar approach in their own study of social order, saying, "We are not writing a history of the world. Some specialist in the times and places we study will argue that we have lifted these examples out of context, and we have. However, our intention is to put these examples in a new context."

4. The original language version (in Dutch) appeared earlier (1938).

5. We admit that the causal order of agriculture preceding religion has recently been complicated by the discovery of the ruins at Göbekli Tepe (Turkey). History is – to repeat – complex.

6. Conscription in the fully developed modern sense of universal active service was seen first in Han dynasty China (200 B.C.–220 A.D.) (Gat 2006, 362).

7. Trust of course existed in previous socio-political arrangements. However, the social upheavals and resulting social dislocation of the early modern/industrial era meant many traditional forms of trust and resulting willingness to die for a group were less viable (e.g. Gat 2006, 541).

8. The roots of command invention/innovation do go back further, but it reached its pinnacle and dominance over other forms of innovation only around WWII.

9. The 1980s RMA in turn led to a whole field of literature, identifying numerous RMAs through history, including some we identify in Figure 2.1. However, we eschew the RMA terminology, following especially Gray's (2002) more evolutionary (versus revolutionary) view of these developments; all emerged over time until the right conditions came together for full manifestation, and all are similar in underlying character to some previous "RMAs."

10. Very briefly and oversimply: Open systems/eras create the very tools that invite monopolization. The innovation process itself leads to the gradual consolidation of a new elite (the innovators), who as they organize tend toward oligarchy (Michels [1911] 1915), forming the basis of a new class to use the tools for the monopolization of violence.

11. As we will discuss, because we cannot know until later whether the shift we are seeing is macro or micro, security institutions should take evolutionary approaches to change and maintain mixed – or hybrid – security systems.

Chapter Three

The Gap between the Contemporary Strategic Context and Security System

Before turning to the present, let us continue briefly with history, returning to a couple of our favourite examples from the last chapters. Since especially the time of Frederick the Great (reign 1740–1786) Prussia had been a rising military power in continental Europe. Following his death, the military reforms he implemented became institutionalized, even idolized: scripture handed down from the man who had brought them greatness. Changing the structures, deviating from the proscribed tactics, was sacrilege. Steadfast commitment to the tools and tactics of Frederick's age continued, helping maintain a domestic status quo, even while the international status quo was changing. The revolutionary period (1789 to circa 1799) and subsequent empire (1804–1815) in France saw that country adopt new technologies, organizations, and ideas which contrasted dramatically with the conservatism in Prussia. The gap between Prussian capabilities and the new strategic situation embodied in the French military led the Prussian military to catastrophic defeat and total disintegration at Jena-Auerstedt in 1806. Yet this was not the end of Prussia, and through failure and crisis the state learned new lessons and adapted, in time rising to be arguably the dominant power in continental Europe.

Prussia's conservatism was not unique. Military innovation entails several risks. Firstly, it can threaten actual military capabilities, as the outcome of any new combination of technology, organization, and ideas is not certain. Powerful states and their military classes thus often hesitate to change, given especially that the military means and strategic ways they currently possess and use are what got them to the top of the international pecking order in the first place. Yet, secondly, even in cases where the military recognizes new capabilities are needed, the political level often kills off any innovative reforms given possible domestic implications. This in turn also ensures the careers of officers clamouring for reform go no further. Thus, the cost of not innovating must be sufficiently high or one's current situation sufficiently intolerable to overcome the status quo biases and preferences for certainty that exist on both the personal and institutional levels. Revolutionary France faced the threat of the combined armies of the European monarchies, even while the domestic status quo had been wiped away along with any certainty about what came next. Thus, they had little to lose by experimenting with new military means and ways. Yet it is rare for a relatively powerful status quo country to recognize in advance that they have a significant capability gap vis-à-vis a threat. The first step to acting in a crisis, whether we speak of individuals or institutions, is to recognize there is a crisis, yet we are often incapable of such recognition until after tragedy. Historically, only following such thorough discrediting of the old ways of doing things were the old regimes, if they survived at all, open to more radical solutions (some of these ideas were drawn from Horowitz 2010, 28, 41; Lipschutz 2000, 54; McNeill 1982; Omand 2010, 310; Posen 1984, 233, 239–40).

A key question then is how can we know whether we are now in a crisis, one requiring risky innovation with possibly revolutionary – in a socio-political sense – implications? Objectively speaking, Steven Pinker (2011), amongst many others, argues that there has been a global decline in violence of almost every form – from crime to war – and at every level – from the family to the state. Yet equally notable scholars such as John Gray (2015) and Nassim Taleb (2015) argue the reverse, and certainly the discourse of insecurity is pervasive, so much so as to be one of the core interests of an entire academic branch of security studies (see also empirical work of Fazal 2014). Many contemporary citizens and even their leaders feel insecure, perhaps best exemplified by the title of David Rothkopf's (2014) book *National Insecurity: American Leadership in an Age of Fear*. This perceived insecurity and the state's apparent inability to do anything about it has in turn contributed its part to what has been called a "crisis of representative democracy." Because this crisis is one not only of actual shortcomings in our capabilities but also of the psyche (both to be examined shortly) it has the potential to be existential in nature, as we see in the ceaseless stream of predictions of the decline, fall, collapse, or end of US power, the EU, democracy, capitalism, and other social institutions that constitute our (though primarily Western) civilization.[1]

The current perceived, subjective crisis began with an objective strategic victory, the triumph of the liberal democratic West over the Soviet-led East. States have long known the advantage of having a clearly identifiable threat or enemy "other" (original idea from Georg Wilhelm Friedrich Hegel; in politics, see Said 1978; Lipschutz 2000, 33, 45). As C. P. Cavafy ([1904] 1975) put it in his famous poem, barbarians at the gate are "a kind of solution."[2] An identifiable enemy gives a state's institutions direction by acting as a clear problem for which they can design solutions. The threat such an enemy poses can help to unify the citizenry, offsetting the fragmentation and dislocation inherent in dynamically evolving and progressing groups. The end of the Cold War brought an end to one such clear and unifying threat and the West's certainty about what must be done, and even how the world would likely end (i.e. with nuclear Armageddon). Russia experienced a similar end to certainty, one with even more severe implications for their state, society, and resulting security arrangements.

Following the events of 1989–1991 the strategic context facing all states changed radically. States and especially their security institutions recognized this fact, but their inherently pessimistic outlook would not allow them to quietly fade away in the fashion of General Douglas MacArthur (on military outlook, see Huntington [1957] 1972). To paraphrase the fictional Stark family, winter would come again and they had to be ready.[3] Thus states, and equally so scholars of security, went on a ten-year search for the threats we would face in the coming century, constructing and then often dismissing a parade of enemies and missions.[4] In the process the very character of war became open for debate: Would it look like Gulf War I (1991), Rwanda (1994), Bosnia (1992–1995), the First Chechen War (1994–1996)? This debate is not merely academic, as the first step to knowing if we lack the necessary capabilities to meet threats is to understand the threat environment, an issue to which we now turn.

THE CONTEMPORARY CHARACTER OF WAR

When most pundits and experts say that war has changed, they mean that its character is different than previous eras, as compared to its alleged unchanging nature. Moreover, the changes they are describing often relate to changes in warfare, that is, in the way war is fought, which relates to how changes in war's character influence the tools, tactics, and targets of war. Understanding these aspects of war in our contemporary era is an essential step before advocating and pursuing any reforms, as we can know what is wrong with our current security system only in the context of the threats it is supposed to defend us from. In other words, this examination will tell us whether our system really needs to change on a systemic level and, if so, give some guidance on exactly how it needs to change. In doing this, the following considerations will remain at a high (e.g. strategic) level, looking at the big picture: the threat environment, not specific threats which are often fleeting in the modern world (though some are mentioned as examples). By focusing on the broad character of war and capabilities we can avoid creating a laundry list of all the flaws – and there are plenty, and many books about them – in our current security system irrespective of the strategic context, actual threats, and what (or whether) viable solutions exist (a focus on "trends instead of gadgets" as in Leonhard 1998, 12).

Following Carl von Clausewitz ([1832] 1976), the nature of war is said to be unchanging, and while some strategic studies thinkers may have more to say on this issue, we will accept this assumption. Broadly speaking war's nature is violent, interactive, and fundamentally political. For our purposes these traits serve as things we must always keep in mind: Firstly, that even if the solutions proposed here (or seen in war) are presented to seem technical, sometimes bloodless, they are violent.[5] Secondly, that these solutions will be met by others with equally violent counter-solutions. Lastly, everything done for security has political implications – as it should have political purposes (immediate objectives or longer-term ends) – both internationally and domestically.

As opposed to the nature of war, its character is not fixed but determined by what Clausewitz called the "spirit of the age," which itself is determined by the relationship between his famous Trinity. This Trinity – variously defined as people, army, and government, or passion, chance, and reason – is a useful starting point, our last chapters having discussed how various configurations (organization) of people, army, and government use reason (technology) and passion (ideas) to reduce and deal with chance (risk) while attaining a purpose (political, but ultimately survival). Scholars of strategic studies have often sought to break down these characteristics further into dimensions of strategy. Colin Gray (2002, 123), for instance, lists seventeen dimensions of strategy, covering many areas, such as technology, law, ethics, culture, and organization, that change across time and place (and which also change based on how long it takes to cross or communicate across space). In that it has so many interacting elements, strategy for war is complex, magnified by the fact that these elements are aggregated intellectual categories, each of which consists of an increasing number of elements itself and is thus internally complex. The precise nature of this complexity and how to address it is the core purpose of strategic analysis.

While "[t]he dimensions of strategy have been stable throughout history [. . .] the character of each dimension and its dynamic role in the 'whole house' of strategy and war, must vary from case to case" (Gray 2002, 9). Yet there is, and never will be, agreement on the exact character of these dimensions of strategy for war in any given era. Their evolution is ongoing, and identifying their combined character, which would give strategic advantage, simply engenders further changes as other strategic actors adapt to survive. A healthy military system will itself debate the relationship between these factors almost constantly as it seeks strategic advantage. As implied, strategic and military thinkers across the globe are themselves at present engaged in such a debate over the proper relationship between the elements of strategy in modern warfare. Capturing the full extent of this expert debate is not possible with a volume that hopes to go on to other issues, with whole books written on the matter (several of which will be cited in the following pages). Thus, we will start by considering (the) two (arguably most) prominent perspectives: network-centric (also net-centric) warfare (NCW) and fourth-generation warfare (4GW). By examining the dominant perspectives, we can see how war is seen by those who fight it, which plays a key role in making war the way it is. In turn, by examining widely different views of warfare and considering how they interact, we should be able to come to some sort of synthesis on the character of war.

Network-centric warfare builds especially on a long American preference for technological solutions to military challenges, mostly on the tactical level (though such obsession with means is not limited in history to America, as we saw in Chapter 1) (Gray 2002, 281; Hammes 2006, 191; Ralph Peters in Singer 2009, 291). NCW is "an information superiority-enabled concept of operations that generates increased combat power by networking sensors, decision makers, and shooters to achieve shared awareness, increased speed of command, higher tempo of operations, greater lethality, increased survivability, and a degree of self-synchronization" (Hammes 2006, 7; original idea from Cebrowski and Garstka 1998). This combination is seen by some as offering the promise of perfect, frictionless war; a belief that chance can be eliminated from the Trinity (Arkin 2015). Moreover, not only chance but also the human, seen as "the weakest link in defense systems," is to be removed (US DARPA official quoted in Singer 2009, 64). Once the human combatant is removed from the operations, and thus from harm's way, the human citizen, the people/population, can also be removed from policy, reducing passion's role in war. War will see no body bags coming home; it will be a one-sided affair and a purely functional objective act carried out "in the background" by the armed forces/security services. NCW seeks to use technology to alter and control the very nature of war, making it less interactive with violence experienced only by one (the enemy's) side.

NCW is thus more a vision of how war should be than a system designed for how war is; it is based on using what we have and have done well, not on an assessment of what we need and what needs to be done. NCW is about continuity with pre-existing systems, it builds on industrial era war and the RMA of the 1980s (details to follow). Such continuity is not automatically a bad thing, and can even be desirable, provided that the strategic context and threats have not changed radically. However, this is not the case, as we saw in previous chapters and will be further elaborated on below. The state as the security object and threat, structured state-versus-state competition in traditional domains, has for now receded somewhat. Nonetheless, because NCW is the approach preferred by the current dominant powers (especially the United States), in some ways war is shaped in its image. NCW sets the paradigm to which others must respond, but its actual application engenders and hastens the adaptation of those on NCW's receiving end. It then becomes a question of whether the continuity (NCW) or adaptation (counter-NCW) makes better uses of the changes in the larger world context: of the new technologies and the shape and ideas of modern society.

While the word "network" appears in the very name of NCW, it applies network principles only to the internal linkage of its tools and people to enable even better command and control; network technology is used to offset traditional problems of hierarchical bureaucratic approaches and the need for information, and knowledge,[6] even while maintaining secrecy. On the other hand, 4GW is internally organized as a loosely coupled network while also targeting the network characteristics of the modern world. A 4GW combatant "uses all available networks – political, economic, social, and military – to convince the enemy's political decision makers that their strategic goals are either unachievable or too costly for the perceived benefit" (Hammes 2006, 2). In this way 4GW is an organizational approach targeting the enemy's ideas, its national identity. It seeks to undermine their subjective security and by making them feel less safe destroy their will (e.g. to continue a given policy). Its proximate (operative) targets are the individuals that constitute the sources of state power today more than ever, as they are both the ultimate principles (authority) in liberal democracies and the increasingly (technologically) empowered agents in the diversified yet interdependent socio-economic systems from which the state draws its resources. To the 4GW combatant nobody is innocent because everybody is a threat or enabler of a threat; thus, everybody is a legitimate target. 4GW takes advantage of the fact that because of technology and the ideas and organization it enables (because the tech was itself designed based on those ideas) "power is becoming decentralized, flatter, and increasingly nongovernmental" (Singer 2009, 266). They use this power for their attacks, but also target this power in those attacks.

4GW is often equated with asymmetric warfare, the use of outdated tools and tactics, but in an often innovative (as well as morally questionable) way, by a weaker actor against a more powerful one, usually in an iterative manner over a long time span as they learn the sensitive points (vulnerabilities) of their more powerful adversary. While much of this is true, 4GW also often makes use of high technology, to the point where scholars have christened the new designation "post-asymmetric war," wherein the asymmetric technological advantage resides with the actor lacking what are considered the other traditional elements of power, including even a state, industrial base, or population.

If we consider what we learned in Chapter 2, and also Clausewitz's observation that war is essentially interactive in nature, then we can conclude that a permanent condition of strategy must be change. If we are to assess whether 4GW or NCW is the way of future war, the key question is the extent, direction, and speed of change. Is it linear or at least logarithmic, or does it represent a radical disjuncture? The former would call for NCW, the latter for 4GW or even more radical innovations. The conclusion of Chapter 2 argued that we have in many areas undergone a major shift from one mode of production to another, from socio-political and economic systems which were more closed to ones which are more open. As the means and way – the tools and tactics – of war originate from technologies and ideas in society, in time these too will become more open. However, historically such shifts originate not in the status quo powers, even if they were the ones to invent the technology and ideas. Rather, it is the challengers who will adopt the open, empowering technology, not only because it is accessible and adoptable (financially and organizationally), but because it is required to shift to the opposite source of power as that which the dominant powers possess and in which they cannot compete (Gray 2002, 272).

Moreover, change is accelerating. This acceleration is largely due to the autocatalytic nature of technology, which is self-reinforcing and accelerating as it builds on itself (as discussed in Chapter 1), and increasing competition (both violent and peaceful) due to an increase in the number of interacting units, whether people or institutions. Yet new technology leads to acceleration not just of innovation but also in other areas; modern technology enables speed in its application: rapid travel, communication, analysis and processing, and manufacturing. One of the most significant changes in the modern world and modern war is in the character of time and space themselves (Paul Virilio in Lacy 2014; see also Bousquet 2009, 22–24; Walsh and Barbara 2006). Admiral Michael Mullen, former Chairman of the Joint Chiefs of Staff (United States) is amongst those who have recognized this acceleration and its impact on the time we have to react to changes (Singer 2009, 434). Increased speed of change is true not only on a system level, but also within the realm of tactical action. Thus the obsession of the NCW camp with speed, though one could say the 4GW camp also focuses on speed, albeit trying to slow events to decades in duration with punctuated spurts of activity. Space, on the other hand, is contracting due to the speed and the reach of modern weapons systems, whether missiles or suicide bombers, but also expanding as new realms for warfare open: space, cyber, and information (Hammes 2006,

31; Lacy 2014; the last realm is quite old, but is receiving renewed attention; see Arquilla 2007).

It is this temporal and spatial expansion that has transformed the realm of war, usually (or ideally) "over there," into the state of security also at home. The field on which war is fought and the times it is conducted have become fluid, even temporarily permanent and omnipresent, echoing earlier anarchical eras of history (related idea in Hammes 2006, 31). The Russian "Gerasimov doctrine" (see below) speaks of "a permanently operating front through the entire territory of the enemy state" (Weiss 2016). Strategic surprise is increasingly likely, as it is possible for action and effect to be far removed, and for the magnitude of one to be out of proportion to the other, while traditional ideas of power may have little to do with outcomes. Because of the complexity of modern socio-economic systems, the interdependence between individuals and different sectors of life and the economy, even minor events can have implications throughout the system. Hitting one seemingly minor target, like the thermal exhaust port on the Death Star, can have catastrophic implications, implications which mean even if the probability of such a bull's-eye is low, strategy must account for the possibility (The Empire did not, with predicable results). Colin Gray (2002, 5–6) describes this as non-linearity, "a condition structurally characteristic of, though not always dominant in, strategy and war that denies authority to the rules of proportionality and additivity [sic]"; that is, there is a "disproportion between inputs and outcomes" (104). Antoine Bousquet (2009, 34) argues this non-linearity is a defining characteristic of contemporary warfare. The problem with non-linearity is that even if things are going well, and our NCW security system is constantly and steadily improving, eventually one of the punctuated spurts of 4GW activities will hit our exhaust port. Our task is to find the best approaches to address such non-linearity: Does it lie in tech, the state, human imagination, or elsewhere?

Despite their radical differences, at their heart both NCW and 4GW are about technology. Both are indeed possible only with modern technology (as their means) and the changes it has engendered in the world (i.e. in targets). Yet in many ways 4GW is better able to use modern technology in a way consistent with its design, one that maximizes the individual – the human element – and the network's power – the organizational design. It then uses this technology in a way that exploits the very openness and technology of (and required by) the target's socio-economic system. Yet it does not limit itself to technology as its means or its targets, but uses it as a force multiplier for all the dimensions of strategy, or put another way, for all the networks it uses. Because of this, 4GW qualifies as a hybrid approach to war (Hoffman 2007). Even while using traditional organization and technology, people and passion have a larger role in using them. It is flexible in its tools, tactics, and targets. It excels at recognizing change, learning, and adapting. 4GW is a more open system, making it more appropriate for today's open world. It does what status quo powers cannot do – change – because of that key component of their name, which defines both their power and the policy objectives: status quo.

Actors adopting 4GW do not do so because they are inherently better in any sense (e.g. better learners, innovators). They adapt and learn, and take risks, because of the harsh realities of their existence. We saw this in the examples which opened this chapter; very often the innovators, those who recognize the change and seek to learn and adapt, thereby further driving the arrival of new modes of warfare, are the challengers, revisionist states, the recently defeated, or militarily weaker actors facing high, usually identifiable, threats. Al Qaeda is one actor that recognized the possibility for a shift in warfare and innovated to suddenly strike deep into the United States. The attacks of 9/11 demonstrated an extreme form of non-linearity: with the power of will and box cutters turning civilian transport into precision firepower, and the immediate death and destruction on 9/11 magnified manifold across society, the economy, and the world over in the following years. The American and allied response to this attack sought not only vengeance, but to prevent a recurrence. However, accustomed to the state-on-state war that had dominated since 1648, the American response floundered in many ways, to put it mildly. While the power of al Qaeda has declined, its first innovative move hastened a new form of warfare. The international jihadi movement continued to innovate in the perfect environment for rapid experimentation that was created by the US-led wars and occupations. The hybrid system that emerged combined the resources of a state with the diffuse power of tech-savvy modern violent political movements, currently taking the form of the Islamic State (which even if defeated by the time you read this, will not be the last creature to evolve from the chain of post-9/11 events).

There are also state actors who have begun adapting their system to the new reality of conflict. This book has already on several occasions quoted Russian Chief of the General Staff Valery Gerasimov, whose thoughts on the mixing of military and non-military tools, tactics, and power form the basis of what many now call hybrid warfare or non-linear warfare (also called contactless warfare, or most recently, gray war). Russia's position as a revisionist power emerging from a time of trauma has made them open to these ideas, and while the Kremlin still seeks to expand its traditional tools of power, its experiments in hybrid warfare puts it on the cutting edge of military innovation (examples in Chapter 5). China may have been even further ahead of the curve, with similar ideas making an appearance in the 1999 book *Unrestricted Warfare* written by two colonels in the People's Liberation Army (Liang and Xiangsui 1999). Recently P. W. Singer and August Cole (2015) offered a fictionalized, yet realistic, vision of how such a war would look in their bestseller *Ghost Fleet*.

Because war is interactive, we – meaning here primarily liberal democracies (with apologies to readers from elsewhere) – must design our security strategy based on our competitors and the threats they may represent, on their capabilities in the current context, not on our capabilities in our preferred context. The world has changed, and those less invested in the old world have changed with it. Therefore, we must learn and innovate, for if we are to fight 4GW enemies, we better be able to do more than one thing well because we have lots of vulnerabilities and the enemy will adapt to what we do not do well. This innovation must construct a hybrid form of warfare using the existing (open) socio-political foundation to create a superior combination of organization, technology, and doctrine capable of surviving and succeeding in the friction of war, friction which may be gone from NCW battlefields (if there ever is one) but which dominates in gray wars. This innovation must be fast to match the speed of the modern world system and one's competitors/enemies, as well as deep and inter-sectoral to sufficiently cover the complex system's many vulnerabilities (and exploit those of any enemy). However, such innovation is complex because strategy for war is complex and the socio-economic system on which it is based and which it seeks to defend is complex. Innovation must thus draw on every network making up society and link these networks. If our enemy is going to attack our water supply or waste treatment facilities, we need the expertise of plumbers and epidemiologists, as well as the experiences and survival strategies of those who've dealt with bad water as part of their lives (whether from the third world or Flint, Michigan).

While this may sound demanding and discouraging, there is also cause for hope. While revisionist state and status quo challengers may innovate based on external environmental pressures, Chapter 2 showed that innovation is most likely in internally open systems, systems the liberal democracies like to think they have and which in many regards they do. Yet Chapter 2 concluded by showing that regarding its current security system, they are not quite as open as they have been in the past or could be again. Following from this, with the broad character of war in mind, we can now turn to examining in more detail how the capabilities of the dominant Western security system (fail to) match up to the current character of warfare and contemporary threats. Hereby, we can identify the gaps we need to fill with innovative security solutions.

THE CAPABILITY GAP: THE LIMITS OF BUREAUCRACY, TECHNOLOGY, AND SECRECY

As we saw earlier, out of the legacy of WWII and the Cold War, the West, and as a result many other states, has inherited a security system that is bureaucratic, (information) technological, and secretive – what we call a BiTS system. Moreover, this system for (security) solutions has been extended and reinforced in the last two plus decades by institutions that very much bought into the ideas of the RMA and NCW, but only to the extent these ideas could be internally controlled within existing institutional arrangements. The BiTS traits characterize all the elements of strategy, from military command and organization, to the way intelligence and information is treated and what tools are best used to perform a given task. Yet these solutions were designed for the security problems of an earlier age, problems which differ in character from contemporary threats in a way which is not purely additive (Bohne, Graham, Raadschelders, and Lehrke 2014, 9; Friman and Higgens 2009, 43). While bureaucracy, technology, and secrecy each have certain capabilities, they also have their limits, limits which are accentuated when the three are combined in the modern context facing contemporary threats. In the following we turn to each of these components in turn, starting with the one from which the others logically flow (thus the order deviates from that of the acronym used, but BiTS makes a more readable acronym than BSiT).

BUREAUCRACY

Bureaucracies are good for efficiently organizing and channelling (relatively) large amounts of resources – including information – over extended periods toward developing, implementing, and maintaining solutions to well-defined problems/challenges that exist within a stable, well-understood system and that have understood optimal end points. They allow leaders to unify many smaller efforts and tactical actions to work toward bigger strategic goals. Because the processes for doing all the above are structured specifically for the task/function in a way proven and known to be successful at that function, they offer a degree of predictability; because the organization is fractal (same patterns within every level) this predictability applies to every element of the organization. Yet these advantages – command and control, continuity and predictability – are intimately connected to several weaknesses. Broadly speaking, bureaucracies tend to be slow and inflexible. From the DMV (Department of Motor Vehicles) to the TSA (Transportation Security Agency), this is hardly a point that needs arguing, though it should be broken down further with consideration for the security context.

Bureaucratic inflexibility can be seen firstly in their decision making, which tends to be constrained by a fixed organizational mind-set derived from years of experience and lessons learned (Zweibelson 2015, 34–35). Because many of these lessons were derived from trauma learning (trauma and its belated resolution), deviating from the lessons is seen as a route to repeating the tragedy. Even when internal deliberation is possible, the range of options considered is truncated, and decisions tend to simply confirm pre-existing preferences, what is called "group think." These problems are magnified in security-related institutions, with the perceived importance of their mission tending to induce a conservative, pessimistic, or even paranoid and risk-averse mind-set (Omand 2010, 292; Huntington [1957] 1972, 63; Leonhard 1998, 6). Contrary to popular perception, glory seeking is less likely than erring on the side of caution, taking the tried-and-true path, even more so for the politically accountable appointees (which include most generals) and elected officials with security portfolios.

These characteristics make bureaucracies good at doing what they were designed to do. Knowledge and expertise are integrated into the actual bureaucratic structure, allowing complexity to be reduced to its components. However, this means adding new knowledge is not simply a matter of updating the library or a database: whole structures would have to change. Because new information threatens the existing knowledge upon which the structure is designed, bureaucracies tend to be unreceptive to dissonant information (Roberts 2004, 74), and the more such information conflicts with existing ideas, the more it is rejected (called confirmation bias in psychology). Thus, while optimization and efficiency are terms we think of as positive, they limit what you can do, make you inflexible, and lead to system fragility (Taleb 2013, 246).

Yet as discussed, today's challenges are difficult to understand given the technology and complexity of the components involved and of the entire resulting system. Moreover, knowledge is accruing at an ever faster rate, while the amount of data out there is growing even faster. As data, knowledge, and science have expanded no one person can know everything known; specialization in a small sector or even one specific technology or process is now the norm. No one person understands the system and its components, and our functional approach to bureaucratic design, with each focusing on a specific sector or task, means no one bureaucracy does either. Attempts to create fusion centres to share information and knowledge have seemingly failed (Mueller and Stewart 2015), as have numerous other information-sharing initiatives (Peled 2014a, 2014b).

As a bureaucracy does not (and indeed could not) incorporate (all) new knowledge and new expertise into its structure, when a new problem arises that is not understood, then old function-specific institutional lessons are even more likely to be applied (Bean 2011, 44; Lipschutz 2000, 51; Leonhard 1998, 8 and passim; Zweibelson 2015, 35). At the highest level of policy the world is seen "in such a way as to reinforce existing predispositions and thereby legitimate them [. . .] [which] in turn, helps to reproduce existing policy or some variant of it as well as the material basis for that policy" (Lipschutz 2000, 56; see examples throughout Singer 2009). We can see this in current US counterterrorism policy, which Stephen Walt (2014) describes as "just doing what comes naturally, instead of doing what might be more effective."

Failure to respond to change and adequately address complexity occurs not only at the policy level but every level below, from the strategic to the tactical. Bureaucracies are designed to reduce uncertainty; predictability in bureaucratic outcomes and performance of tasks is something we rely on. They are boring by design. Yet it is not only the customer-facing service desks that are slaves to procedure. Even analysts in security institutions have, according to Hamilton Bean (2011, 83; see also 82), been turned into machines, with "automation-like processes" focused on producing outputs rather than using "imagination" as was called for by the 9/11 Commission (2004, 339–48). William Arkin (2015, 84) goes further, suggesting that "our entire system of national security was [is] in its way becoming autonomous and unmanned." These features had their upsides in the chaos and fog of industrial-era warfare with their unreliable communication, and even in the envisioned nuclear wars to come, but in the "long war" of today they have large downsides. Established bureaucratic practice leads to "automatic reactions" that are designed for previously known threats; thus they have only a few tricks, ones that modern adaptive competitors can easily learn after a few uses (Schneier 2003, 170). In reducing their own uncertainty, security institutions have made themselves more predictable. In the introduction we mentioned the criminals from the *Die Hard* movie franchise, who knew every move the police would make in response to their own first moves. Real-world terrorists make similar calculations, though the most successful such predictive adaptations are seen in hybrid actors like Hezbollah, full-scale insurgencies, and states using hybrid tactics, such as Russia (for examples on the latter, including its moves into Syria in 2015, see Galeotti 2015a).

Bureaucratic predictability in action is mirrored by inadaptability in structures. Even if the adaption required is not on the level of social reorganization, bureaucracies are still constrained by the need for "agreement and coordination and – in some instances – a lengthy bureaucratic procurement process" (Schneier 2012, 229; see also Lynn III 2014; Slayton 2013, 219). The latter need, for not only a new technology (e.g. a weapon) but also human resources (i.e. training), implies a period of at least several years before an innovation, even once given the green light, can diffuse through the entire system (Lehrke 2013, 1; for theory, see Darby and Zucker 2003). More paradigm-shifting innovations, on the other hand, can take from thirty to one hundred years (Garstka 2009, 64; Richard Simpkin in Leonhard 1998, 241; more broadly, see Krugman 1994, 28–29).

Moreover, "rapid developments in technologies can outpace the time it takes to alter organizational structures, modify processes, and teach new skills" (Friman and Higgens 2009, 52). Thus, reform, even if enthusiastically pursued, may never be able to keep up with the rapid incremental development that characterizes modern innovation (Slayton 2013, 219). Even tactical "urgent operational needs" that are clearly identified by troops on the ground have often taken too long to field to be of value. Matthew McClure (2014) illustrates this in the context of improvised explosive devices (IEDs), discussing how American counter-IED innovations were slow and costly and never able to keep pace with the cheap, rapid iterative innovations of Iraqi insurgents. The problem is even more pronounced for larger strategic needs given that current strategic challenges and direction, problems and threats, are not well understood. Command innovation simply does not function as well with open-ended, undirected research. It is hard to design a weapon when we do not know where it will be used, against whom, with what other assets, and so on.

A current preference (largely cost driven) for platforms capable of many different roles may somewhat offset this problem, a welcome adaptability feature, though not one universally liked in the military services and which has proven difficult for them to adopt (for the example of the US Navy's now largely abandoned mission-based modular system, see Axe 2009 and Beckhusen 2016). Additionally, some military labs can get around the rigid bureaucratic procurement system (Singer 2009, 145), and this process also has leaked over into procurement for certain high-technology products to meet urgent needs (for example, see Arkin 2015). These exceptions are important, as they demonstrate that reform, such as that called for herein, is not impossible and can even build on current initiatives (more on this later). A constitutive feature of bureaucracy, its fragmentation into sub-organizations with functional missions, can introduce points of flexibility into bureaucracies; these sub-organizations can become promoters of innovation if they can find allies to support their cause vis-à-vis (intra-)organizational competitors. If we look at Russia, it has a quite fragmented and competitive organizational framework, which may be a reason it has produced successful hybrid tactics. However, unless the political leadership prioritizes external goals over domestic power consideration, fragmentation has drawbacks: hindering full institutional adoption of an innovation and disconnecting tactical applications from a consistent strategic goal.

Despite the preference for internal bureaucratic solutions, most militaries now recognize not everything can be done in-house. Current complex security tasks require tools and skills government actors do not have and, moreover, which they cannot afford in the age of austerity. Thus, the military and intelligence agencies have increasingly resorted to outsourcing even sensitive functions as their missions have expanded beyond their ability to handle alone. Yet there are (inter-related) reasons why outsourcing alone cannot solve objective security problems (to say nothing of subjective security at the moment). It begins with the obvious observation that outsourcing is generally done to for-profit institutions. This means profit maximization, not the public good, is their primary interest. With short-time horizons set by their contracts and a desire to secure their renewal, the contracted firms have an interest in producing results, and thus perpetuating need (for their services/product), even if there are no (good) results (see Bean 2011). Even if we assume the regular contractor (e.g. analyst) has the best intentions, and that pressure from management is absent, there will be psychological pressures to demonstrate performance through tangible evidence. For the contractor, not crying wolf would require immensely difficult "inhibitory control" to counter their training, willingness to risk missing something important (a false negative), and totally selfless placement of the public interest over the personal. Moreover, many contractors have security background, which means hiring them does little to counter the pre-existing way of thinking. Even if the contactor is a true outsider or has been sufficiently civilianized, working for pay "crowds out" intrinsic motivation, reducing passion and creativity, both which are essential when addressing security issues (called the overjustification effect; see, for example, Dignan 2011, 65; *Hackers Wanted* 2009; originally proposed in Morris 1962). These issues of independence and motivation must be borne in mind when we later consider how to engage citizens as an alternative to in-house and outsourcing solutions.

. . . PLUS SECRECY

To recap, secrecy is seen as increasingly essential because in the modern context anybody – not just agents of the enemy state – is possibly a threat and information would empower them further. Secrecy, as we understand it here, is not just a system of classification; it is an idea about who has a right and need to know and, thus, where authority and power lie, and even what constitutes legitimate knowledge (e.g. information labelled "secret" is considered by many to be superior to open source information). Secrecy within a compartmentalized bureaucracy means the hand often does not know what the foot is doing and likely nobody knows what the whole is up to. However, bureaucracy – through its established procedures and flows – helps ensure a system can function as a whole even in this context. Nonetheless, secrecy also magnifies some of the internal bureaucratic tendencies discussed above, while exacerbating also inter-bureaucracy tensions. The contribution (but to be clear, not full responsibility) of such internal system pathologies to catastrophic failure during 9/11 and Hurricane Katrina are well documented and, furthermore, continue to exist despite reforms (Peled 2014a, 2014b).

The first of these aggravated side effects of the system is reduction in knowledge and thus in the quality of decisions and actions. As Julian Assange pointed out, secrecy in an organization "induces fear and paranoia in its leadership and planning coterie. This must result in minimisation of efficient internal communications mechanisms [. . .] and consequent system-wide cognitive decline" (quoted in Leigh and Harding 2011, 46). Moreover, the more sensitive an issue, and thus more important for national security, "the more completely the experts are excluded while harassed senior generalists take over" (Roberts 2004, 74). That is, the more important an issue is to our survival, the less the people who need to know, who could solve the problem, are provided with the information they need to do so. Thus, internally, secrecy can amplify the bureaucracy's tendencies to inhibit collaboration and information sharing and result in poor analysis and decision making (Peled 2014a, 2014b; Roberts 2004, 70). The system of vertical organization, in which compartmentalized data and information proceed slowly upward through various hierarchies before knowledge and orders cascade back down, thus, according to Thomas Hammes (2006, 193, also 192), offsets the "premier benefit" of the information age.

These communication issues are amplified in the case of inter-bureaucracy information sharing. Max Weber's posthumous landmark *Economy and Society* ([1922] 2013, 991–92) touched on this issue of bureaucratic secrecy. Weber claimed that bureaucracies seek to bolster their power by keeping their knowledge secret beyond what is functionally necessary. One need not even sink into cynicism to believe this is the case. It is natural that an institution believes in its own importance and the superiority of its solutions; nobody would want an institution with an inferiority complex providing an essential service like security. Because it believes in its mission and expertise, it seeks to maximize its resources and power, of which information is especially today a key component. Thus, they are hesitant to share their information, and sometimes equally unwilling to admit the validity of others' information. It is unclear if recent trends in putting many organizations under one institutional roof, like the American Department of Homeland Security (DHS) (established 2002) and Russian Federal Security Service (FSB) (especially from 2016), will counter these tendencies (though the author is doubtful).

Externally the problems of bureaucratic secrecy are equally pronounced. Secrecy, as seen in Chapter 2, often leads to the adoption of internal solutions that are inferior to those which could be found in the private sector. Secrecy even pre-empts such innovation, as transparency is needed to create a market for innovation to improve security (Colaresi 2014, 28; Schneier 2003, 131). As was pointed out by Vannevar Bush, "Our ability to overcome future enemies depends upon scientific advances which will proceed more rapidly with diffusion of knowledge than under a policy of continued restriction of knowledge now in our possession" (Piotrowski 2010, 26). He said this in 1945 as President Roosevelt's key scientific advisor, an opinion reiterated by the Tolman Committee assessing declassification of Manhattan Project elements, the very program that served to inaugurate the era of the BiTS security system. Yet at least the technology of this era could be monopolized and thus to some extent kept secret, given its high cost and organizational complexity plus a generally highly trusted and resource-rich state that still could attract the best and brightest minds. On the other hand, contemporary cutting-edge technology is much cheaper and thus more widespread, resulting also in innovators being widespread. As such they are harder to control, resulting even in the criminalization of those forms of innovation least easily controlled, with the innovators labelled as "hackers."

The innovation-quashing implications of secrecy apply not only to hardware and software but also to ideas and analysis, which feed into security and military doctrine, strategy, tactics, and organization. In a recent polemic, leading terrorism expert Marc Sageman (2014), who has worked both within and outside (the U.S.) government, lambasted the secrecy and lack of information sharing as contributing to insufficient analysis and thus ineffective counterterrorism policy. Even ex post analysis is constrained, with secrecy preventing independent monitoring and evaluation of policy and performance, while internal evaluations are often politically suspect, and sometimes severely scientifically flawed (for example, see Albrecht 2008, 40). A recent case in point are revelations, revealed from senior internal sources, that the US Department of Defense's Central Command was painting an unjustifiably positive picture of progress in the fight against the Islamic State (and possibly also earlier against the Taliban) (de Luce 2015a, 2015b).

Possibly the most important implication of secrecy is how it inhibits collaboration not only with private sector innovators but with the wider public, preventing them from helping in any way. As noted by the Congressional Joint Inquiry into 9/11, "The U.S. Intelligence Community was involved in fighting a 'war' against Bin Laden, largely without the benefit of what some would call its most potent weapon in that effort: an alert and committed American public" (quoted in Roberts 2004, 79). In the most traditional sense an alert public can act to prevent or mitigate security threats, as seen on numerous occasions since 9/11, such as citizens' roles in thwarting the so-called Shoe and Underwear bombers (2001, 2009) and, more recently (2015), the gunman on a high-speed French train. An alert and informed public is also more resilient, mitigating the social and economic disruption that threats and attacks can engender. Such resilience can even deter such threats in the first place, as attackers may seek other targets where the effect of their attack will be more pronounced (Gearson 2012). Yet as we will see, these "soft" contributions can be matched with "hard" citizen contributions to security capabilities.

The above focused on the effects of secrecy on task performance, but secrecy also impacts the institutional structure(s). As Joseph Stiglitz argues, secrecy "is based on a mistrust between those governing and those governed; and at the same time, it exacerbates that mistrust" (Bean 2011, 61). Trust is not only some fuzzy emotion that can play second string to security. In a democracy mistrust can lead the public, through their representatives, to hamstring policy through legal restrictions and withdrawing needed financial and other resources (Colaresi 2014, 13, 15). This in turn can increase insecurity despite everybody's best intentions. Michael Colaresi (2014) outlines how such a process prevented inter-war France from capitalizing on new innovations and split its intelligence apparatus, resulting in its falling behind, and then falling to, its Nazi neighbour (see also May 2000; Posen 1984). This situation is most dangerous when a population suddenly discovers the state is engaging in something which they did not and would not approve, typically something contrary to their values. Moreover, today, sudden discovery, through leaks and hacks, seems to be the only way we discover anything – and these leakers and hackers have an interest in revealing the worst, which our media then spin and filter further into sensational stories.

The question many security institutions need to ask in this context is whether they would rather have a secret system that they lose when its existence is leaked (or otherwise exposed), or a publically known system that they can keep, but which the enemy – knowing of its existence – may adapt to counter? Yet one must consider also the natural corollary to the second part of this question: How much can the enemy adapt more than they already do?[7] Because security actors err on the side of caution, secrecy does not prevent adaptation. Competent terrorist organizations, for instance, already assume their communications are being monitored and adapt as much as they can; yet they are also constrained in how much they can adapt and still compete. They cannot go back to hand-delivered messages and still launch spectacular attacks capable of affecting their enemy's will. States behave similarly; Russia takes precautions even against secret, thus unknown, American systems, yet they still use radios and computers despite the associated risks of monitoring or hacking. They accept perfect secrecy is not possible; perhaps we also should build this idea into our institutions.

. . . AND TECHNOLOGY

The public is excluded also from involvement in the information technology that is the third pillar of the contemporary security system. As discussed, technology leads to complexity. While some internal security experts may understand the technology, they are increasingly limited in number as well as often excluded from higher decision making given that most military and security career systems focus on producing and promoting generalists (Hammes 2006, 235). Neither the compartmentalized experts nor the senior generalists can deal with the overall complexity and resulting fragility that requires equally complex solutions. Thus, while bureaucracy helps to channel information and maintain system knowledge even in the face of secrecy, technology is increasingly used to capture knowledge and then determine or even execute actions in a complex world that bureaucratic institutions alone could not address. That is, faith for dealing with the complexity technology created is increasingly placed in the technology itself, through further augmenting and linking together the data, algorithms, and automation (for extensive critique of US technological focus, see Hammes 2006; for a specific case, see Slayton 2013). This information focus, seeking even to create (artificial) intelligence, is the core of technology today, including for security; it distinguishes the information-driven NCW ideology from the computer(chip)-based RMA that preceded it. The core of our security system and its technology is either designed for total information awareness or depends on that information for its operation. Thus, this information-as-enabling-technology will be our focus, with specific hardware deficiencies resulting from this brought in as examples (with other specific capability gaps – a better ship, plane, etc. – left to others to identify).

Despite the faith put in how information can be used to automate everything, there are severe limits to this ability that raise real dangers when put in practice. Until the prophesied "technological singularity," a belief which we will briefly address later, technology is limited in its ability to adapt to and learn from the very system it constitutes. Current technology lacks intuitive thinking and the ability for creative strategizing, is not yet good at spatial reasoning and pattern recognition and thus associated tasks, and most importantly does not exist separate of human psychology (on some of these, see Franzoni and Sauermann 2014, 11). Technology simply uses pure computational power to find patterns in sensor-gathered data that match previously known and logically reducible patterns that are correlated with an outcome of interest. The two key requirements here then are information (data), as well as filtering out the "noise" from the important data, and knowledge to make sense of it. The following will focus on these aspects.

Existing knowledge forms the foundation of the algorithms that form the brain of our current, imperfect artificial intelligence systems. Herein is a quandary, as this implies algorithms can only be as smart as we are (albeit as smart as the smartest among us gathered together). Yet even the best of our existing knowledge is incomplete and often laden with assumptions, biases, and values that thus find their way into our algorithms (Mindell 2015, 10; Pasquale 2015, 35). For example, incorrect algorithmic assumptions about, inter alia, (economic) value, incentives, behaviour, and thresholds were a key contributor to the 2008 financial crisis (Pasquale 2015). Yet these assumptions were made in the fields of economics and finance, a permanent social realm in which we have vast data and experience upon which to build knowledge and our resulting models. When we speak of the security realm, we have significantly less data given the lower frequency of many security events (e.g. attacks); yet the impact of a security event, or even a single data point in a collection of variables indicating something of interest, is even more significant in survival terms (Taleb 2013, 240). In other words, the more important the issue, the less we know about it. Averages and thresholds fill in where the knowledge is missing – if value *x* is over threshold *y*, then the object is a missile not an airplane; if traits *x*, *y*, and *z* exist, then the subject is a terrorist.

To help us get around the problem of limited knowledge we have learning algorithms, when machine learning devises its own rules, based on a training data set, thus creating its own algorithm. As mentioned in Chapter 2, an entire field of these, called genetic algorithms/programming, even attempts to use the rules of evolution, of imperfection and survival, to learn. Scientists are also turning to nature and the swarm logic of honey bees to learn how to efficiently solve particularly difficult algorithmic problems (e.g. the so-called travelling salesman problem; see Chapter 5). Another group is attempting to map the human brain and, by learning how we learn, be able to teach algorithms how to learn as well. Despite all these efforts, we are some way off from developing a general-purpose learner that is totally free of assumptions and which does not result in biases that limit it to specific well-defined tasks.

Until we discover such a "Master Algorithm" (as Pedro Domingos [2015] calls it), and perhaps even after, the overall problem (in addition to the problems within each approach to algorithms) is that these learners are based on what we know about learning. It seems unwise to trust an algorithm built only on what we understand about ourselves and our survival needs (idea following from Gilbert 2013). We can be sure some of our mind's traits are adaptive, derived for our survival through the process of natural selection. Yet if they are subconscious and not yet scientifically understood, they will not be put in an algorithm or given the correct weight (importance level) within them (in Bayesian algorithms). Even worse, some traits may seem ill-adapted, not "fit" in survival terms. These will also be excluded (even in genetic algorithms, which tend to eliminate diversity). Yet as pointed out earlier, what may seem ill-adapted for survival today, may prove essential tomorrow; whether we are talking about biology, social institutions, or military tactics, "some bugs are features." Our universal learner may thus turn out to itself be ill-adapted for survival even if it is by some measure objectively "perfect."

The exemplar of such innate knowledge/skill whose functioning we do not understand is pattern recognition and association. For instance, while a computer cannot even make out a single word from a CAPTCHA used to protect us from bots, humans were able to identify the authors of the letter (the *bordereau*) that broke the Dreyfus case (in 1896) and the Unabomber manifesto (in 1995) based on handwriting and writing style, respectively, two famous security-relevant examples that, moreover, were made possible only by these documents' public release (i.e. transparency). While lacking pattern recognition sets important limits on computers' abilities to collect and analyze some forms of intelligence, even more important is its role in limiting their ability to recognize the social context of specific situations, an area identified as perhaps the last that computers will be able to understand (Marvin Minsky and Ralph Peters in Singer 2009, 131 and 296, respectively). Yet security and conflict are largely made up of social phenomena and interactions, which in turn are rooted in individual thoughts and beliefs that come together to shape emergent group thinking. Understanding social context is essential if our surveillance is to have any value; the subtle nuances of a situation (e.g. celebratory gunfire at a wedding) must be understood before action (e.g. a drone strike) is authorized. Thus, current technology, with sensor-gathered data fed into algorithms that decide on pre-determined automated actions, cannot "dynamically react to complex security situations"; it is ill-suited to deal with adaptive competitors and the "arbitrary complexity" of ever changing human institutions and systems that possess no hidden underlying logic (Schneier 2003, 123; Fred Brook referenced in Slayton 2013, 200). The trajectory of an incoming missile and thus the converse requirements of our anti-missile are logical; the reasoning behind why that missile was launched though is based on a bounded logic that is equal parts information, preferences, biases, emotions, and errors.

When algorithms are linked to our weapons systems, as they have been for decades even if the final "shooter" was still human, further problems arise.

While it is unfair to take old examples given how rapidly technology has progressed, bear with us a moment. In 1983 nuclear Armageddon was avoided when Soviet Lieutenant Colonel Stanislav Petrov ignored warning alarms of an American missile attack because the computer's data-driven conclusion conflicted with his own knowledge of what the context of a nuclear attack would look like. Jump forward just five years to 1988. The American Navy cruiser USS *Vincennes* shot down an Iranian passenger jet over the Persian Gulf when their system told them it was a fighter jet; even though they had data saying it could not possibly be a fighter, "they trusted what the computer was telling them more" than they trusted their own conclusions (Singer 2009, 125). The issue with algorithms is not that they are not perfect – nothing is and they certainly are useful; it's that people "go from plausible suspicion to way overconfidence" when it comes to technology (Google engineer in Mindell 2015, 202; see also O'Grady 2016 and Robinette, Li, Allen, Howard, and Wagner 2016). We easily buy into the myth of technological infallibility and solutionism, just as some in the US military believe that technology can offer perfect, frictionless war and thus pursue designing a system with this end state in mind.

Even while trust in the technological solutions continues to grow after initial resistance is overcome, in most security situations we still keep humans "in the loop" as a final control in the event of error. Yet the irony is that humans left in as a last resort and check on the system are not able to act in such a role because their own skills and knowledge have atrophied, as automation has been doing it all for them (Bainbridge 1983; Mindell 2015; also Morozov 2014 and Carr 2015). Such a degradation effect was first noted in our physical capabilities as machines took over our physical labours, but has been found also regarding mental and analytical skills, while Christopher Coker fears it may one day also affect our ability to make "critical judgments" (in Singer 2009, 324). However, despite this degrading effect, it is worth pointing out that technology can also be used to enhance human skills *if designed to do so*, a subject considered in Chapters 5 and 6.

The *Vincennes* incident was a problem with the algorithms, but algorithms are only part of the software that in turn is only part of a system that is often linked to hardware. The missile warnings that Petrov ignored were due in part to problems with the sensors providing the data and then how this was interpreted by the computers. In a more recent case, in October 2015 US aircraft accidently conducted a strike against a Médecins Sans Frontières (MSF) hospital in Afghanistan. The error here was attributed primarily to network problems connecting the information, command and control, and "shooters" (the AC-130 gunships) (Gallagher 2015b). The human is not the weakest link; it is just one of many links liable to failure. While proper networks are resilient against the failure/removal of any one component, net-centric warfare is not really a network.

One of these key links is data, as "no matter how good the learning algorithm is, it's only as good as the data it gets" (Domingos 2015, 45). Due to how easily data collection is scaled up, with declining costs for ever increasing storage space and cheap sensors capable of filling it (Smith 2002), the response to the shortcomings of our systems has very often been calls for even more data to be fed into the system. These calls are justified by unproven (or even disproven) claims that such data-intensive systems have helped prevent attacks (Bergen et al. 2014). Yet for several reasons more does not mean better data or better outcomes.

For many intelligence purposes new data will come from the Internet and other electronic communications. Yet if an algorithm learns from the Internet – as, for instance, some stock pickers do – then we are in trouble. As (most) humans have learned, "I saw it on the Internet" does not make something true. When the Associated Press's (AP's) Twitter account was hacked in 2013, the hacker posted a false report of a bombing at the White House, a report re-tweeted thousands of times. This information was picked up by trading algorithms that then wiped $136 billion off the value of the S&P 500 in seconds, with follow-on effects in futures, bond, and currency markets.[8] While in this case the recovery was quick, not all systems are so liquid or can self-correct. Fake facts and news on the Internet has become a major problem within politics, which responds notoriously slowly. Hackers *cum* leakers have also started mixing fake news in with real news to complicate efforts to separate the two (Groll 2016). Even once information is shown to be false, "cybercascades" make removing it from every corner of the Internet impossible, and inevitably it re-emerges (Sunstein 2007, 84–86). Despite the best efforts of Snopes.com (or EU Courts with their "right to be forgotten") people continue to spread long disproven rumours about our favourite celebrities, new Facebook privacy rules, or Hillary Clinton.

The above approaches to attacking data were targeted, but it can be even more effective and easier for attackers to take a diffuse route to confuse the algorithms through generating excess information to increase "noise." This can be done firstly for short-term tactical gains, to hide what is really going on, like what we saw citizens in Brussels do in 2015 (Singer 2009, 277). Terrorists reportedly used this tactic during a heightened period of alert in 2010, burying their real plot in a sea of fake plots to distract police and send them off chasing ghosts (Lehrke 2016; Arquilla 2007, 8–9). Noise can also be used in the longer strategic term, with terrorists working toward throwing off the learning algorithms themselves, comparable to what we see now in the "endless cat-and-mouse game of 'search engine optimization'" in the business world (Pasquale 2015, 65). By inserting false information into their communication, or even meaningless actions into their preparations, irrelevant variables could become associated with terrorist acts, which can lead the state to chase irrelevant (and innocent) individuals.

Yet bad data resulting from noise need not be the result of purposive manipulation by terrorists, trolls, or political partisans. In late 2015 Google Translate, which learns from the Internet, started translating the Ukrainian words for Russia and Russian into "Mordor" and "occupiers," respectively, due to the tone of Internet conversations following from the tensions between Ukraine and Russia in recent years. One saw a similar phenomenon, somewhat more purposive, when a Microsoft chatbot *Tay* was within a day of its 2016 release taught to swear and make inflammatory racist remarks (Wakefield 2016). An algorithm trying to learn about terrorism from today's Internet is likely to see as many pictures of Presidents George W. Bush and Vladimir Putin as of Osama bin Laden.

Regarding less well-known figures, you and me, the information about us on the Internet is, as Jaron Lanier points out, "semiautomated self-presentation" where we must overly define ourselves downward to fit the templates (Lanier 2010, 19, 52). Our online presence and activities represent only a collection of "fragments" which when divorced from the larger, offline context are of questionable value for deriving anything more than basic demographic conclusions (Ibid., 21, 53). Moreover, many of our online fragments are a fiction created for social reasons, profiles and posts fine-tuned to make us seem cooler, happier, and sexier, or to make others seem less so. If we, or rather our online selves, are the normal from which deviance – people engaged in acts that threaten our security – is judged and detected, it will be a very odd picture of normality. As citizens make more adaptations to protect their privacy in the wake of revelations about the violation of that privacy, these pictures of the online user will become even more fragmented.

Even if we can feed the system more relatively reliable data, quantity does not always offer qualitative improvement in outcomes (i.e. in the conclusions drawn from the data). Computers, like humans, can see faces on Mars and animals in clouds, a phenomenon called "inceptionism" (Mordvintsev, Olah, and Tyka 2015; called pareidolia in people). An artificial neural network is trained using examples, but "features that are entered bias the network toward certain interpretations," leading it to over-interpret an image; simplifying, if the network was trained to see something – say a threat – it is more likely to see it (Mordvintsev, Olah, and Tyka 2015; Nguyen, Yosinski, and Clune 2015). Scientists have even fed networks random-noise images (i.e. images with no pattern) and still got an identifiable output from the network. More data doesn't resolve this problem, as more data means more noise and thus a greater chance of seeing the non-existent pattern the computer was looking for.

This problem is true not only of image recognition; "overfitting is the central problem in machine learning" generally (Domingos 2015, 71). This is exactly what happened in Operation RYAN around the same time as Colonel Petrov's decision not to start Armageddon: a faulty model (based on the 1941 Nazi invasion) was fed data that did not make sense to it (because that data was from the modern 1983 context). This resulted in the system warning that a NATO attack was likely, which led the Soviet Committee for State Security (KGB) to feed the program even more data, which simply worsened the over-fitting. The computer and the KGB became convinced of an imminent attack, resulting in the USSR going on a war footing. There is thus a danger of a network "looking into the emptiness of its data feed and . . . seeing enemies everywhere" (Gallagher 2015c). Even in cases where the false positives – seeing a threat where there is none – are not so apocalyptic, and thus where some may say it is worth the risk (e.g. flagging one person as a terrorist), we must bear in mind that false positives require time and resources be diverted from other areas so they can be investigated (e.g. Brooks 2015; Herridge 2015).

This last point relates to a larger issue: the interventions that the state engages in based on its data can also throw off algorithms, as the "digital alchemy creates new analog realities" (Pasquale 2015, 32; see also 114). Algorithms lead to interventions which alter reality and in turn alter what the algorithms know or need to know. Even legitimate interventions against real threats can simply catalyze the action they were intended to prevent: a terrorist cell is discovered, leading to a drone strike, which while preventing them from plotting attacks leads to a backlash and radicalization – to more and/or new terrorists who then do things differently than their "droned" predecessors. Our interventions act as natural selection, killing off the less capable terrorists, while teaching the competent ones something new with every strike. Simultaneously, as interventions alter outcomes (e.g. no attack from killed terrorists, but one from new terrorists), they alter the (data) patterns associated with that outcome (the new terrorists use new, unknown methods), undermining the algorithms' predictive ability.

Yet when inceptionism combines with interventions is when we really create our own threats. Once a non-existent pattern is detected by our computer algorithms, our actions, interventions to stop the outcome, can make the pattern manifest and become real. Just as the USSR's belief that war was imminent could have led to actual war, our actions that follow from a belief that a person is a terrorist could make them a terrorist, our belief somebody is planning an attack could lead them to start planning one (for an example, see Mora and Hayes 2015). Moreover, this self-created reality in turn changes what patterns are associated with the outcomes to the false pattern we initially acted upon; thus our algorithms increasingly associate the wrong pattern with our outcome of interest, creating more interventions that create more terrorists, and further reinforce our bad algorithm. The more actions we take to make ourselves safer, the more the utility of our tools declines or even backfires. Security, like war proper, calls for economy of force, not total information and pervasive (over)use, as well as for adaptable tools that can be changed once their initial usefulness is past.

WAITING FOR THE SINGULARITY

Several arguments could be advanced against this critique of the current security approach. These revolve around the acknowledged fact that the system is in transition and not perfect. Strong technologists, including within military and security institutions, would argue that we should continue the transformation as it is currently envisioned by them. They claim that the system simply needs continued resources and more time. If these are provided we will reach what some call the singularity: "strong AI" that is capable of general learning and thinking. However, this point is still some way off; decades even if all goes well. While some algorithms and associated systems have developed advanced capabilities, "they are generally incapable by themselves of extending beyond the very specific tasks they've been programmed to do" (Goodwins 2015). Virtual reality pioneer Jaron Lanier (2010) doubts the required perfect software to run such algorithms can ever be attained. Moreover, hoping that if we keep feeding data into learning algorithms eventually they will evolve into strong AI themselves (a held, but not widely held, belief) seems rather optimistic given the data we are feeding them is incomplete in critical ways, sometimes blatantly wrong, and often confusing and contradictory because we ourselves are confusing and contradictory.

On the hardware side, faster processors to enable such a leap are also not likely to come soon. The well-known Moore's Law, which states that processor speeds double every eighteen months, has limits set by physics, and we are pushing up against them, perhaps reaching them by the mid-2020s. Adding more cores is not a solution, as few computing tasks can be efficiently split to run across multiple cores. While quantum computers are oft touted as something which could provide for a breakthrough, these also are some years and perhaps billions of dollars in investment away. In ideal circumstances it has been claimed we can perhaps develop them in ten to fifteen years (Morgan 2015), conveniently coinciding with the end of Moore's Law; two or three decades is more reasonable, especially given current economics do not favour such investment. Moreover, even once invented, supporting hardware and radically new quantum algorithms will still be needed.

What makes this search for the perfect hardware running the perfect software even more difficult is that, as even believers in the singularity acknowledge, we must "get it right the first time," as there is little room for "non-recoverable errors," tech lingo for disaster or even extinction (Singer 2009, 434). The closer we get to strong AI, the harder it will be to reach because as the depth and speed of technological change spreads and increases, it will have further destabilizing effects, creating just the type of social problems that the current technology cannot solve (Schwab 2016; World Economic Forum 2016; see also Cave 2000; Cookson 2016; Richard Clarke in Singer 2009, 293). All this effort and cost, risk and destabilization, will occur with no guarantee the final product can address human security problems along not just objective measurements, but also subjective ones.

THE SUBJECTIVE (IN)SECURITY GAP: PEOPLE, PERCEPTIONS, AND PARTICIPATION

Society has been affected by the same factors that have altered the strategic context that the military faces: a technologically driven change in time, space, complexity, and non-linearity. Technologies have empowered people, yet they often struggle to use these tools for more than immediate conveniences and objectives; technology has made our lives more complex, the boundaries of our time and space (for instance, between work and play) have become unclear; the amount of information is often overwhelming and makes it difficult to form preferences, reach decisions, or even identify the ultimate goals these should work toward. Yet this context is not all that affects subjective security/insecurity. People's perceptions of security are simultaneously affected by the state and its security institutions' response to the strategic context: the bureaucratic, information technology, and secrecy-driven system outlined above. The citizens' sense of subjective security that results from the context and state response to it is important not only in itself, but because these feelings subsequently feed into objective security. Society is the basis of the resources upon which state and security depend; the people are a defining characteristic of what it means to be a state and the carriers of the nation's identity. As such, the people are the ultimate object that the state must defend, whether as individuals or aggregate groups.

Given the importance of the human, societal dimensions of security (Gray 2002, 280), we must turn to why contemporary society feels insecure in many ways, keeping in mind that society is neither a homogeneous nor unitary actor (which is in fact, central to the argument to follow). Moreover, even proving the existence of insecurity is difficult despite its clear manifestations in media coverage and election results. While any exploration of society is thus necessarily complex and filled with qualifications and exceptions, we will consider the reasons for current feelings of insecurity along five lines. We feel insecure because:

1. We are insecure.
2. Messages from the media and politicians make it seem worse.
3. Conflicting messages lead us to mistrust the government.
4. We do not think the government can make us safer.
5. We cannot personally do anything about our insecurity.

Beginning with point one, how unsafe are we? The citizen is generally not as concerned as soldiers with how modes of warfare match the character of war; they do not feel insecure because of capability gaps per se. Rather any feeling of insecurity is based on their own vulnerabilities, provided a threat matches (as in, is capable of exploiting) these vulnerabilities. The vulnerabilities of the average Western citizen today are not usually immediate; most (but not all) need not fear for sustenance, shelter, or soldiers at the door. Rather, the average citizen's vulnerabilities relate to the complexity of their lives as engendered by the complexity of technology and our socio-economic system. As discussed, alongside the benefits, this complexity makes a system more fragile (Dennett 2013, 8; Omand 2010, 13–14, 324; Lacy 2014, 5; Taleb 2013, 246). A complex system means firstly many components, which means many points of failure, that is, points to attack. Moreover, these components are tightly coupled, forming an interdependent system, meaning an attack can cascade through the system. The effect thus is non-linear, as described above, meaning a simple attack could possibly bring down an entire system (or a sizable subsystem). Because our socio-economic systems are based on efficient specialization – of tools and people – there is little to fall back upon when part of the system fails: we have few redundant backups, which would be too costly; people are skilled at one thing but lack general survival strategies.

The point of this discussion is to highlight that subjective insecurity can be and usually is constructed based on objective facts (Bean 2011, 148; Lacy 2014, 28; Lipschutz 2000, 49). While from day to day mostly unrealized, there are real threats out there and we have real vulnerabilities. Given the way the liberal order's components (individuals, companies, goods, and tools) are linked together, these threats can even be existential: threats to the very existence of our states and societies. Of course, the probability of such an existential threat's manifesting is low. Yet the mere possibility is enough, as the severity of the consequences swamps the risk assessment (which is based, simplifying, on probability times severity).

Yet vulnerability alone does not explain insecurity; many more vulnerable people than us get on with life just fine. Rather, the vulnerability must be made salient by being communicated to the vulnerable (i.e. us) either by events or narratives. Within academia the latter is seen as a driving cause of what is called securitization, the expansion of security logic to other sectors and areas of life (Buzan, Waever, and de Wilde 1998). Often cast in a negative light, from the perspective of the securitizing actor – the government security or military organization – it makes perfect sense: it is better that the narrative highlights your vulnerability than an actual event (e.g. a terrorist attack). Our system of democratic debate and politics, coupled with media transparency, even means a discussion of insecurity is necessary before a resolution is reached. Yet once the discussion is begun, the first securitizing act/move is made, the contemporary audiences – people and politicians – are especially easy to convince to move from "speech act" to security action. Security events, and speculation, are exactly what the (Western) media are designed to cover (Pratkanis 2007; see also Nacos 1994). Modern communication technology acts to "inform us just how insecure each of us should really feel" (Lipschutz 2000, 45). It shows us images and provides information on diseases, crime, rogue states, and terrorism. Yet on the other side of the stories the media cover are the consumers – the citizens that sought those stories. People seek out such news not necessarily because of disaster voyeurism, but because of hedonic asymmetry. This means negative information and experiences receive priority over positive news because, from an evolutionary perspective, threats demand more attention (than enjoyment, leisure, etc.) if we are to survive (Reeves and Read 2009, 188).

Beyond biology, insecurity stories are effective because the knowledge available to modern educated society allows threats that would have been intangible to previous eras to resonate: the average citizen understands just enough about biology, politics, psychology, etc., so that they understand the dangers presented to them and have opinions on how to solve them (and, as we argue, even actual capabilities to help solve them). Moreover, unlike previous eras, modern Enlightenment-inspired ideas of progress (and arguably its realization), coupled with the artificial safety (stability) of the Cold War, have made the modern audience less accepting of risk and insecurity than generations before (related, see Gat 2006, 597–600; ideas from Moore 1978). Predictability is "central to contemporary life" for citizens, markets, and status quo states (Lipschutz 2000, 158). Our own security makes us more susceptible to messages that threaten the loss of that security or that show the world inhabited by those less fortunate (Lacy 2014, 50), perhaps justifiably since the average Western urbanite would have a hard time surviving even a week if routine socio-economic activity were to suddenly cease. Our own comfort and knowledge, fear of uncertainty, hedonic asymmetry, mass media, and democratic governance have all combined to make the average citizen hyper aware of security messages.

This burst in information and knowledge accelerated greatly at about the same time as our security institutions were going through their post–Cold War search for meaning and purpose. Academics and politicians competed to create the narrative that would define the new era in the same way George Kennan and containment dominated the old Cold War era. To these previously, mostly conceptual, threats of a "coming anarchy" and "clash of civilizations," 9/11 gave a concrete manifestation. The near concurrent birth of Web 2.0 and explosion of media outlets meant this message, images of the planes hitting the towers, could be repeated and replayed endlessly. If we relaxed too much because things were too quiet, al Qaeda would release a threatening video to put us on edge, even if their promises of death and destruction typically came to naught. In this way information and knowledge, springing from democracy and associated rights (press, information, etc.), have not made us feel safer. Observers have noted increased anxiety in contemporary societies about many risks (Breakwell 2014, 132), something which US President Barack Obama even commented on in his final report on the State of the Union in 2016. This is reflected in the discourse of insecurity mentioned earlier – in the news we watch, the books we read, even the television shows and movies we enjoy.

As the state securitized more and more areas of social and economic life, matched only by the media's enthusiasm to connect threat messages to their viewers'/readers' personal lives, optimism bias (the belief that something cannot affect or happen to you) gradually broke down. Both the state and media had an interest in showing that the threats really could affect you personally (Lerner and Keltner 2000). For the state this was particularly necessary. The state was already facing a citizenry that had grown increasingly distrustful of social institutions over the past decades, in part due to technology and information itself (figures for United States in Gallup 2016; generally, with figures, Lerner 2014, 7–10; for reasons, see Breakwell 2014, 158). Society had become increasingly heterogeneous and fragmented, economic specialization had led to social differentiation and political polarization. As a result the rural Caucasian male, the urban African American male, women, and every other identity group all faced different security concerns. The (democratic) state had to address them all, at least in words, to get enough support for the enhanced security measures that it hoped would increase confidence in the state's ability to make you personally safer.

Yet this effort by the state to address all our interests and fears did not have the intended effect. While the blanket coverage raised awareness, it served only to increase anxiety; the fact that the state was talking about a security concern did not translate into people thinking the state was doing something about it. This was because technology had multiplied the messages a citizen receives, and many of these conflicted with the state's message. If the government said something was a threat, the opposition would inevitably say it was not; if the state claimed success, a counter-narrative would soon present it as a failure (though the state provided lots of fodder in this regard). When a person receives such conflicting messages, the result is that they estimate risks as being higher; they feel more insecure (Breakwell 2014, 167). Moreover, by drawing attention to even one security concern – such as terrorism – the message induced thinking about all other security threats, what is called "associative anxiety," when feeling of anxiety spread from one area to another in the same general (policy) area (Nakayachi 2013). In this way efforts to increase trust by increasing the message, to show the state was addressing your specific security concern, only increased anxiety about security broadly.

In turn, this anxiety about security spread to anxiety about the state's response to that security. Such actions picked up notably following the attacks of 9/11, after which terrorism became the crucible upon which modern security was built. Yet the reactive legislation passed in the wake of the attacks and the tactics of the War on Terror – state secrecy, mass surveillance, rendition, torture, and assassination – conflicted with the values of most citizens of liberal democracies; whether left- or right-wing, the laws and tactics were so broad that everybody could find something to be unhappy about. Trust in institutions after such negative events can be maintained only if the values of the state institution remain in line with those of the nation's citizenry (Cvetkovich, Siegrist, Murray, and Tragesser 2002). Instead the combination of "experiences" of negative events – even if mostly via media – and value differences led to a further loss of trust in institutions. For some citizens the state's new (lack of) values contributed also to negative experiences, through discrimination, militarization of the police, or the mistaken targeting of an innocent person as a terrorist.

Moreover, even the use of tactics inconsistent with our values seemingly did not provide security. Promises of security competed with images of cities in ashes, images the media were eager to show even if distorted or imagined in investigative *cum* speculative reports. Yet these reports "generate psychological and social responses that can be every bit as consequential as responses to people and places in the real world" because the brain has not evolved to distinguish the real world from a virtual world (Reeves and Read 2009, 192–93). Meanwhile, assurances by the state of progress had to be taken at their word given rules of secrecy, making state claims easily refuted by pundits who often could point to actual (even if cherry-picked) events to counter state claims, as when the US military reported good progress in the fight against ISIS shortly before they took over Ramadi (2015) and routed the Iraqi army (de Luce 2015a). While we should not equate such a tactical setback with a strategic one, and there are many explanations for the DoD's optimistic reports, the contradiction opened old wounds of distrust from the intelligence fiasco surrounding the 2003 invasion of Iraq as well as more recent feelings of unease following the Manning and Snowden leaks. The state seemed less a "protector" and instead, at best, merely "a belated and essentially futile avenger," at worst, the source of the problem itself (Arendt 1963, 15).

Moreover, many people believed they knew why the state had failed. The approaches the state was using were old and ineffective. Citizens largely share the state's affinity with technology, and even marvel at many modern weapons, but nonetheless many see the state's approach to the use of technology as outdated. The scientific system today has evolved to be more in line with the values of liberalism, rejecting any claim to a monopoly on knowledge or exclusionary right to a technology. The nature of modern technology and the science it is built upon sees solutions as arising not through command innovation, but through diffuse actors arriving at solutions through network and/or swarm (stigmergy) logic. The subsequent use and application of technology is thus also maximized by its democratization. It was designed by the network, for the network, as the network is the legitimate source of knowledge and what technology should serve (e.g. Lanier 2010; Morozov 2014). Herein is the roots even of current trends in anti-intellectualism; liberalism implies equality of knowledge, and legitimate outcomes of knowledge – solutions to problems – thus required *your* knowledge (e.g. Ezrahi 2004). The rationalist methods the state uses for threat and solution identification therefore lack process legitimacy.

Thus, trust in the state has declined along two dimensions: general institutional trust fell and with it trust in the messages the state provided, and specific trust (often called confidence) in the state's ability to provide security declined. New technologies aggravated the long-term trends in declining trust; continuous and conflicting messages created anxiety. With the most recent advances though, filtering the information you receive has become possible. It is possible that soon people will reduce anxiety by filtering out the security news or views they do not like. However, such a development would not be good for security; people would either withdraw or polarize. Security policy would suffer the same fate we are now seeing in democracy generally (on filtering and effects, see Sunstein 2007; Pariser 2011).

Lack of specific trust in the ability of the state to provide security is possibly even more problematic. Lack of security directly increases anxiety, further undermining socio-political functions, including general institutional trust given the social contract is based on security provision. In Thomas Hobbes's ([1651] 2010, 21:21) original words, "The obligation of subjects to the sovereign is understood to last as long, and no longer, than the power lasteth by which he is able to protect them." As we have seen, this lack of trust due to subjective insecurity can then even undermine objective security as the public deprives the state of tools needed for their defence, such as we saw in inter-war France. Objective security failures can result, seemingly confirming that the feeling of subjective insecurity was correct (a form of both confirmation and hindsight bias).

Yet considering our discussion in Chapter 2, things that threaten our survival should receive not only our attention, but should lead to a response – to an action to control the risk. Why, if there is fear, worry, and/or anxiety, resulting in increased interest, has there been no action or effective pressure on the state to act? This brings us to our fifth and final point on people's insecurity. Lack of action comes down to lack of individual self-efficacy, both regarding ability to influence the state generally, and to provide for one's own security personally. Unlike the 1950s and 1960s, with its civil defence messages delivered by Bert the Turtle or a young Gene Hackman, the state has not provided a constructive message to its citizens about how they can help provide security. In the absence of such direct instruction, general feelings of connectedness to security providers can suffice. A citizen need not become a soldier, spy, or civil servant to meaningfully participate; it simply requires a person's decisions be meaningful in that they can see their influence on the environment (see especially Chapter 4). Such feedback can be directly provided by the state ("Look what you did to help our victory!") or inferred through perhaps spurious yet still tangible connections ("Johnny came home, my victory garden must have helped"). Moreover, self-efficacy can be vicarious; provided an individual can identify with the agent that is bringing about security they can feel they have done it themselves (Reeves and Read 2009, 73–74). Yet as discussed, the modern citizen is largely disconnected from security provision given its bureaucratic structure and secrecy imperative.

Without a feeling of self-efficacy, vicariously experienced or through viable options for self-protection, feelings of anxiety and fear, real or induced, are more likely to lead to withdrawal than mobilization (Girandola 2000; Weinstein, Lyon, Rothman, and Cuite 2000). Those who have the means opt for self-help through private solutions – gated communities and guards – that give a (albeit useful) feeling of control if not real security (Virilio's "priva-topias" in Lacy 2014; see also Lipschutz 2000, 140, also 132). Those who lack such resources retreat into compensatory control mechanisms, such as religion, magical thinking, superstition, or belief in a coming singularity (sources at Amsterdam Uncertainty Lab 2017, e.g. Wojtkowiak and Rutjens 2011).

Rather than the result of some dramatic event, the interconnected increase in subjective insecurity and decline in specific and institutional trust are the result of increasing secrecy from the state, increasing information from the media, and the citizens' disconnection from security. The technology and openness of the information age have thus combined with the closed state to create subjective insecurity on top of the complex objective insecurity. In-transparency feeds apathy – we do not know what we need to know; bureaucracy compounds this – what we know does not matter because we cannot do anything.

Yet despite this discouraging trend, this is only the first part of a story still in progress. Society's interest in security is real, and is increasingly so as the state extends security to every realm of everyday life. With each security failure this interest grows and the political narrative intensifies, often further polarizing with promises of security through walls, lists, and deportations. Yet each tragedy has also shown that despite modern trends toward fragmentation and individualism social solidarity is still real: from "We are all Americans" (*Le Monde*, 2001) to "Je suis Charlie" (2015). The diffuse nature of contemporary "wars" – omnipresent and eternal – as well as the speed which images travel and even the state's failures have made citizens increasingly aware of their own embeddedness in a larger context. As philosopher Bernard-Henri Lévy (2015) put it in his essay "Thinking the Unthinkable: This Is War" following the Paris attacks of 2015, "That leaves you, me and society, both collectively and individually. Each of us, this time, is a target, a front line, a soldier without knowing it, a cell of resistance, a locus of mobilization and of biopolitical fragility." Interest in doing something is high; it need only be met with openness and opportunities for participation from the state.

CONCLUSION

Complex technology and a complex world system have created complex security problems that the current system is stretched to meet. The world has shrunk, in that space and time are less barriers than they once were. Capabilities and threats have dispersed throughout an interdependent system wherein actors are increasingly enabled materially while unconstrained philosophically. Nowhere is this exemplified better than on the Internet.

This security environment was engendered by the technologies and social innovations of the previous era that were created to solve the security threats of that era. Yet these approaches – bureaucracy, (information) technology, and secrecy – cannot meet the current threats in their current configuration. Bureaucracies are slow and inflexible, subject to group think and being stuck in patterns of old thinking. Secrecy compounds these problems, preventing both internal communication and limiting adaptive potential and collective problem solving. Instead of participation this system places faith in automation and algorithms, despite that many modern problems cannot be predicted or solved based on such solutions and that automation can have negative effects on the human and social world. This system cannot address the unknown, fast, adaptive, innovative, fluid, and networked threats of the modern world and puts humans in a position where they also know little about the security realm and can do little in it. Moreover, modern ICT makes every security failure or near miss clear to the citizens even if they are secure, and in the end the images of possibilities outweigh the facts of reality.

The perceived failure of security has resulted in a further loss of trust and confidence in the state that is supposed to provide that security, to the breaking of the social contract and a crisis of representative democracy. On many levels this has led to a search for new sources to which one can be loyal, whether selfish individualism, localism, nativism, or transnational networks. Modern technology has made the turn to such alternative identities increasingly possible: political revolutions are driven on Twitter by both democrats and demagogues. Some individuals have become threats in themselves, joined threatening networks (Anonymous), or sworn loyalty to new anti–status quo groups (ISIS). Yet state actors have yet to democratize the security technologies they largely created (e.g. the Internet itself) and continue to rely mostly on professional security and military apparatuses. Current policy reflects a hammer-nail approach, using the traditional capabilities of bureaucracy, technology, and secrecy and simply scaling them up (using new tools in a "sustaining" fashion, see Horowitz 2010, 216, 220). By using the capabilities we now possess it "make[s] it easier for our leaders to skirt the more fundamental questions about interests and strategy. It allows them to 'do something' even when what is being done won't necessarily help" (Walt 2014). More radical solutions that could alter power relations and social structures are thus avoided, until the inability to meet the threats breaks down those very socio-political institutions while leaving only anarchy and self-help in its place.

Yet while new technologies are the source of many threats and many of our vulnerabilities, might they also be the source of our security? Is the "cyber"-weapon possibly the new dominant weapons system? If it is, will this too be dominated by "elaborately trained and equipped individuals," as in the vision of net-centric warfare (McNeill 1982, 20)? Or can it enable broad-based participation in a new adaptive, more effective security system, thus disarming the "securocrats" of their expertise-based arguments for their monopoly on information and policy and restoring democratic control over security? This book now turns to arguing that the latter possibility can be realized, that we can design our technology in this way and thereby influence our social structures and security. Despite our present uncertainty and self-doubt, this is a feature, not a bug, of our liberal democratic systems. It allows for the system's flexible adaptation, for reform without the need for revolution (RFE/RL 2015c; similar but broader points in Sommermann 2015, 5–7; for a new source in this vein, see Roberts 2017). From the 1930s to the 1970s to today, the questioning of our security and state-society system has and can again lead to its improvement. Such improvement is not assured or inevitable; but provided criticism and discourse is allowed – that is, the system is open – the likelihood of such innovation is high.

NOTES

1. While too numerous to cite, see such popular titles as *After the Empire: The Breakdown of the American Order* (Emmanuel Todd, 2003); *A World in Disarray: American Foreign Policy and the Crisis of the Old Order* (Richard Haass, 2017); *Democracy in Retreat: The Revolt of the Middle Class and the Worldwide Decline of Representative Government* (Joshua Kurlantzick, 2013); *Democracy in Decline?* (ed. Larry Diamond and Marc F. Plattner, 2015); *Buying Time: The Delayed Crisis of Democratic Capitalism* (Wolfgang Streeck, 2014); *The Unwinding: An Inner History of the New America* (George Packer, 2014); *It's Even Worse than It Looks: How the American Constitutional System Collided with the New Politics of Extremism* (Thomas E. Mann and Norman J. Ornstein, 2013); *After the Fall: The End of the European Dream and the Decline of a Continent* (Walter Laqueur, 2012).

2. Entitled "Waiting for the Barbarians."

3. From *A Song of Ice and Fire* by George R. R. Martin, on which the television series *Game of Thrones* is based.

4. A more critical perspective would claim this search for threats was purely about power (resources and authority). While there may be some truth in this claim, there is no need to retreat into such cynicism to explain why military/security actors would search for a purpose (we all search for purpose), and the underlying causes of this search are not relevant to the argument herein (though they are important to other arguments and thus worthy of study by others).

5. Violence is defined in the *World Report on Violence and Health* as "the intentional use of physical force or power, threatened or actual, against oneself, another person, or against a group or community, that either results in or has a high likelihood

of resulting in injury, death, psychological harm, maldevelopment, or deprivation" (Krug, Dahlberg, Mercy, Zwi, and Lozano 2002, 5). This is largely consistent with strategic thought and international relations theories (e.g. in considering violence's actual and threatened use and its different scopes, scales, and application).

6. Herein, we understand information as essentially data, presumably objective and true; information then feeds into knowledge creation, which is about patterns in information that enable generalization and thus informed decisions and action, sometimes called foresight.

7. A further question is how much of the details (and in what format) must really be revealed? This will be considered in Chapter 5.

8. A similar incident occurred in 2008 when a malicious individual posted a report on a citizen reporter platform that Steve Jobs had been hospitalized following a heart attack, wiping 10 percent of Apple's stock value in minutes.

Chapter Four

Openness and Open Government

Limits, Possibilities, and Approaches

When many people think of Estonia, the first thing to come to their mind may be something like "Where is that?" Yet this well-educated Baltic republic of 1.3 million, the birthplace of Skype and Playtech as well as numerous niche tech start-ups, is at the forefront of applying technology to enhance state capabilities and improve state-society relations, to create what Estonian president Toomas Hendrik Ilves calls a new "Lockean contract" (Keen 2016). With the establishment of a national online ID system and the creation of an integrated national database containing its citizens' information, Estonia has created "a new kind of digital civic operating system" (Keen 2016). Through this system citizens can access hundreds of online services, while the government also has access to its citizens' data. Rather than anonymity and privacy, personal data protection is based on a system of mutual transparency: the owner of any data (e.g. a citizen) can see who has accessed that data, thereby preventing abuse and engendering trust. Based on its own variant of Blockchain technology (BBC News, Business 2016) this e-government system has a decentralized/distributed structure that ensures security, scalability, cost savings, and integration with older systems (Bershidsky 2015). The system is a source of pride for both the Estonian citizens and their government. Moreover, as we shall see in Chapter 5, Estonia's integration of technology and citizens has not stopped at the civil realm, but extends also to national defence.

Capabilities like what Estonia has developed are how challenges and threats are met; matching existing or emerging capabilities to the nature of the current gap that prevents threats from being met is the key in defence and security transformation (Jasper 2009a, 2009b). In the recent past these capabilities have been monopolized, as required by the highly structured context, clearly defined threat, and well-understood solution to that threat. Yet the nature of the modern era, its unstructured environment and diffuse threats, its problems with non-linear solutions or even no optimal solutions, requires capabilities of a different sort. While these capabilities currently do not exist in any single machine, or any person, they can still be captured through an organizational approach which unifies the machine and the human to draw on the full network of technology and persons available.

States can, and often have, drawn these capabilities from outside the traditional military sector (and should do so again according to Omand 2010, 290, referring especially to the intelligence sector). The ability and necessity of doing so depends on the locus of innovation at the time, which often depends on the nature of that innovation: Is it expensive with no or uncertain wider applications beyond the defence sector, or inexpensive with wide applications in many sectors? Currently the locus of innovation is in the private sector and, moreover, is focused on the production of technological goods for the mass market (though business to business also remains important).

At the cutting edge of private sector development is the idea of openness, from open source software and code, to open innovation, open science, and peer production. These modes of knowledge, goods, and service production are – to recap from the introduction –organizationally centred on the idea of networks and swarms (versus hierarchical command and control), technologically focused on systems designed to enhance and complement human capabilities and to meet their needs (rather than designed to replace humans or meet the needs of pre-existing technology), and based on the idea of openness for empowering individuals to contribute to the fulfilment of their own needs while also releasing the emergent properties of individuals working together. Through these approaches organizations seek to innovate faster with less risk and resources by capturing diffuse creativity and unifying the producer and consumer (the equivalent of means and ends in security terms) in one person (a so-called "produser").

Despite their slow bureaucracies, states have begun to catch on to this trend. Their command solutions and centralized solutions were becoming increasingly insufficient in the context of new problems and social demands. Governments looked with envy on the seemingly nimble private sector and its use of distributed power and production to meet human needs. It was a seductive idea, one consistent with their own liberal ideas, with both the market and democracy. Thus some states began to experiment and deploy new technologies enabling openness and participation to many sectors of government and numerous policy areas. These initiatives fall under the collective policy of open government (OG), a concept that goes beyond transparency and accountability and calls also for deeper participation, deliberation, and even co-production to "promote efficiency and effectiveness" (United States, White House 2009). It is thus based not only on the historical (or natural) rights of man in a liberal democracy but on "the wisdom of crowds" and distributed task performance, swarm logic that can now be mobilized through modern technology. Moreover, the state sees in OG the potential for participation to translate into social cohesion, to restore a sense of community through the subtlety of organizational socio-psychology rather than outdated tools of universal education, conscription, and national media.

Yet in contrast to the openness espoused, even if not always realized, elsewhere, the state has argued that security is a "special domain, where the normal calculus of open government does not apply" (Roberts 2004, 69–70). Instead, as we saw in Chapter 3, national security policy is incubated by "securocrats" inside massive rationalized bureaucracies and implemented through technological solutions requiring absolute secrecy. Regarding transparency, most governments take a minimalistic position, considering its useful and desirable extent to be limited to that necessary for the purpose of basic oversight and accountability, typically through representative approaches rather than directly democratic ones. Indeed at one time such accountability mechanisms seem to have been sufficient, allowing the states using them to accrue some of the benefits of openness even while keeping secrets (Colaresi 2014).

Yet as times change, threats and capabilities change, and the nature of transparency and oversight "must evolve to keep pace" (Fung, Graham, and Weil 2007, 181; also Colaresi 2014, 15, 242). As shown earlier, the existing organizational approach toward security is inconsistent with modern technology and modern science, with the cutting-edge way of knowing things and thus solving problems and doing things. Technology has changed the dynamics, leaving decision makers less in possession of the needed tools and knowledge (even if they cling to as many fragments of data/information as possible). Power – which equates to capabilities – has diffused into the increasingly specialized and diversified socio-economic sector. Meanwhile, the complex world is increasingly understandable only in a non-linear, even chaotic (scientifically speaking) way, requiring solutions to problems that cannot be organized through traditional command and control approaches. The state can recapture the capabilities suitable for addressing current challenges only through new and original approaches that embrace the emancipatory potential of current technology, enabling broad-based participation in the provision of security.

Yet total blanket transparency, which is often what laypersons understand openness to mean, may not be the solution. Our critique of the current system does not imply or justify an automatic swing to the polar opposite of what we currently have. To come to a more balanced solution, we need to see how far openness has come beyond its occasional appearance in history; that is, what does the current system look like and what problems does it have. We need to also interrogate what further openness would mean, whether there are other risks beyond the accusation it alerts our enemies of our secrets, a risk turned to in Chapter 6. Only then can we consider the benefits: how openness can be, and has been, given structure in various approaches currently applied within the open government movement and other open approaches. In light of these approaches, and the mechanisms behind them, we will then be in a better position to understand the role that open participation can play in security and how it can be designed for the unique character of security problems, which is turned to in the following two chapters.

PROGRESS IN OPENNESS: TRANSPARENCY AND ACCOUNTABILITY AND THEIR LIMITS

In Chapter 2 we saw some pre-twentieth-century developments in openness, ones which at first involved more participation (action) than information, though the people participating had no reason to doubt what their priests and kings told them – their information and authority were often widely accepted to be valid. Over time there was a gradual shift toward releasing more information, especially when the state needed other means of gathering support and getting people to participate. Information proved to be a valuable resource for states to increase their power. Over time, citizens came to demand such information in exchange for their role in providing that power, even coming to see some information as a right. Information became more important in modern societies the less direct participation there was, a necessary element to allow for trust between actors unknown to one another but dependent upon one another: whether the Chicago meat industry, capital city politician, or Wall Street banker.

The first modern era of openness – focused on transparency – was primarily inspired by economic and related social concerns, with of course, consideration of how these would affect politics. In the United States, this took the form of the progressive-era fight against the so-called robber barons and was led especially by the Supreme Court activities of Justice Louis Brandeis, author of the well-known trope "sunlight is the best disinfectant." These activities translated into laws such as the Publicity Act of 1910 (regarding politicians and campaign donations), the Securities Act of 1933, the Securities Exchange Act of 1934, and the Administrative Procedure Act of 1947 (out of which the Freedom of Information Act [1966] evolved). The essence of these right-to-know laws, and subsequent ones in the following decades, was to inform the public about the inner workings of government, with this information then being used to hold officials accountable ex post through the participatory mechanism of elections. The larger, essential point here is that "the linchpin of effective transparency was [and is] the connection between information and action" (Fung, Graham, and Weil 2007, xiv). The right to information and the right to vote, and perhaps other rights (to be explored), are inseparable.

Despite our previous generalization, over time national security secrecy has lost some of its allure as states realized secrecy can undermine security and may increase the chance of war (e.g. Jervis 1988; Watson 1978, 31). The first Freedom of Information law in 1766 (Sweden) was itself driven by security-relevant foreign policy concerns. On a geo-strategic level WWI discredited secret treaties and alliances, leading to more open diplomatic practices. The times when the Cold War almost went hot led to arrangement for transparency and openness in weapons and military disposition, the birth of monitoring and verification as an international practice. On a national level, in the United States the *Pentagon Papers* inaugurated an era that, even if not more open, at least required more justification and persuasion in policy making. "Secret" weapons proved to be illusionary or, when possible, expensive and quickly outdated, sometimes even before they were fully operational and deployed. Many never even realized their kinetic potential (i.e. saw actual use), while the secrecy surrounding them meant their power could not even contribute to diplomatic or psychological goals. Meanwhile, in the intelligence sector the secrets acquired often gave no advantage, winning the spy game did not win you the war, covert operations backfired spectacularly, and false negatives (failure to know, e.g. the collapse of the USSR) and false positives (incorrect "facts," e.g. missile gaps with the USSR, WMDs in Iraq) led to strategic surprise and costly strategic miscalculations, respectively. With each scandal came hearings, investigations, and increasing oversight, though still typically by a limited circle of the people's representatives meeting behind closed doors (Colaresi 2014, 246). Through these events and processes we arrived at our modern system: by accident and reaction, not foresight and design.

THE MODERN POLITICAL PARADOX OF TRANSPARENCY AND ACCOUNTABILITY IN SECURITY

In his elaborate analysis Michael Colaresi demonstrated that "retrospectively transparent democracies" can and do keep secrets and are thereby able to accrue significant benefits in foreign and security policy while preventing abuses. To rephrase, ex post release of information to the public can be effective at disciplining national security decision makers due to fear of ex post accountability, from losing re-election to facing jail time. Yet his analysis acknowledges that as technology advances, the scale and vectors of potential abuse of secrecy change, thus requiring innovation in oversight as well (Colaresi 2014, 15, 242; see also Fung, Graham, and Weil 2007, 181). The past several years have revealed the extent of both technological change and the secrets that governments are keeping, with just how much we do not know about our governments and their policies becoming especially evident following the revelations made through WikiLeaks (circa 2010 onward) and Edward Snowden (2013 onward). These secrets and their inevitable revelations have directly impacted US national security, not due to exposure of our agents and methods as the state contends, but by undermining trust in the state.

The insufficiency of traditional transparency and accountability mechanisms in the modern context is rooted in the interaction of three factors: 1) the speed of the world and a resulting need for quick decisions and actions; 2) the secrecy behind decision making and action in the security realm; and 3) the ex post transparency and accountability mechanism itself in light of the desire of politicians to stay in office and civil servants to keep their jobs, to which we could add the people's need to hold somebody to account – to blame somebody – when something goes wrong.

As highlighted in Chapter 3, one of the key variables that has changed due to technological advances is speed and interconnectedness. Modern threats – terrorism, cyberattacks, disease – are increasingly offensive in their nature and travel quickly through unexpected and uncontrollable vectors, making defence increasingly impossible in a porous, target-rich environment. Addressing security problems has thus increasingly required proactive measures, measures which current technology encourages by seemingly offering the ability to strike quickly, in a visible way with low cost (casualties). In this world the loop from information (observation) to decision to action is too fast for traditional internal democratic control mechanisms, such as court orders, congressional approval, or even knowledge of one's direct supervisor. The fact that actions need to be taken quickly requires thinking quickly, meaning the resulting decisions will fall back on existing institutional lessons (see Chapter 3); in other words, they will be rooted in established bureaucratic, technological, and secretive practices that operate almost automatically.

Yet the decider is somewhat protected in that the decision-making process itself, and even implementation remains in-transparent. Internally, the decision maker is protected by compartmentalization within the bureaucracy and secrecy between the different compartments. Externally, secrecy is also the default position, with ex post transparency possible only "via a reactive, delayed, emergency-oriented, history-driven, confrontational, judicial, do-it-yourself, cost-driven mechanism" (Peled 2014a, 172). Indeed, in the decision maker's defence, sometimes the process is even in-transparent to them, laid down long ago in procedures and templates, guided by black boxed algorithms.

With this system in place it is the default position of policy makers to err on the side of caution in security issues. Yet caution in modern security matters does not mean inaction. Instead the system reinforces the tendency to take proactive measures consistent with available technological tools, established practices, lessons learned, and the nature of the threat. If the system of surveillance is there, the space for storage free, the drones already hovering over areas of interest, they will be used. Because the solutions adopted and actions taken remain hidden even when they are ongoing practice – distant drone strikes and virtual snooping – there is little to no price or cost for the policy (until there's a leak), so the logic is why not do it and see if it works (idea somewhat related to Singer 2009, 321, referring to the work of James Der Derian). The secrecy will hide false positives (e.g. falsely accused terrorist), useless policies, and unknown counterfactuals (what might have been with a proper tactical assessment) allowing the policy makers and implementers to claim success with selected illustrative examples.

Yet while the secrecy of the process hides what is happening while it is happening, if something goes wrong, if there is a security failure or a leak revealing socially frowned-upon tactics, then afterwards somebody will be held accountable, if not legally then at the ballot box (Albrecht, 2008, 15; Garfinkel 2004; Indridason 2008; for theory, see Arce, Croson, and Eckel 2011, 379; Jervis 1978, 208). Ex post transparency will ensure a responsible party, or a scapegoat, is found. Thus, there is a "political logic of response" (Jervis 1978, 208) that requires a "do something" approach (Walt 2014) for the decision maker to keep their job, an approach encouraged by the tools the decision maker has at hand. This political logic of response has the potential to turn the advantages of retrospective transparency and accountability on their head, leading not to careful consideration of policies in the public good but to reflexive actions to ensure that when the time comes for accountability, evidence that "we did everything possible" can be selectively produced while blame can be placed on invasive or automated systems that did not receive funding by Congress/Parliament, approval by the courts, or support by the public, perhaps ultimately because of a Snowden or Manning.

As security threats become more offensive due to permanent war and hybrid operations, security measures have necessarily become more proactive, even pre-emptive. To ensure these measures are effective and in the public interest, oversight needs to become the same. Given our system's potential to make any threat, even the inevitable accidents and normal failures (Perrow 1984; Virilio in Lacy 2014, 34), into an existential one, we need more than ex post accountability after the ashes have settled; we need better a priori solutions. Yet to ensure proper accountability requires also putting the citizen as well as many civil servants back into the increasingly automated decision processes and resulting actions. Active oversight of disempowered bureaucrats and officers by disconnected citizens would mean little.

THE LIMITS OF TOTAL TRANSPARENCY

Many people equate openness with transparency due to the choice of terminology, though the "open" concept comes from ideas of open source (as in software), not open filing cabinets. Given this belief the solution to current secrecy is often held to be its opposite: less secrecy, in other words more transparency. However, there is no guarantee that more openness earlier and throughout the security-making process will necessarily result in better policies. There can be such a thing as too much information (and too much choice).[1] The public has only so much capacity to absorb and analyze information, and even less if this comes in the form of raw data; this is why so many such tasks are delegated to the state in the first place.

The insufficiency of pure, unstructured openness was illustrated by the failure of WikiLeaks to crowdsource the analysis of raw data dumps and create their envisioned "open-source, democratic intelligence agency" (Julian Assange quoted in Leigh and Harding 2011, 52; on failure, see 61). The data on WikiLeaks did not really reflect any given truth; it was not knowledge about some area of life. It was fragments that need exploration to start building a fuller picture (Ibid., 108, 182–83).[2] Yet the people proved uninterested in following the bread crumbs on their own. This led WikiLeaks to essentially abandon the "Wiki" part of its philosophy; rather than using the people they made a partnership with international mainstream media outlets to help put the material in context and give it meaning that would resonate with the public and thereby impact policy. Organization of transparency is required for transparency to have meaning. As will be shown shortly, governments have even used unorganized transparency to create information overload and thus conceal the real facts.

Additionally, the mass release of security information can lead to not just analytical but also emotional overload, increasing fear in society due to knowledge of all the threats out there and all our vulnerabilities (Lacy 2014, 34). This can serve to acclimatize the population to "life in the state of emergency" and normalize insecurity (Ibid., 83; on normalization, see e.g. Borell 2008; Galeotti 2014a). While this can have advantages, creating a more resilient (or fatalistic) society and even having deterrence functions, it can also be used by the state to prove to the public "why you need us." An example of such a policy can be seen in Putin's Russia, where authorities want people horrified but not moving from their couch; appalled but passive (Pomerantsev and Weiss, 2014; RFE/RL 2015a). Transparency can thus link to inaction just as much as action.

Thus, regardless of whether it is a natural or legal right, transparency itself is not sufficient for more effective policy making, just as secrecy alone is not necessarily bad for democracy (on this logic, see Colaresi 2014, 237). Nor can transparency alone induce the trust necessary for subjective security. While transparency is an important predictor of trust, trust is a complex phenomenon.[3] It requires also expertise, independence, and shared interests and (especially) values (Frewer, Howard, Hedderley, and Shepherd 1996). Currently, citizens have doubts about all these requirements for trust when it comes to their governments, in part because transparency has shown them not to exist. The discovery of how states conduct their wars, as we saw in the "Collateral Murder" video released by WikiLeaks, or of how states are monitoring their own populations through programs like PRISM, has shown how the values of state and citizen diverge. The fact that despite these tactics we can still be (arguably) losing our wars and subject to attack at home calls into question the state's expertise.

Rather than total transparency, what is needed is structured transparency, which is a necessary precondition for effective participation (Nakatsu, Grossman, and Iacovou 2014, 11; Spina 2014, 179).[4] The resulting informed action is in turn what is ultimately required if policy making is to be both effective and accepted, thus increasing both real and felt security, respectively, and thereby also faith in the political and technological system which brought that security about. Openness is a means to participation, which is a means to security, which together facilitate trust, by which all are in turn reinforced. The state's task is to devise ways to initiate this process in the face of a sceptical citizenry, civil service, and soldiery.

OPEN GOVERNMENT

So if it is not just about tossing non-redacted classified folders onto the Internet, what does or should openness in government entail? The most recent trend in this regard goes under the moniker open government (OG), which while continuing to build trends in increasing transparency, is intended to go much further, moving from simple transparency-enabled accountability to full participation realized through Web 2.0 technologies. It is a tool not only to protect representative democracy like many older transparency systems, but to enable a transformation toward upgraded versions of democracy, sometimes called liquid, direct, participatory, or deliberative democracy (Gamper 2015, 83). Action in the new system is not centred on rights enabling citizens to take actions directed at the government if they so choose, but actions by the state to create opportunities for actions by citizens that contribute directly to governance itself. In this way they resemble a positive right the state must create (versus negative rights they must abstain from), but which in turn creates a civic responsibility, one good citizens should engage in (even if they are not legally compelled to do so). The implementation of these participatory rights/responsibilities is taking a gradualist, evolutionary approach, represented in the United States by specifying phases of open government as OG 1.0, 2.0, and 3.0.

Governments the world over have come to embrace the idea of OG, from the Obama administration's Open Government Memorandum in the United States (United States, White House 2009), to the 2011 Open Government Partnership (2015), which now has sixty-seven member states, to recent charters and statements by both the G8 (in 2013) and G20 (in 2014). Nonetheless, despite its viability, potential, and political support, open government programs have thus far led to governments that are at most slightly ajar. While there is more information now available to the people, "there is limited genuine deliberative public engagement, collaboration, or co-production of public services and/or policy" (in the United States, see Blomgren Amsler and Foxworthy 2014, 195; Dixon 2010, 440; for some other countries, see Sandoval-Almazan and Gil-Garcia 2012; globally, see World Wide Web Foundation 2015). This failure seems to result from both sides of the state-society; the state is not fully developing OG opportunities, while the citizens' levels of engagement in the existing programs is "underwhelming" (Wojtczak and Morner 2015, 30; see also Larsson 2013). However, the onus lies mostly with the state: many organizations are still not sharing their most valuable, and thus critical, information assets (Peled 2014a, 166). Institutional and organizational resistance has led many online OG platforms to fail (Chadwick 2011, 21). Thus, the citizens' lack of engagement is rooted first in the lack of real opportunities to make meaningful, informed contributions to areas in which they have high interest (some of the above draws also on Min 2010, 32 and passim).

For the security sector, OG has gone even less far, with participation limited to "comments and suggestions" which "do not generally equate to substantive influence" (Bean 2011, 105; see also 144), this despite that Defense Advanced Research Projects Agency (DARPA) programs have shown the "value of increasing the number and diversity of problem solvers" for resolving problems that are "insolvable by conventional means"

(DARPA 2011; more in Chapter 5). The US Department of Homeland Security's (2014) OG 3.0 plans do not seem to advance OG much further either. The vast majority of its transparency programs focus on financial aspects, not to downplay the importance of those records, whose budget lines investigative journalists often can follow to discover more about the bigger picture. Yet people with less time on their hands may find these records less useful. The section on participation and collaboration is less than two pages and discusses only two programs, one with the Commerce Department to ensure the security-trade nexus and one "Loaned Executive Program" to provide the DHS with unpaid experts. Nonetheless, some other countries, and even some individual American organizations, have come further, a topic turned to in the next chapter after we explore what this whole openness idea is all about.

HOW OPENNESS AND PARTICIPATION WORK

How can opening participation to the citizens help to provide security, and not in a way that turns every citizen into a soldier or spy but allows them to be tinkers and tailors too? This section starts to explore modern participatory approaches, starting with the mechanisms behind how they work. This conceptual discussion will broadly raise many points, while the following section on specific applications of open approaches will go into more details on them. The conversation will be couched, to the extent possible, in general terms of open approaches and open government, with intermittent reference to security to help the reader keep their eye on the ball. As a note, because each approach has numerous sub-approaches we can cover only the largest of these. However, the next chapter will discuss some more fine-tuned approaches that may be of special applicability to security.

Any Web 2.0 (i.e. user created and focused), OG, or OPS system must first provide information and a platform (the opportunity) to enable a person to participate in a given activity of interest to them. As the individual engages in the activity and interacts with the platform, and thus directly or indirectly with other persons, the system provides *feedback* to the individual that evidences their *autonomy*[5] and progressive *ability* to *influence* (success) their environment, giving them a *relatedness* to a larger context and community. Contributing to the activity, whether solving a problem or performing a task, in this way then alters the person, giving them internal feelings of control, or self-efficacy, which in turn motivates continued and deepened engagement in the participatory act. This continuation intention, the permanent development of what techies call "perpetual beta," is what distinguishes true open approaches from the use of technology for meeting internal organizational needs/goals, though many organizations do not recognize the difference.

Open approaches are used to tackle tasks or issues which an organization/institution does not have the resources to tackle alone. This may be because the organization cannot afford the needed means (e.g. a supercomputer), because the desired outcome is inherently external to the organization (e.g. marketing), or because the task simply cannot be done by any existing means that can be captured internally in an organization (e.g. hard non-linear problems). By opening the task to wider participation the organization is seeking to capture the diverse interest, knowledge, creativity, and/or skills dispersed across society and the specialization-driven economy. The problem is thus solved, task performed, product produced, or outcome attained through decentralized means, though the exact nature of these means and how to aggregate or integrate the solution/outcome vary by approach (some of the above builds on Reeves and Read 2009, 146). The solution devised is then fed back to the participants – as a product, service, or information – in a way which promotes engagement with that solution, thereby feeding into developing the next solution. This is a core part of the concept of a perpetual beta system: one being simultaneously used, tested, and improved.

Yet as the introduction to this chapter touched upon, OG, as well as Web 2.0 and many other computer applications generally, seek not only to solve problems and perform tasks. It is hoped that they can also build a community. This is most clearly demonstrated and realized in social networking sites (SNSs). Research has shown that online interactions on SNSs lead to feelings of social closeness, which in turn lead to more positive emotional states, with these then encouraging continuance of the online interactions (Neubaum and Krämer 2015). If these interactions occur in a collaborative task-oriented environment, such as with many massive multiplayer online games (MMOGs), then feelings of belonging and group identification, and identification with the task, are further strengthened (in OG see Wojtczak and Morner 2015, 36) (elaboration [and full referencing for academics] to come, especially in Chapter 6).

Moreover, building a community means not simply gathering together people already bonded or predisposed to have social relations. To be successful SNSs and OG want to create a new identity, to transform the person and their behaviour: to create consumers/citizens who willingly produce what they use and seek to deepen and expand their engagement in this process. The extent to which a Web 2.0 platform engages in changing their users varies by site: from the educational to the addictive to what some call "nudging" and others manipulation. Tech pioneer and philosopher Jaron Lanier explains how technologists "can change how you conceive of yourself and the world [. . . and . . .] tinker with your philosophy by direct manipulation of your cognitive experience" (2010, 6). "It is impossible to work with information technology without also engaging in social engineering" (Ibid., 4). The behaviour engineered is often designed to transfer across your virtual behaviour as you surf the Web as well as into the physical world. Thus, through gathering together, bonding, and transforming its participants, "virtual civil society appears to have many of the same benefits for citizen norms and political involvement as traditional civil society" and has "the potential to be an important new source of social capital formation in the contemporary age" (Kittilson and Dalton 2011, 641, 642).

But of course building this community requires its components: individual actors. The greatest challenge in open government is, much like with any innovation, getting people and organizations to adopt it and then getting them to continue to use it. Naturally, the technology needs to be there, but also the interest needs to be there on both sides of the state-society; people need to offer their time and governments their information (and to an extent vice versa) (Min 2010, 32). As we saw in previous chapters, interest in an issue increases when that issue begins to negatively affect a human need, increasing its salience (Bovaird, Loeffler, van Ryzin, and Parrado 2014, 123–24; Myers, Henderson-King, and Henderson-King 1997). This kicks off seeking behaviour as we try to find ways to reduce or manage the risk the issue is posing to our survival needs (Panksepp 2004; see also Dignan 2011, 24–25). States go through a similar process in their own assessment of threats and how to meet them, albeit on a macro-level.

In such situations of high interest in solving problems that are threatening our needs yet are unamenable to existing solutions, people and organizations are open to learning and innovation. This does not mean that interest needs to be universal; it rarely will be, and universal interest can actually even be detrimental to project success because too many actors with vested interests and established ways of thinking and cultures try to get in on the project or set up their own independent projects (for the example of public affairs [information warfare] units in the military, see Rid and Hecker 2009, 40).[6] More typically, some actors – whether a state, (sub-)organization, or person – will be first to see their survival threatened. If they are provided with or themselves develop an innovation, they will be the *lead* adopters. For problems crossing sectors, like many today, and which thus require cross-sectoral solution, these lead adopters form the initial constellation of actors that can build and develop a platform without resistance by vested interests to the point where it is developed enough to attract *early* adopters and advocates who set the tone of the project in a way that promotes *mass* adoption (framework derived from the development of Wikipedia in Karpf 2011).

To get people interested and put the idea of openness into practice, the technology and how it will be applied to a problem/task needs to be properly organized. Initial design and its development determine the experience the users will have, and the process plays a big role in whether people will continue usage after initial exposure and continue that use after extended exposure (versus giving up because it is too difficult, or stopping once it gets too easy, the idea of "flow" [Csikszentmihalyi 1975, 1990]). Many adopters, in business as well as in government, tend to have a "field of dreams fallacy," that if they build it the consumers, users, or participants will come (Karpf 2011). Yet there are numerous reasons OG platforms can fail, like any product or service. Risk of failure due to lack of effort and engagement by the designer is high in the case of OG because you have a non-tech-savvy actor who buys into the modern myth that technology offers quick, easy, and cheap solutions/satisfaction. As the technologically savvy know, technology is none of these; there are hidden R&D (research and development) costs, maintenance and support, hundreds of lines of code, and numerous sub-operations that run in the background that seemingly produce an instant response when you hit a button. OG cannot be an easy solution because if you build an online platform badly, people will not stay. Moreover, even if initial design is elegant and content rich, if it does not evolve (and not just scale up) as the number of participants grows to address changing needs, the participants will not stay; but change it too much and the critical lead adaptors may drop out. Web 2.0 platforms require continued investment like any infrastructure as use of that infrastructure expands and changes.

APPROACHES TO OPEN GOVERNMENT

Open government, and thus the proposed open participatory security, has several constituent approaches. A broad conceptualization of these is presented in Table 4.1, along with minimal and maximal examples and the current prevalent mode (in the author's view). While these approaches share much in common in the way they work, as outlined above, there are important differences in their operationalization, in how far they take participation, and thus in their impact on outcomes. Each approach is thus appropriate for a different set of tasks, as determined by the time for task completion, structure of task, and nature of solutions. Tasks can require quick action or be an extended or even permanent process. The structure of a task can be easily divisible into sub-tasks or require iterative or fully collaborative efforts (Franzoni and Sauermann 2014). Solutions can be facilitative, selective (and selected in different ways), or integrative (Nakatsu, Grossman, and Iacovou 2014, 4). In these

Table 4.1. Open Government Approaches and Examples

	Minimal Example(s)	*Maximal Example(s)*	*Current Dominant Mode (For Security)*
Transparency	Ex post pull request (e.g. FOIA) for accountability; manipulating/ placating information	A priori available in accessible format and educational (push informing)	Secrecy preference; free media initiative for investigating; redacted ex post information
Participation	Elections (representative); issue-specific referenda; suggestion mechanisms; military service	Active advocacy; e-referenda (full cycle); liquid democracy; citizen service (for support and oversight)	Support via voting, paying taxes, producing/consuming; participation via political party or civil society organizations
Deliberation	Town hall meetings	Web 2.0 (permanent, ongoing, integrated with policy)	Closed-door, limited circle; public comment and suggest; occasional meetings
Co-production and *Open Innovation*	Observe and report; feedback	Volunteering (provision); crowdsourcing; competitions	Outsourcing to military-intel-industrial complex; limited observe/report
Gamification and *Serious Games*	Advertising (propaganda); educating; informing	Problem solving; prevention; meta-analysis of play	Intra-military war gaming; some games for recruiting

ways each approach can contribute to lesser or greater extents in the different areas of policy making, problem solving, and even practice and provision. The following sections will discuss these aspects with regard to each of the approaches, including some OG examples as well as some first hints to how they may apply to OPS.

TRANSPARENCY AND RIGHTS-BASED PARTICIPATION

As discussed, transparency alone is not sufficient for inspiring citizen interest in engagement or for helping in effective task fulfilment. Transparency is not simply throwing open the filing cabinets for the crowds to rummage through; it must be proactive, ongoing, sourced/contextualized, and structured. In this way it will be enabling; specifically the information provided will enable the individual to take the proper action. Transparency that does not have a corresponding action that can be taken, and is enhanced, in response to the released information is mere propaganda. Thus, transparency is linked in most modern democratic political systems to participation. Most commonly, this participation takes the form of rights, though there do remain also some responsibilities. This issue aside for now (returned to in Chapter 7), we will call this "rights-based participation" to distinguish it from other forms of participation.

In democratic systems, even many partial or qualified democracies, the most visible right to participation is the right to vote, as discussed above. The right to vote links information (about performance and promises) to accountability, thereby establishing democratic control over state organizations and their agents. Indirectly, the rights of free speech, free press, and peaceful assembly also are important, as is the right to fair trials (e.g. the right to sue in a court of law). These actions in themselves contribute to at least a minimal level of individual self-efficacy for the citizens, a feeling that they have some control over policy and their future. These rights are justified on the basis that the population has not only the right to influence their future, but that they have the information required to rationally do so.

When transparency is no longer provided, it undermines the justification for the rights, the action the information is to enable. For without information the actions will not be appropriate. Lack of information has often been used to deny participation, and it can be used to deny rights; a passive population does not need rights, only protection (ideas drawn from Leonhard 1998, 24, who draws in turn on Alan Campen). Dictators have long used such logic to justify their rule of a population "not ready for democracy." Also, in democracies, rights have been easily withdrawn in times of insecurity, and without (accurate) information there is little protest when this happens, if the people even know it has happened. Moreover, the cycle is somewhat self-fulfilling: if rights are exercised independent of information, they result in inappropriate actions that undermine the government, its policies, and even the state. Even the most well-intended plans can be undermined by the ignorant masses the government created, creating yet more reason for the state to withhold participation rights if it is unwilling to stop withholding information.

To enable appropriate actions, the proper exercise of rights and perhaps even the fulfilment of some social and state responsibilities, requires information be released proactively (i.e. before the exercise of rights *cum* actions). Moreover, proactive release offers the clear advantage of allowing the releaser (e.g. the government) to set the "anchor." On a given issue, the first piece of information a person receives has an overly large influence, with adjustments to this anchor made afterwards based on new information being smaller (anchoring is also called the focusing effect/illusion, see Breakwell 2014, 89–90). This effect becomes even more important in light of the modern mass media and online communication. Corresponding to the general increase in speed in the modern world, "speed to air" is critical for media. Thus, if the government has not provided information, the media will seek to fill the air with pundits or will repeat less reliable reports from actors who better understand the news cycle. Media, reflecting general societal views on secrecy, are prone to believe these false reports because they assume absence of information reflects incompetence or a cover-up (Ibid., 175). By the time government gets their side of the story out, society has already anchored its beliefs on the false information, while the media have often moved on if the event is fast developing, while more durable reports (for instance, on a scandal) are retracted late in the next day's newscast or on the back pages of tomorrow's papers. While all this sounds like bad news for governments, this context has a positive side in that modern media "are ripe for proactive information delivery," especially as the sector fragments and budgets decline, including resources for deep investigative journalism (Ibid.). This race to air, of course, does not justify the release of false or purposely manipulative information *cum* anchors, which is of course why a system of accountability exists alongside transparency, as well as why both a priori and ex post transparency (for verification) are needed (Fung, Graham, and Weil 2007, 154).

Following from this, modern transparency must be an ongoing process. To be effective it cannot be one-off or intermittent, as it often is in contemporary stand-alone ex post transparency systems. Firstly, this is simply because such an approach is not conducive to coherent policy, even in a minimal participation system involving only constitutional rights, while it would be even more detrimental if a state wanted to take advantage of the capabilities of more advanced forms of participation since citizens would be providing solutions based on incomplete or outdated information. More importantly, ongoing transparency is required to provide "feedback" on OG approaches, on how progress is going and the outcomes and results attained. Such feedback is essential for an actor to continue engaging in the action that followed from the transparency (e.g. on importance of feedback systems, see McGonigal 2011). Failure to provide consistent feedback would mean the next wave of information in an intermittent, punctuated release system would be ignored. Consider information release as a market in a staple good. This requires slow and continuous supply to the market. No supply and the good (information) is sought elsewhere (from mass media, pundits, rumour mills, etc.). When a new supply comes in again from an unreliable provider, the consumers no longer require it. Nor do they trust it since the good provided last time proved to be lacking in substance; it did provide what it was needed to provide: a means to maintain and further a human need and survival.

Moreover, the current ex post system is often scandal driven. For many actors in government this has led to the perception that transparency is always a bad thing. Transparency is "more likely to be sustainable when some disclosers perceive benefits from increased transparency" (Fung, Graham, and Weil 2007, 178). Feedback can provide the information that shows the benefits of the initial transparency and encourages further transparency. This need not imply every actor must benefit every time, but an ongoing and proactive market for information means even if you do not come out a winner this time, you can next time. While such cynical political calculations may not appeal to the more critical readers, institutional change does not happen overnight; evolution is the typical course of such transformation, as has been made clear throughout this book. States are approaching OG the same way, and OPS will have to be similarly developed. Resistance to any transformation will be encountered, from citizens as well as entrenched interests, and needs to be realistically managed; market-based ideas may appeal most to those most invested in the status quo systems and ideas (for such market-based solutions, see Peled 2014b).

Transparency also implies not just providing the information, but also collector's identity and intentions to the greatest extent possible (and no, identity does not mean we need the name of our secret agent in Tehran; more on this in Chapter 5). We saw this above: openness alone is very important, but expertise, independence, and shared values and interests are important as well, and these can be known only if data is sourced (i.e. its producer identified) and its purpose clear. Effective communication of intentions is especially key, as it can offset concerns over the means used if they conflict with values in the short term (in part, see Oulasvirta, Suomalainen, Hamari, Lampinen, and Karvonen 2014). This allows the state to use these means until they can provide evidence of their effectiveness – though this must be provided in the medium term. The US Patriot Act is a case in point – initially accepted, later questioned, but still in force; the NSA's PRISM and related surveillance programs are the counter case – secret, then leaked, resulting in outrage and the program's disappearance. Citizens have amazing patience and acceptance when it comes to a state's using extraordinary measures to address emergencies, whether security related or not. States and security providers thus can benefit from active, contextualized transparency in a way that civil rights activists may bemoan, but this is simply a reason for the latter to stay on their game, especially to point out when the emergency is past.

Lastly, the WikiLeaks incidents discussed above illustrate the importance of structured release. The amount and complexity of information produced by modern bureaucracies make its absorption and thus translation into action difficult. In this context transparency requires more than "simply placing data in the public domain. Instead, it means requiring the provision of content that is useful, customized, and interactive" (Fung, Graham, and Weil 2007, 181). A case in point in open government, one which borders on purposeful obfuscation, was the release of Minister of Parliament (MP) expense reports in the United Kingdom following a scandal about improper claims. The government then released, or rather dumped, one million forms and receipts that were scanned as unsearchable images, leading the media to dub it "Blackoutgate." Such releases seek to demobilize not out of fear like in the above case of Russia, but out of frustration. Yet in Blackoutgate we saw something else, which segues to the next form of participation.

PARTICIPATION 1.0

The Blackoutgate incident revealed the power of electronic media when the *Guardian* newspaper launched the "Investigate Your MP's Expenses" website to crowdsource the mining of information from the records. The investigations and reports that followed resulted in twenty-eight resignations or statements of intent to not seek re-election, criminal proceedings against four MPs, new codes and laws, and money being repaid (McGonigal 2011, 220). Transparency, once structured, led to analysis by interested persons, which led to results.

Where did this interest come from? What made the people level up from consumers of information to active participants in its analysis and advocates for accountability based on that analysis? As has been mentioned, participation most easily arises when something blatantly wrong is threatening a human need, whether a physical or higher psychological need. These threats inspire action, provided someone provides the means to action. Violation of norms in Blackoutgate threatened such higher needs in that the government was not acting in the people's interest, while the media provided a means for citizens to regain control and repair the threatening environment.

Participation such as this represents a scaling up and expansion of those rights-based participatory mechanisms enshrined in constitutions and other founding documents. Often, they include an appropriation/seizure of a function of government which is not being performed or being performed properly, such as oversight. This appropriation is typically welcomed by the government, at least publically. Thus, it does not constitute protest action, nor does it constitute the soon to be discussed co-production approach, which has more approval and active involvement by the government. For ease of reference we will call such participation "Participation 1.0," distinguishable both from rights-based participation and more advanced forms of participation that have their own specific designations. Participation 1.0 activities give a feeling of control, versus the feeling of ownership that other soon to be discussed forms of participation inspire. While good for promoting self-efficacy then, it is less useful (though not irrelevant) for building community. Because it largely works within the existing system and processes, these participatory approaches tend to be easily accepted by governments.

Though often provided for by law, citizen referenda and related forms of direct democracy are a good example of Participation 1.0. While long a tool of governance, with conflicting and various purposes, modern ICT has made citizen's referendum less a cynical tool of government, or spoiling tool for opposition parties, and more of a grassroots tool to seize the legislative function from the government. Referenda can now be initiated and organized more easily through online platforms, developed in a collaborative manner to build a base of support prior to being put to the general population. However, the dysfunctional condition of governance in some places (California perhaps) demonstrates the danger of such forced, outside intervention in government versus a more cooperative, co-productive approach. States are increasingly burdened with more mandates while starved of resources due to populist referendum: more services with less taxes is an easy way to get yes votes. Yet technology could be used to ensure referenda are not simple plebiscites. By putting them online they can be more routine, thus better integrated with the policy-making process and able to easily display (visually) more complex options. Ideally, they would also be iterative, with the first outputs becoming inputs for new rounds of referenda (ideas here draw from Franzoni and Sauermann 2014; James Fishkin in Sunstein 2007, 91–94).

The mobilization following Blackoutgate represents another form of Participation 1.0, in this case taking over the oversight function typically performed by judicial branches and ombudsmen. Oversight here took the form of crowdsourcing, a term introduced by technology journalist Jeff Howe in 2006. WikiLeaks in many ways aspired to be a crowdsourced anti-corruption/abuse-of-power platform, in this case one not welcomed by the state given especially its foray into areas of national security. Though a very unique organizational case, the International Campaign to Ban Landmines (ICBL) also represents a case of citizen involvement in a national security issue, the seizure of a diplomatic function falling usually within the executive branch. The ICBL's efforts resulted in so much pressure on states that in 1997 they adopted the *Convention on the Prohibition, Use, Stockpiling, Production and Transfer of Anti-Personnel Mines and on their Destruction*, which entered into force in 1999 and as of 2016 has 162 (state) signatories (ICBL 2016; United Nations 2016).

Not all Participation 1.0 functions are so confrontational though, and there are some citizen initiatives that seek to be more supportive by providing information to government service providers. For instance, the platform "FixMyStreet" in the United Kingdom allows reporting on road conditions; there are even apps that now track and report potholes automatically as you drive. Assisting the government in these tasks borders on the co-production discussed below, though true co-production tends to require a greater contribution from the citizen than mere reporting. This of course illustrates the deficiencies in any academic classification system; participatory tools rarely fall neatly into a category, as they are adapted to meet local needs and preferences. Take for instance participatory budgeting, an idea born in Porto Alegre, Brazil, in 1990 but now used in 1,500 cities worldwide (Lerner 2014, 45 and passim). In some places such participatory budgeting resembles a simple reporting of preference for government spending; more often though it involves the development of the budget through deliberation, while in other cases even the final budget documents and oversight are co-produced by both citizens and their government.

Participation 1.0 is clearly limited in its ability to improve processes and outcomes, as well as to build communities. It is intermittent even if ongoing, a sort of punctuated participation. However, it is perhaps the easiest form of participation for states to build and for people to engage in and thus the most prevalent today. It builds on the foundation of direct democracy and thus has a pre-existing basis for legitimacy. Moreover, it exposes people to participatory mechanisms and thus can help feed into further participation as people seek to level up to deeper forms of participation, following the same hedonistic levelling up that rights once took (Josh Lerner [2014, 205] observed such a process in his own case studies). We turn now to some of these higher forms of participation.

DELIBERATION

Deliberation can be most simply understood as participation in the process of developing and guiding governance, the rules under which we live. Deliberation between citizens, other stakeholders (e.g. businesses), and government officials has two purposes and one side effect, though this too may actually be an intentionally sought even if unspoken outcome. First, deliberation is intended to arrive at better solutions to policy problems. This is based on the idea that a policy is only as good as the policy options offered up when it is being formulated. Specifically, it seeks to counter the lack of specialized knowledge of decision makers and counter the internal bureaucratic tendencies discussed in Chapter 3 (e.g. group think, fixed mind-sets) by providing civil servants and politicians with the knowledge and perspectives of the entire community of stakeholders. Secondly, it is intended to promote acceptance of the outcome. It does so by ensuring that the outcome appropriately balances the interests of all stakeholders through raising awareness of all perspectives, searching for common interests, and reaching compromises. In addition, because the process of deliberation, of being included and taken seriously, is itself perceived to be normatively good, the process is accepted, which often transfers over to acceptance of outcomes reached through that process, even if they conflict with one's personal preferences (Boedeltje and Cornips 2004).[7] This process of creating acceptance is what the participatory literature describes as creating a sense of "ownership" (Baker, Addams, and Davis 2010, 119; Burby 2003). The participants feel not only that they have more control over outcomes, like exists also with even basic participation (rights based and 1.0), but that they helped to build those outcomes. Lastly, because deliberation is based on interactive problem solving and development of integrative solutions, it also can be more effective at building trust and creating communities than Participation 1.0, which solves problems primarily by aggregating individual actions to arrive at selective solutions (exemplified by voting) (agreeing, see Sunstein 2007, 193–95).

Traditionally, deliberation has been limited due to the need for co-presence (i.e. the ability to gather all relevant persons together in the same place and time). Both participation and the issues to be dealt with are thus primarily at the local level. Moreover, to maximize the benefit of such deliberations experts recommend long-term citizens' panels, which in the pre-online era created undue demands on people's time (Kathlene and Martin 1991). Technology has removed these constraints, even while outcomes in policy quality and acceptance as well as community building have been maintained. Technology can even improve on these by using better metrics for measuring and comparing ideas, versus "let's see a show of hands," and working toward narrowing down ideas through selection and/or integration over time. Nonetheless, technology does not remove all barriers, and outcomes (policy and trust) are improved the greater the human contact aspect, such as through co-presence (i.e. people being online at the same time) (Altschuller and Benbunan-Fich 2010).

Despite the technical possibilities, many existing ostensibly deliberative platforms are actually just simple comment and suggest platforms. To be truly deliberative a platform must link and integrate ideas and thus persons. Additionally, these persons must include government officials, ones given the necessary training, career incentives, and authority to be transformational leaders. Alongside providing policy information, the officials can provide also a centre around which the discussion can focus, or serve as a moderator if needed. For deliberations of a more technical nature, the appropriate technocrats, engineers, and scientists can serve a similar function. These people are also responsible for, in conjunction with the metrics used to measure an idea's popularity ("likes"), filtering and linking ideas for the next round of deliberation. To encourage such ongoing and iteratively progressing debate, many platforms now adopt game elements, which we will discuss separately.

Historically, the timing of deliberations has also been an issue, beyond scheduling a time slot. Rather than involving citizens early in the process of problem identification or need assessment, public meetings have often been held late in the decision process (Baker, Addams, and Davis 2010, 121). In this way a few pre-vetted ideas, or even a single plan, are presented fait accompli, with any possible changes being confined to the margins. People tend to accept such default settings, whether presented on a computer or a social site or by a local government planner (Thaler and Sunstein 2008). This tactic is using ex post transparency – presenting a well-laid plan against which alternatives cannot compete – to short-circuit genuine participation.

However, even with technology not all persons will have the time and interest in engaging in deliberation. It is for this reason deliberations are best extended over longer durations, as an extended process allows for fountaining and cascading effects. In the former, information fountains up from the community to the deliberation participants; in the latter, information cascades down from experts through the participants and then to the general community (Breakwell 2014, 167). Fountaining allows deliberation to capture the wider community's knowledge and preferences to contribute to better outcomes; cascading allows the knowledge of the process and outcomes to be shared broadly, which can also result in a shared appreciation and acceptance of both. In this way a certain level of participation is all that is required to gain wider objective and subjective benefits, similar to how only a certain number of a population must be inoculated against a disease to provide "herd immunity."

Not all deliberation will necessarily come to a conclusion. Yet even if they do not, deliberations can still serve a valuable role, acting as a sort of mediation process that reduces polarization (Sunstein 2007, 81). Even if de-polarization fails, the deliberation can still increase tolerance and awareness of other ideas that can prime a person to be more receptive to future information. If all else fails, OG deliberation can serve as an arena in which legitimate (non-violent) competition can occur, channelling people's time and energy toward engagement in directly democratic processes, keeping them involved, linking them with other like-minded persons and with a loyal opposition. In doing so, government-linked deliberative platforms could actually prevent individuals from turning to other outlets to express their social dislocation, ones which can lead to crime or radicalization (the risk that such individuals could undermine OPS will be turned to in Chapter 6).

The sceptic may point to the level of the current discourse in websites' comment sections as an argument that deliberation for OG will equally descend into trolling and Hitler references (latter referred to as Godwin's Law). The easiest way to prevent this is to not allow anonymity, which leads to drastically more civil conversation. Anonymity was never necessary for the Internet, but this design choice somehow became locked in as a right (Lanier 2010, 68). This is not to say all platforms for open government should require personal identification; anonymous spaces can still have value depending on their purpose, but there is no reason to turn OG or OPS into 4Chan. A second, more challenging but more inclusive, way to raise the level of discourse and encourage pro-social behaviours is to take a page from online game designers and make reputations matter. Even if your online identity, or avatar, is not the same as your real-world identity, if the online identity has value over time, then a person will work to retain their (avatar's) reputation to maintain that value. The key to this approach is to ensure an identity is transparent, persistent, meaningful, and current, all which build trust (Reeves and Read 2009, 75–78).

The state's responsibility does not end with the deliberations. Like with all participation, feedback is needed. In the short term there must be feedback on the outcomes of the process (i.e. the revised plan, ideally with a report on the deliberation itself). In the medium term there must also be further information on the success or failure of the project or task that was the subject of the deliberations. Feedback on the two aspects will, firstly, help maintain interest in participating in deliberations and, secondly, allow for learning to improve future deliberations; it shows participants they made a difference and how to make a greater difference in the future and may even inspire them to level up to other forms of online, or even offline, participation (on transfer to offline action, see Kahne, Lee, and Feezell 2013; Vaccari, Valeriani, Barberá, Bonneau, Jost, Nagler, and Tucker 2015; Vissers and Stolle 2014; more on this in Chapter 6).

CO-PRODUCTION AND OPEN INNOVATION

Co-production is when citizens actually participate in the service provision itself, though if considered broadly it need not imply performance of the actual final task but also contributions to supporting processes, techniques, and organization. Essential is that "all parties make substantial resource contributions" (Bovaird 2007, 847). Thus co-production importantly is not privatization or outsourcing, as it requires also the government contribute to the task, nor is it a public-private partnership (i.e. government-corporate), as citizens must be more than mere consumers. Co-production also requires "long-term relationships," thus distinguishing it from intermittent one-off forms of participation (Ibid.). Neighbourhood watches, adopt-a-highway litter collection, and social service volunteering are traditional examples. As mentioned earlier, some participatory budgeting initiatives also reach the point of co-production.

While, generalizing, basic Participation 1.0 gives a sense of control; deliberation adds a sense of ownership on top of control; co-production gives an even higher form of ownership, one which academics have not yet designated with a term, a feeling of creation. As the producer/provider, the feeling associated with the object made or service provided goes beyond acceptance and identification to affective commitment, to being attached to the object or service and considering it to be better than what otherwise would have been produced. Michael Norton, Daniel Mochon, and Dan Ariely (2011) call this the "IKEA effect," the increased value persons attach to things they made themselves, which they consider to be of the same quality or value as something made by an expert. This high valuation in turn helps magnify the self-efficacy that co-production creates; with a high opinion of how well they have done, the person feels a sense of even greater control and skill. This in turn leads to greater self-identification with the task, appreciation of the outcome, continuation intention, and connection to fellow co-providers and the community which our creation serves.

Open innovation is a subset of co-production that is generally more technical and involves small groups that come together to compete to offer a service or product to the state (or another actor) that was previously provided internally or by traditional corporate actors. Open innovation remains more popular in the private than public sector, from the development of Linux through an international network of volunteers to Wikipedia. Open innovation is closely related to peer production, with slightly different emphases on development versus building a product/service (in the above, Linux is more the former, Wikipedia the latter, while user-generated content for video games, for example, is somewhere in between). Within the state, the US Digital Service is a possible example, though currently of limited vision; it seeks only to recruit techies to update and modernize the government's online presence (i.e. websites) (United States, White House 2016; see also www.usds.gov). Some open innovation initiatives go around the state completely, using the start-up culture to provide a public service the state is unable, or claims it is unable, to provide. We still consider them co-production, though, since the service the people create in such cases is intimately linked to a service the state *is* providing, even if the linkup occurs only after the citizens create the supplementing service. An example of such co-production initiated first through citizen-led open innovation is the development of a public transport app for the Baltimore (Maryland, USA) area. The local transport authority had claimed it was unable to develop such an app, as it would have cost an estimated $600,000. Yet a few "civic hackers," scrapping the data off the transport authority's website, and a commercial development team made such an app in less than a week for no cost (Gallagher 2015a).

Related to open innovation, but tending to be more inclusive, is open science, also called citizen science (though the two are sometimes conceptualized differently). Open science distributes tasks to crowds and subsets of people based on the tasks' characteristics and skill sets required to perform the task, thereby contributing to data collection and coding (classification) as well as individual, aggregated, and collective (integrated) problem solving (Franzoni and Sauermann 2014; Nakatsu, Grossman, and Iacovou 2014). Many open science initiatives also make use of gamification, which is possibly the highest form of participation in terms of complexity and impact (discussed below). In open science's simplest form laypersons volunteer their computers' processing power to help conduct scientific tests and exhaustive searches. SETI@Home is a long-established example.[8] The Great Internet Mersenne Prime Search is another, with more tangible results that have contributed to fields such as cryptography and hardware testing (GIMPS 2016). However, these examples border on simple crowdsourcing, while actual open science requires more sharing of intermediate outputs, which become new inputs that feed into the final outputs (conclusions); that is, it is much more open regarding data and process (methods) and involves more interaction between the participants and the scientists involved (Franzoni and Sauermann 2014). Zooniverse (2016) is currently the largest such open science initiative, with some 250,000 participants contributing in various ways to forty-nine (as of January 2017) projects in numerous disciplines.[9] Its astronomy projects are currently the most successful if judged by output, including scientific publications. These projects mostly leverage the earlier discussed human pattern matching skills to, for instance, classify galaxies or find exo-planets (planets around stars other than our sun), with the latter's Planet Hunter project being known for identifying star KIC 8462852, whose untypical and unexpected dimming – making it unidentifiable by algorithms – became the talk of astronomers and alien hunters alike in 2015. While open science does have applications to solving technical military issues, when transferred to security applications, often the method of open science takes the moniker of open intelligence, which will be discussed in detail in the next chapter.

GAMIFICATION

Gamification, or to gamify a task, is a rather new concept. The term itself is controversial for many reasons,[10] not least because of our cultural association of games with play and fun, something to waste time. Yet research on games over the past decades has discovered that there is more purpose behind games, in that they both serve a functional (objective) purpose and give us (subjective) purpose. Games played a role in structuring and ensuring the survival of hunter-gatherer societies, Greek city-states, and Prussian armies (see, respectively, Gray 2009; Herodotus *The Histories* in McGonigal 2011, 5; and [for example] van Creveld 2013; full history in Huizinga 1949; for much current research, see the *American Journal of Play*). They are not about wasting time but "enlivening time" (Tal Ben-Shahar quoted in McGonigal 2011, 33); even if they are a form of escape, they are "*purposeful* escape, a thoughtful and active escape" (McGonigal 2011, 6).

Brian Burke helps to clarify gamification itself by saying it is not about fun per se, but about using the "science of motivation" to get things done and done better (Burke 2014, 29). Games are thus a "means," as Aaron Dignan puts it, using fun to fulfil the needs in Maslow's hierarchy (Dignan 2011, 30). Jane McGonigal makes the same observation, that "computer and video games are fulfilling *genuine human needs* that the real world is currently unable to satisfy" (McGonigal 2011, 4). In this sense these scholars see gamification as a solution to both objective and subjective needs, both appearing in Maslow's hierarchy. These scholars argue that purpose-designed games or game elements incorporated into existing processes/tasks can provide (subjective) esteem, meaning, and a sense of community while contributing to accomplishing a (objective) task.

Games and gamifying other tasks utilize the same mechanisms as basic participation outlined above, motivating an individual to engage in a task by providing feedback on their progress in the context of a larger community and environment. The medium of games though can take these mechanisms further using "hard fun," which targets additional areas of our biology and induces additional neurochemical responses as other forms of participation (Dignan 2011, 24–26; McGonigal 2011, 48). They do so by exploiting our minds' inability on a subconscious level to distinguish between the virtual and real worlds, in the same way modern media contribute to feelings of insecurity as discussed in Chapter 3. In this way they tap into the same mechanisms that encourage learning survival skills and evolutionary progress, as seen in Chapter 2.

Through these intrinsic reward mechanisms, games, especially interactive games (Lee 2015), are more able to promote a feeling of self-efficacy, a sense of capability and responsibility that arises from making what McGonigal calls "meaningful decisions," choices that make us feel in control in that they progressively influence our environment in an observable way as our skills develop (McGonigal 2011; Dignan 2011, 145–47; on support for underlying self-determination theory, see Kazakova, Cauberghe, Pandelaere, and De Pelsmacker 2014). Thus, games, the skills and self-efficacy they teach, can help individuals develop an internal locus of control by which "we become better able to protect and strengthen our quality of life, regardless of external circumstances" (McGonigal 2011, 47, referring to work of Sonja Lyubomirsky; see also Hans 2000; Reeves and Read 2009, 81). Indeed, the psychological and even physiological responses to gaming are so strong that gamification has been used to treat cancer, chronic pain, anxiety, and post-traumatic stress disorder (PTSD) (literature review in Sulea, Soomro, Boyd, and Wiederhold 2014).[11] Chapter 6 will go into more depth on these processes as they relate to security, as well as some further design features that games use to reinforce them.

Turning to gamification in practice, it is currently most commonly used by corporations seeking to solve business problems, especially to promote product usage and thereby increase revenue. However, the application of gamification to solve collective-good problems and complex problems has great potential and has seen initial usage, primarily at a grassroots level (for example, see McGonigal, 2008; offline games for same purposes, see Lerner 2014; several networks/organizations have emerged to support such efforts, most notably Games for Change; see http://www.gamesforchange.org). Looking forward, the US White House has acknowledged the potential of gamification for government tasks, holding a conference of government employees from twenty-three agencies in 2011 to begin exploring the issue (Steinkuehler Squire 2011).

In the simplest approach to gamification, game elements – points, leader boards, challenges – can be added to traditional processes and tasks to make them more enjoyable to perform. Such games can occur entirely in the virtual world, or can link to the physical world by requiring actions in the real world to progress in the virtual world, so-called "alternate reality games" (ARGs). For example, First Aid Corp developed an app in which the users are given "secret missions" to find and map out the location of public defibrillators (McGonigal 2011, 250–51; a game type called "geocaching"). Thus this app seeks to capture knowledge people have that they do not know is valuable (where a defibrillator machine is).

On a more advanced level, new games can be purposely designed specifically to harness human cognitive traits for problem solving. This can include designing scenarios and simulations closely modelled on reality, what are called serious games. Luis von Ahn (2006) has advocated and designed what he calls "games with a purpose" (GWAP) to "solve complex computational challenges through the medium of online entertainment," specifically in his field of computer science. Microsoft has followed the same logic, but reversed it: creating a platform (*Project Malmo*, formerly *Project AIX*) to train an AI within the popular *Minecraft* game, though its current target audience is programmers and researchers, making it more a gamified open innovation initiative (Linn 2016; Walton 2016; see Chapter 3 on training algorithms). Within the field of medical research, the University of Washington (USA) designed a highly publicized puzzle game called *Foldit*, which leverages human pattern-recognition skills and creative intuition for rapidly narrowing large property spaces toward solutions to look at protein folding, an essential step in combating many diseases. Approximately 240,000 users registered for the game, and a 2010 paper in *Nature* credited 57,000 of them with providing useful results (Cooper et al. 2010). In 2011 these gamers decoded an HIV protein in three weeks (Praetorius 2011). In 2012 the project moved from decoding to the more difficult problem of designing proteins, also with valuable results (Marshall and *Nature* Magazine 2012). *Phylo* is a similar game for decoding the genetic code of diseases, wherein players can even choose which disease to help unravel (see http://phylo.cs.mcgill.ca/).

Turning to internal effects, which of course can have external manifestations, gamification has been used extensively for educational purposes (see especially the journal *Computers in Human Behavior*). This educational role is especially valuable in that education is, if not a prerequisite, then certainly a very valuable enabler of participatory processes, even more so for electronic ones, and can greatly improve outcomes (Min 2010, 32; wider digital literacy call in Taleb 2007). There are currently many video games being released, also by small developers and yet often still of high quality, which are designed primarily to raise awareness and interest (sometimes called "editorial games"). Themes covered include poverty, third-world development, Alzheimer's, psychological disorders and treatments, elections and politics, and many different issues relating more directly to security, and which will thus be discussed in the following chapters. A good list of many such games can be found at the website *Purposeful Games for Social Change* (see http://purposefulgames.info).

Games are especially useful for correcting mental maps (i.e. re-education) by creating a safe environment where people can experience an inconsistency in their beliefs themselves, experiment with solutions, and thus naturally and easily adjust their mental models (Klein 2013, 214; Lacy 2014, 89; Pellis and Pellis 2009). This is often done in simulation games for professional skills. In addition to education and skills training, games can improve transferable soft skills, such as the spatial and cognitive abilities that feed into learning as well as into general situational awareness and attentiveness (on general transferable learning, Eichenbaum, Bavelier, and Green 2014; specific examples in Dale and Green 2016 and Reeves and Read 2009, 209–10; case studies in Green and Bavelier 2003 and Stroud and Whitbourne 2015). Games also get individuals used to competitive situations, teaching them to take risks and face fears, but also to deal with failure and thus to learn (Dignan 2011, 45–46, referring to research of Andrew Weaver; Reeves and Read 2009, 30). Moreover, and importantly, there is good evidence that all these traits learned virtually are applied in the offline world, a topic we will save for the next chapters.[12]

Yet games are not all about competition; many, and certainly the most popular, online games require cooperation and teamwork if the individual is to progress, appealing to our cooperative socio-biological nature. The strategies that gamers develop to succeed in their virtual worlds transfer to the real world as social skills useful for team building, providing and seeking social support, and active conflict resolution (Lobel, Granic, and Engels 2014; Reeves and Read 2009, 30). The need for cooperation also promotes social values, such as meritocracy and mentoring relationships over supervisory ones (Reeves and Read 2009, 30). Moreover, while there are often anecdotal claims that violence in video games may acclimate players to violence, and thus even promote violent behaviour, most of the scientific findings and community find this is not true (Coulson and Ferguson 2016, passim, but specifically 67 and 70). Indeed "committing 'immoral' virtual behaviours in a video game can lead to increased moral sensitivity" as feelings of guilt increase "the salience of violated moral foundations" (Grizzard, Tamborini, Lewis, Wang, and Prabhu 2014). Some violent games even penalize players for killing other players who do not fight back (e.g. *Lineage*); amongst them is a jihadist-made video game that chides the player, "Mujahid Brother, you have hurt the innocent civilians by mistake" (Peck 2014).

These psychological effects take place not only through the player's interaction with their environment or other players sharing that environment, but also through the player's own online representation, called the avatar. As mentioned in Chapter 3, self-efficacy can be experienced vicariously. This is true also online, with the feedback, even the physical characteristics, of a person's avatar having a so-called Proteus Effect on the real person (see Stanford University 2015 and Yee 2014; see also McGonigal 2011, 161; Reeves and Read 2009, 73–74). Energetic avatars increase energy levels, fit avatars improve body image, avatars accomplishing something "epic" (as the gamers like to say) make the player feel proud.

The combined effect of all these (socio-)psychological mechanisms is, as Kittilson and Dalton (2011, 641) put it following Robert Putnam's famous book, that "multiplayer online gaming may also have the same social capital potential as bowling leagues." Katherine Isbister's (2016, 118) comparison to summer camps, with their greater team and task focus as well as punctuated yet possibly continuous (i.e. only in summer, but every summer) temporal character, may be even more apt. Gamers who have come together in one game have even moved together to new games (Isbister 2016, 128–29; Pearce and Artemesia 2009). This spirit of the gamer community is reflected in the online support communities (e.g. Wikis) built around games such as *World of Warcraft* and *Halo*. The latter has also seen these used to mobilize the entire *Halo* community to accomplish missions of epic proportions against their virtual enemy. The players of *Eve: Online* are arguably even more dedicated, engaging even in outside-game propaganda campaigns to recruit other players to their team, as well as – less desirably – launching DDoS (Distributed Denial-of-Service) attacks on players they know to be on an opposing team to knock them offline during critical battles (Cowen 2016). However, even in games that are largely individual centred, "playing alone together" gives rise to the sensation of sharing the same space with other people. This leads to "ambient sociability," which while not creating direct bonds, allows one to feel connected to others (McGonigal 2011, 90). Thus, gaming has for millions taken over the role that the nightly news used to play in the pre–cable television era (Ezrahi 2004, see Chapter 6).

CONCLUSION

While it has far to go, our knowledge and practice of participatory approaches has already come far in the past decade. Yet the continued existence of old modes of ex post transparency remains a large stumbling block in participation. The lack of relevant and timely a priori information, when combined with the perception of the status quo as unalterable and unamenable to outside influence, has resulted in a public which, despite interest in an issue, withdraws into alternative arrangements to better their lives, protect their interests, or at least calm their anxieties. Nonetheless, many governments now have road maps to try to alter this situation and are releasing more information, thereby building rather than redirecting the interest that citizens have in areas affecting their survival needs. This information must next be supported with better platforms enabling participation, allowing the interest to be translated into actions to improve policies, solve problems, and even directly assist the state in tasks. As an additional benefit, the interactive nature of the participatory process can help to build trust between citizens, between citizens and their government, and in the tools, systems, and processes of governance. To realize these transformations in the state-society the government, through its system of governance, must provide feedback. The feedback should evidence the progress made in a given area due to citizen participation, thereby motivating continued involvement by both citizens and state institutions, as well as highlight areas needing improvement, thereby encouraging learning. This will allow the gradual scaling up of open government initiatives, in terms of their number, rates of participation, as well as complexity, and the progressive expansion of the scope of issues covered.

Nonetheless, before moving forward an important consideration to keep in mind is that open government and the proposed open participatory security are not (yet) a replacement for traditional government or traditional security. It is the use of technology precisely to reintroduce the human element to government/security and act as a force multiplier for existing institutions. This fact does not mean existing institutions do not need to reform radically, but it does mean they will not be swept away in the near term by bottom-up governance and security. Indeed, the expertise already in the state is needed to structure the approaches and corresponding technological platforms and interfaces, to co-produce their share of the task when citizens are engaged in other essential socio-economic functions, and to provide transformational leadership through encouragement and feedback. The need for the integration of these elements cannot be understated. Any participatory system must be integrated with the democratically elected authorities and the civil service. Failure to do so "paves the way for the emergence of incoherent parallel structures of *demos* [people] and democracy" (Gamper 2015, 83), leading either to the new participatory system undermining the legitimacy of the traditional authorities, and thus democracy, or the old system working against the new system and thus undermining its success and sustainability (for case studies, developing and developed countries, respectively, see Lange 2008 and Jansson and Ó Erlingsson 2014). In security the dangers of two parallel systems are even greater; yet diversity within a unified system is necessary for security. The next chapter will turn to how the approaches described in this chapter can be applied to fill the gaps in our security system, while the following penultimate chapter will turn to how they also can fill us with a sense of security by using technology to integrate the state, soldier, and citizen under a new social contract.

NOTES

1. In this section we deal with just the "more/total openness" argument; other weaknesses of transparency – including limited transparency – will be discussed further on.
2. Moreover, Colaresi (2014, 4) claims that such leaks lead to a "false sense of transparency," which can dilute calls for real transparency, or even delegitimize and thus demobilize calls for further transparency. The pros and cons of leaks are somewhat on the periphery of this book's scope but covered in depth by, for instance, Rahul Sagar (2013).
3. Trust research, falling largely within public administration but also many areas of sociology, is a huge field and will not be done justice herein. Nonetheless, our conception of trust will be outlined in Chapter 6.
4. It is secondly also a sustaining condition for participation, in that further information, in the form of feedback, is required to create engagement loops that ensure participation continues and even expands. More on this later.
5. Autonomy, which is causal agency through control over meaningful choices that have consequences, is not the same as independence. Thus, it does not conflict with the relatedness component.
6. Though, conversely, many organizations with pilot programmes in a new innovation can also create healthy competition and drive superior outcomes.
7. These concepts are also referred to, depending on one's academic discipline or profession, as procedural versus substantive legitimacy, or input versus output legitimacy.
8. Available at http://setiathome.ssl.berkeley.edu/.
9. List of projects at https://www.zooniverse.org/projects. For publications with meta-analysis of the citizen science processes, see "Meta Studies" on Zooniverse (2016). For a review of these and other projects, including design, see Franzoni and Sauermann (2014).
10. The term *gamification* was coined in 2002 by Nick Pelling, a British consultant, allegedly to be deliberately ugly.
11. Many articles of this sort appear in the journal *Cyberpsychology, Behavior, and Social Networking*.
12. For a popularized discussion that includes some of these points, see Steven Johnson's (2006) book *Everything Bad Is Good for You*.

Chapter Five

Filling the Security Gap

Open Participatory Security for Objective Security

Narva is a small city of some 60,000 plus souls on the far eastern border of Estonia, a country we saw in the last chapter. Yet despite the city's small size in a likewise small country it has become known as the city that could end NATO, just as it once (in 1700) saw a battle which nearly broke the power of the most famous Russian czar.[1] With a population mainly of ethnic Russian stock and high tensions along the Russian border, Western military planners worry this will be the next target of the Gerisomov doctrine of hybrid warfare that was so successful in Crimea in 2014.[2] Yet the battle, if it comes, will not be so straightforward for Russia as it was in Crimea. Following a concerted and massive cyberattack on Estonia in 2007 the country realized its vulnerabilities and began seeking to bolster its defences while also strengthening its social cohesion. The broad-based e-government program seen in the last chapter was part of this effort to forge a new nation, as is the new Russian-language TV station established (2015) to serve as an alternative to Russian (mis-)information sources. Yet there is also a hard edge to the new policies. Citizen militias have expanded, with their personnel now numbering five times that of the active Estonian military, including a unit focused on cyber defence (discussed further below). While Estonia is not yet secure and has much more to do to integrate all its citizens, it has come far in filling its capability gap by engaging its population and getting them in turn to engage in their own security. Estonia is unlikely to be a quick and easy target for any Russian adventures.

Just as with all innovations, the idea of open participation security (OPS) was not born overnight; Estonia may be an innovator, but they are not an outlier. Even in security issues there is a long tradition of participation which was often linked to openness in the traditional sense of information provision (for mobilization) and occasionally even transparency (for accountability [control] and trust), as discussed in Chapter 2. The evolutionary development of ever more participatory and open technologies and thus security has, through peaks and troughs, led to our contemporary world and its myriad challenges, outlined in Chapter 3, but it has also seen the development of possible solutions, presented in Chapter 4. While these solutions, the new capabilities of openness and participation leveraging modern technology, have not yet come far in the field of security especially, the system has attained enough maturity for pilot proposals and projects, as well as some real-world programs. We are thus now at the point where the multiple futures that current technology can bring about are beginning to manifest. This development requires that we examine the current state of the art and trends so that we can influence the design of the emerging system and nudge ourselves in the direction of the future we wish to see.

It is important to keep in mind that the following discussion of the possibilities of OPS does not imply simultaneous and sudden adoption of all OPS approaches for all security tasks. This book has made clear, and will continue to do so in the conclusion, that innovation and adoption should be evolutionary and iterative processes. Neither current military and security actors nor the public has enough interest, or lack faith in the current system, to throw the doors open wide for OPS; even if they did, such revolutionary transformations historically bring more disruption and insecurity even if they first seemed like good ideas both technically and normatively. Cheap iron was cheered by the kings of Mesopotamia, but led to centuries of anarchy; the Dreadnaught class battleship seemed to herald the continued dominance of Britain at sea but instead fed competition and new innovations that left the Royal Navy behind while contributing to war and the eventual end of their empire.

Moreover, in the realm of security, the dual existence of two (or more) generations of warfare is common, even necessary. While information warfare or even cyberwarfare may arguably be the fronts of the (near) future, traditional fronts – air, land, sea, and space – will almost certainly continue to exist, requiring older capabilities be maintained to defend those fronts. Infantry did not disappear with the advent of the tank; nor did all ground warfare become irrelevant in the face of air power. While OPS can contribute to victory on traditional fronts – providing better tools, methods, and intelligence for tactical needs while ensuring consistency with strategic and policy goals – the warrior caste and their high-tech tools will still be needed. While OPS may be excellent for addressing distributed attacks (for example), public deliberations or an open competition will help not when a missile is inbound (though it can ensure those missiles are met with the best anti-missile missiles and soldiers with the trust to use them). OPS will coexist with NCW and 4GW in modern non-linear hybrid conflicts.

Yet it is equally important to keep an open mind towards the possibilities of OPS so that we have a clear policy objective – an end state to structure our interim policy decisions; set operative (near-term attainable) objectives; and guide decisions on procurement, career incentives, training, and so on. Such a strategic approach ensures the smooth development and eventual attainment of an integrated system. Without this vision, and associated changes at the policy and institutional levels, military organizations may adapt the means, the tools of OPS, but will be unlikely (or even unable) to make associated organizational and doctrinal changes on their own. Yet OPS cannot be treated as a mere tool of war; it is a way of war/security. Just as dropping an aircraft carrier into your fleet raises more risks than capabilities, OPS requires also the development of supporting systems, organization, and ideas. The result may look unlike anything we think of as a military, so we need a plan to get there (see Tom Ricks and Rosa Brooks in Foreign Policy 2015b; related ideas in Singer 2015 and Arkin 2015, 283).

In addition, vision is necessary so we do not deviate into versions of OPS that are inconsistent with larger political ideas and value. The technologies of openness and participation can be underpinned by ideas and organized in a fashion not conducive to liberal values, as we saw in the history of older information technology from the printing press to radio. In some so-called managed democracies, exemplified by Russia, we already see examples of the use of such tools to selectively mobilize and demobilize select citizens for selected issues (discussed below). Many in the West have a different, but equally limited, view of the role of information and society. Here, the people are still largely conceptualized as a front to be won through public relations to facilitate preparations for war (i.e. provided resources), rather than as a tool or agent to help win in war proper (Rid and Hecker 2009, e.g. 42). Nonetheless, contemporary thinking and practice regarding civil affairs operations in 4GW, such as seen in Afghanistan and Iraq, show that the military can be more open to engaging civilian populations, even though ironically this is currently more likely to be practiced in wars abroad than for security at home.

The sections that follow will discuss how the various OG approaches seen in Chapter 4 are currently and can be further applied to the different security tasks of policy making, problem solving, and provision. Each approach will be recapped and occasionally expanded on with sub-approaches that may be of special value for security. The chapter draws on existing experimental and pilot initiatives that fall directly within the security sector as well as functionally equivalent private, academic, and corporate initiatives. It will also occasionally expand on existing ideas to propose viable future programs for certain tasks that are well suited for open solutions. For general organizational purposes the chapter is structured along the lines of the open government approaches, with their value for given security tasks, and inappropriateness for other tasks, discussed under these headings. Given this capabilities focus, attention will be placed on socio-technological feasibility, with wider social and political issues being reserved primarily for Chapter 6.

Throughout the following discussion the information requirements – especially relating to how information can and should be structured – to facilitate open participation in given tasks will be mentioned. While doing so we hope to also diffuse the main concerns of the pro-secrecy camp about the dangers of openness. Nonetheless, after discussing the approaches to participation there will also be a section devoted to transparency to show what a broad information policy for OPS would look like. While some may find this order of presentation atypical, being accustomed to seeing transparency get top billing, it follows the order of precedence this book advocates: that the extent of viable and valuable participation determines the extent of the necessary transparency when dealing with security.

NOT YET A PERFECT PLEBISCITE: THE LIMITS OF REFERENDA FOR SECURITY

From the perspective of liberal representative democracies the seemingly easiest step towards openness after facilitating some level of transparency is to implement referenda for decision making by popular vote. Organizing an election, and lobbying for a specific vote, is something with which democracies have experience and seems to offer legitimacy by building on the existing constitutional order while also paying homage to the system's direct democratic Greek origins. Yet from both an effectiveness and truly democratic perspective referenda have their limitation, something which one could deduce in observing that referenda are a favourite tool also of less democratic regimes. Moreover, referenda are limited in their potential to build a community or trust. Voting is for many people an individual and private experience (thus the secret ballot), aside from the already politically active who join in campaigning for an issue on the ballot.

As was pointed out earlier, our current system of openness tends to release information, and allow comment when applicable, late in the policy cycle. Referendum and the likes, even if put online, would simply reflect this problem. The choices would be those pre-vetted and approved by those currently making policy. A similar problem exists for referenda as a check on existing policy. The public may accept a given policy once the agenda is set; a policy already implemented and with the power of the government spin machine behind it may be supported despite not being the best solution (Blomgren

Amsler and Foxworthy 2014). Because of status quo bias and the anchoring effect, ex post approval is more likely than ex post disapproval (see Chapter 4; some of the above draws from Berggruen and Gardels 2013).

Allowing for citizen-driven referenda is seen as offsetting some of the above problems of government control of the process and the resulting lack of community-building potential. However, citizen referenda are self-selected and often driven by the persons making the most noise, who are often not those most in need, insecure, or disempowered. Citizen referenda can also suffer from the same manipulation as government initiatives, albeit by media and business interests. Looking at Switzerland, which has a comprehensive referenda system, citizen-driven initiatives in the security realm tend to be either unrealistically utopian or very limited in scope (i.e. special interest). These traits, combined with the momentum of the status quo with the government behind it, lead most such referenda to failure: in the Swiss case, of the (circa) twenty-four referenda on citizens' initiatives with security-related themes since 1848 only one has passed. The most recent such citizen referendum (2016) sought to reject a law passed in parliament that gave new surveillance powers to the country's intelligence agencies: the status quo won with over 65 per cent of the people supporting the parliament's decision on enhanced surveillance.

Additionally, citizen (and possibly all) referenda simply adopt the majority solution as the "best" solution, when it is just the most popular solution. While the outcome may capture the wisdom of the crowd or at least provide a utilitarian solution, it may also merely reflect the best advertising campaign, selective release of information to favour a preferred outcome, or clever wording or formatting of the ballot to nudge opinion. Referenda as traditionally designed are not based on modern ways of knowledge production through networks, stigmergy, or openness. They do not consider the structure of the problem they purport to address and correspondingly alter the format of the process for devising a solution. Thus, a large crowd is left to resolve an issue through selecting one of two options, yet our problems are rarely so straightforward.

Lastly, the fact that referenda are on individual issues also has implication for effectiveness. They do not reflect system thinking and do not individually aggregate into a coherent policy or strategy. In referenda-driven polities this can lead to an inflation of demands (e.g. for services) even while the tools to provide such services are stripped down (e.g. less taxes) (for example, see Micklethwait and Woolridge 2014, 127). This risk of stripping resources from national security providers would be especially pronounced if referendum were suddenly introduced in a political context where there is subjective insecurity and lack of trust in existing institutions. Such occurrences have already been seen even in representative democracies, exemplified by inter-war France as discussed in Chapter 2. More recently, leaks regarding government use of surveillance in the United States led to political pressure to curtail (or better, hide) the mass collection of data, regardless of considerations of its effectiveness. Had the citizens known in advance who was collecting for what purpose, even if the specifics ended there, trust possibly could have been retained and the policy kept in place, at least partially (on theory, see Oulasvirta, Suomalainen, Hamari, Lampinen, and Karvonen 2014).[3] The sudden discovery that the tactics being used conflicted with values, coupled with the leaks that showed the government was not even able to keep its secrets, showed the system to be both normatively bad and technically ineffective; trust declined, and use of the tool was restricted. Referenda would likely accelerate this process in the current political and insecurity climate.

This is not to deny, and even highlights, the role that referenda can play in certain questions at the (grand) strategic or policy levels, particularly for issues which touch on national values and therefore on the identity that the state is built upon and sworn to protect. Policy makers themselves often lose sight of such seemingly intangible yet essential ends, pursuing only short-term *realpolitik* ends (often with a time horizon matching the election cycle) or even focusing only on the means (e.g. air strikes), which offer visual evidence of doing something. The result is a tactic-strategy mismatch that often leads to defeat/insecurity, or in the event of victory/security preserves only the physical traits of the state while emptying it of its philosophical *cum* constitutional content. These system-level and foundational issues are ultimately what all else is built upon, and direct citizen approval of given value choices would give the policy maker much greater assurance that their chosen means has a priori approval, giving them greater flexibility and range of action to respond quickly (Colaresi 2014). Limiting referenda to such core issues would also offset the problem of the preparation (debate, education) required to obtain a valid outcome since national identity and values are already inherent in the population.

Moreover, such referendum could benefit from the use of modern technology. The popular mood is not constant, varying with events in the environment. Thus, the timing of a referendum can be used to nudge its outcome in a certain direction. Just as bad, and even more likely, the outcome of a referendum can be determined by unrelated, external emotion-inducing events occurring especially in the weeks prior to a vote that push public opinion temporarily in one direction (on general phenomena, see Sjöberg and Engelberg 2010). The terrorist attacks of 11-M prior to the Spanish elections of 2004, which shifted the expected winner, is an example, though one in which attempted government manipulation of the facts/narrative also played a role. Referendum can and should be designed to get around these temporary shifts and capture the baseline around which opinions fluctuate, much like the deliberative opinion polls designed by James Fishkin to provide more than a "snapshot" of a given moment (Sunstein 2007, 91–94). This takes on special importance since a party elected, legislative act approved, or action taken in the heat of the moment cannot be so quickly ejected, revoked, or extricated from as it is entered into. Temporary tends to become permanent especially in the security realm, in large part due to the political logic of response and accountability (see Chapter 4; on permanence, see Albrecht 2008, 16, 40; Oehmichen 2008). Nobody wants to be the one to lower an alert, release detainees, or restore privacy only to have, even if just by chance, a security failure to immediately follow. Ironically, the likelihood of a security failure being blamed on a relaxation of security policy or posture increases the closer the former follows from the latter; yet the existence of an actual causal relationship is less likely the closer the failure (e.g. a terrorist attack) follows the reduced security act (because the planning for the attack goes back much longer).

The issue of citizen preparation – that is, education – if they are to make an informed decision in a referendum draws attention to the other irony: that despite that referenda are often seen as the first step in participation, their actual full value may be realized only after the exercise of other forms of participation. While a basic education, one that can be gleaned simply from being raised in a polity, may give the citizen the knowledge to vote on fundamental issues (i.e. at the policy level), security still has aspects requiring specialized knowledge – something advocates for monopoly never tire of pointing out. A concerted education program on security issues is neither likely nor desirable; people should focus on their own personal interests and professional expertise. However, the necessary experience and knowledge can be gained through other participatory approaches. This would not endow every citizen with the technical knowledge of every platform and tactic, but has the potential to redraw the mental map of citizens to the security way of thinking (on the latter idea, see Schneier 2003).

OPEN DELIBERATION FOR POLICY AND PRACTICE: JAMS, SWARMS, AND ENCLAVES

Older forms of deliberation took the form of town hall meetings and other similar face-to-face exchanges to facilitate debate and discussion at various points of the policy cycle. Today such deliberation has more potential to be inclusive by being based on Web 2.0 platforms, which open the geographic and temporal scope for participation. Technologically enabled deliberation has both problem-solving and community-building characteristics, both of which contribute to objective security while the latter also contributes directly to subjective security (the former does, however, contribute indirectly; see Chapters 6 and 7).

As discussed, deliberation is firstly based on the insight that decisions about policy are only as good as the policy options offered during the policy formulation phase. Given especially the inter-sectoral nature of modern security challenges, and the distribution of knowledge in a specialization-based economy, bringing together people with different education and experiences can contribute to building better solutions, and help foresee and prevent problems during implementation. Deliberation is based secondly on the view that inclusion in policy development leads to higher acceptance of the resulting policy, even self-identification with said policy. As many security policy problems do not have optimal solutions, objectively speaking, such acceptance leading to commitment and confidence can be determining for policy success. They ensure a policy is sustainable over the longer term, and get citizens to contribute time and resources more intensely to a policy.

Current examples of organized open deliberation in the security sector are limited. The best example is the Security Jam operated by the Security & Defence Agenda (SDA) and its sister think tank Friends of Europe and sponsored by IBM's "innovationjam" Web 2.0 platform. In 2014 this event brought together 2,300 participants from 129 countries during a forty-eight-hour debate, leading in 2016 to its expansion to a four-day discussion (almost 2,500 participants from 131 countries) (Ames 2015). Participants include many high-level government and inter-governmental organization leaders (in 2016, forty-eight official VIPs and a global coalition of over fifty partners). Active participation is encouraged through the integration of elements of a game that create motivation and feedback loops, for instance ranking an individual's quantitative contributions or the popularity (reflecting, we hope, quality) of their contributions. Through a systematic process the Jam contributions are shaped and reduced so they can be developed into a final report with key recommendations. This report is then presented to NATO and the EU's European External Action Service (i.e. the EU's diplomatic service). The attendance of both organizations' second-highest-ranking officials at the report release reflects the seriousness with which they treat the report. Aside from this program there are a few DARPA projects that have a deliberative Web 2.0 character. However, they also have other characteristics that make them more advanced forms of participation and thus will be discussed below.

Most of the issues dealt with by the Security Jam, and those likely to be best addressed in future Web 2.0 deliberations, are on the strategic and operational level, with the latter dealing also with some tactical guidelines that apply to a broad operational environment, but not with proper tactics (i.e. temporally sensitive decisions made on the ground by the leaders present). To enable such tactical intervention, information would have to be provided in much more detail and at high speed, but this could compromise the persons on the ground and their mission. However, more limited Web 2.0 deliberations of this type – restricted to vetted circles – is a promising area to test. At a slower pace, there are internal military and security deliberative platforms – such as companycommand.com and Intellipedia – that promote information sharing and collaboration, though these largely run parallel, and secondary, to official channels (see Rid and Hecker 2009, 222).

Military thinkers have also begun discussing the advantages of "swarm logic" over traditional hierarchical decision making for fast-moving environments, though also here their swarm is still traditionally confined to the military (e.g. Steinman 2016; Zweibelson 2015). Swarm thinking goes somewhat beyond deliberation in that the person being informed by the deliberations would not see the entire conversation thread; rather the knowledge from the swarm (of citizens) would be integrated – with the help of technology – to provide a seamless and rapidly executable solution. To be truly effective this approach would require robust and secure individual-level information systems on deployed security/military personnel. While these were once envisioned, most were a victim of budget cuts over the past decade. However, such fast-paced deliberation could still be viable in somewhat slower-paced operations such as peacekeeping (or, more negatively, occupation). The development-security nexus of these operations means they require expertise in many different fields, expertise that could be better attained remotely (the best experts are unlikely to sign up for deployment to war zones).

Why is it that we do not see more deliberation on security issues? Consider first that the examples we do see are focused on the first purpose of deliberation, that is, the generation of new ideas and options for attaining objectives. These initiatives have thus been floated by actors with functional focuses, military and security institutions, and the participants limited more to self-selected communities of interest. These initiatives thus approximate (not always perfectly) what has been called enclave deliberation, which gathers together (relatively) smaller groups of persons like minded along at least one major dimension of an issue. Such enclaves are better able to generate new ideas since they do not require the long process of coming to agreement, which entails coming to the middle, where one usually finds the status quo (generally, see Sunstein 2007, 76–80). Moreover, this deliberative design can help offset issues of voice – the suppression of minority opinions and loss of individual creativity – by starting smaller and then working towards larger group deliberation (which may or may not include the persons in the earlier rounds of deliberation). Regarding minority voice, for example, when Black Lives Matter deliberate, their purpose is, and must be, the generation of new ideas; coming to agreement can come after only they have these ideas to bring to the larger community and local security providers, that is, the police. Regarding creative voice, the maintenance of enclave ideas is as essential for social progress as the maintenance of genetic diversity is for biological evolution (related idea in Schirrmacher 2009). While a goal of OPS is to build a stronger community, it should not be a homogenizing force in all respects. If lack of variation and new ideas is the key problem for security (rather than lack of consensus), then this form of deliberation may be not only more feasible in the near term but also more ideal. As a caveat though, because OPS takes on the truly challenging inter-sectoral issues, integrating different enclaves into a network of enclaves will be essential, as will ways to ensure self-selection (to participate) include those experts and stakeholders in an issue that we need to be involved to develop solutions.

Turning then to the second purpose of deliberation, we see few initiatives focused on creating acceptance, which requires the deliberation be structured for coming to agreement and thus must include more participants.[4] This purpose falls on the political and policy level. Thus, we have a situation that at first seems counter-intuitive: the political level and its policy making, which should be most connected and open to the citizens, is seemingly more closed than the military/security sector. Yet this situation reflects a common pattern of development seen throughout history. Functionally oriented military and security institutions open, at least in part, to participation to meet the needs required to perform what it believes to be its survival-critical mission; the political level only opens following citizen participation in the task of security. Citizen engagement with the "middlemen" of security is essential to enable access and eventual control of the executive security makers. Indeed, it is better these security persons are the ones handing a role in security to the people, both functionally since they know where they need help and for trust since the military opening is voluntary. On the other hand, one should worry when a top political leader promises to hand security directly to the people.

OPEN INNOVATION: COMPETITIONS AND CROWDS FOR NEW TOOLS, PRACTICES, AND TEAMS

Open innovation represents an attempt to return to the (admittedly idealized) version of more open competition between private innovators in the development of security solutions that existed prior to WWII. The consolidation of the military-industrial firms following the end of the Cold War has approached a level where viable competition cannot occur, with many contracts having only one bidder. Inferior or drastically overbudget solutions have often resulted, with some projects being dropped even before full deployment/implementation. Many leading technology firms, as mentioned in Chapter 3, have no interest in security-related contracts. Individual innovators in security, on the other hand, are more likely to be labelled as threats – criminal hackers/crackers – than to be cultivated and brought into security making. Yet their inclusion is exactly what is needed, as has been argued for instance by John Arquilla of the US Naval Postgraduate School (*Hackers Wanted* 2009).[5] Rosa Brooks of Georgetown University similarly views the best defence in the future as likely to come from private persons and groups, pointing out that law journals have even begun discussing how a relationship between the state and such security providers could be formalized in a modern version of the "Letters of Marque and Reprisal" once issued to commissioned privateers (Foreign Policy 2015a), in other words, pirates for the cyberseas. The US Department of Defense has even recently started taking this advice seriously, announcing in 2016 that they would invite hackers to do penetration testing on their cyber defences (BBC News, Technology 2016).

Even before this announcement, various US military suborganizations have been experimenting with open innovation; indeed, these experiments' success may be why the larger institution has become more open to open ideas. Specifically, the US Defense Advanced Research Projects Agency (DARPA) and other military labs have increasingly been issuing small contracts and grants to innovative researchers and entrepreneurs to develop new ideas and military tools (technology). As part of its attempt to capture such solutions DARPA has since 2004 routinely organized "Challenges" to "reach beyond the traditional defense performer base and tap into the ingenuity of the wider research community" through a "prize-based competition to attract novel performers and ideas and encourage collaboration across diverse fields" (DARPA 2014). This represents the introduction of a new participatory element into security innovation and issues; yet its 2009 Network Challenge took participation a step further. This Challenge examined "how broad-scope problems can be tackled using social networking tools" by encouraging teams to build networks and gather information on the Internet to locate ten large red balloons at undisclosed locations across the United States (DARPA 2009). The winning team completed the task in under nine hours.[6] The Shedder Challenge, in which teams had to reconstruct shredded documents, saw 9,000 teams register to participate in a challenge for which "experts were skeptical that a solution could be produced at all" (DARPA 2011). It took the winning team thirty-three days to reconstruct the five documents shredded into more than

10,000 pieces. Dan Kaufman, director of the DARPA Information Innovation Office, stated that "The most effective approaches were not purely computational or crowd-sourced, but used a combination blended with some clever detective work" (Ibid.). In a less team-oriented effort DARPA organized the Anti-Submarine Warfare Continuous Trail Unmanned Vessel (ACTUV) Tactics Crowdsourced Simulator to help develop new ways to track enemy submarines (see http://archive.darpa.mil/actuv/). Most recently, the Cyber Grand_Challenge invited teams to create automated cybersecurity computers to hunt for cyber vulnerabilities, with the final real-time competition being held at the DEF CON 24 hacking conference in 2016 (see http://archive.darpa.mil/cybergrandchallenge/). While this Challenge's goal of automation seemingly runs counter to OPS, the open and participatory way in which the system was developed – and the spectacle of its testing – has the potential to endow it with more trust and thus enable its more effective, even if automated, use. This issue will be turned to again in Chapter 6.

Drawing inspiration from the Network Challenge, graduate students from six countries, with the support of the US Department of State and Institute of International Education, organized an even more ambitious endeavour in the TAG Challenge (Rahwan et al. 2013). Herein, teams had twelve hours to locate and photograph five persons in two American and three European cities based on their photos (and a competition shirt, for verification purposes). The successful team located three of the five persons in the time allotted for the game. The implications of this, for crime fighting as well as for privacy, need no elaboration. Indeed, using social media to find wanted persons by targeting specific communities has already proven an effective replacement for wanted posters: in October 2016 Syrian refugees in Germany captured a suspected terrorist who was on the run from police based on information from online media targeted at their community, and moreover they then sought the social network's advice on how to deal with the situation.

When looking beyond current pilot projects it is best to fall back on our old capabilities approach to see where new efforts in open innovation should be applied. For instance, we have seen that algorithms could use some improvement, that they lack creativity, a trait we humans have in plenty (even if to differing extents or in different areas). We can see here a perfect situation in which OPS can be used to improve BiTS security (to refresh your memory, BiTS is Bureaucracy, [information] Technology, Secrecy). Rather than the citizen just being a data point to teach algorithms, citizens could help teach them, as is done even now – for better and worse – with many online algorithms. As discussed in Chapter 3, to learn, algorithms are taught with a training data set. Afterwards, to see if the algorithm learned well enough, a test data set is used. Citizens could be involved in either part of the procedure, helping to train an algorithm by providing the needed data, or testing algorithms with their own data. The collective creativity of groups of non-scientists – scientists themselves often not being the most creative of persons – should ensure a more comprehensive data set for training and testing. While such open development raises the risk some persons could attempt to undermine the algorithms, this should not be feared: if it is so easily undermined, we probably should not be using it for our security. Beyond improving the technology though, as Domingos points out, "the greatest benefit of machine learning may ultimately be not what the machines learn but what we learn by teaching them" (Domingos 2015, 281). In the 1980s classic *War Games* it was up to the humans to teach Joshua (the computer) that there was no solution to global thermonuclear war, but in the process the generals also learned something from the interaction between Joshua and a teenage Matthew Broderick. In addition to learning things to feed back into the technology and policy, another key thing we will learn by improving our algorithms is to trust them more, just like with the Cyber Grand_Challenge previously discussed.

Yet not all open innovation need be so technical. Take for instance the needs of soldiers deployed for operations. Often lowest-bidder hardware proves insufficient for their needs, or new needs are discovered during the operations, ones the bureaucratic procurement process cannot rapidly meet. These are often not highly technological needs, but simple reconfiguring of gear to make it more functional. Indeed, solutions for many of these problems may already exist in other units, having been discovered by previous generations of soldiers, or thrown together by overly enthusiastic parents optimizing their camping equipment. A simple platform for compiling these needs, and then opening competition for the public to develop solutions, would more quickly and cheaply be able to meet such "urgent operational requirements" (as they are called), as well as create the political pressure to budget for them.

These examples show that innovation is not just about building better, more technologically advanced tools, but about innovating new organizational strategies, tactics, and teams that can then be adopted by traditional security actors, which in doing so will often be required to open their organizations to wider participation. Much of current open innovation is driven by teams from business or academic communities, but there is clearly scope for expansion to other groups. For the development of new tools, technical knowledge is often (but not always) required, which in turn requires also the state be more open with its technical secrets (on innovation, see Chapter 3). However, open innovation of new practices and organization requires primarily just creativity, which is widely distributed across society.

CO-PRODUCTION: PARTICIPATION IN PRACTICE AND PROVISION

Co-production can be seen as a replacement for outsourcing and public-private partnerships (PPPs), which have large downsides, such as conflicting incentives, motivation and creativity suppression, and trust and accountability issues. Instead of one corporate partner, in co-production the state has many distributed citizen partners who nonetheless can often make more of a contribution to task performance, while also realizing other subjective advantages. For sensitive security tasks such distributed task production may be even more secure than the servers of any potential corporate provider; the latter need fail at only one point and then all their information is out there; in the former, information is distributed up to the point when it is integrated, selected, or realized as a solution.

In keeping with what the history (and subtly introduced theory) covered in Chapters 2 and 3 would lead us to expect, some of the most innovative participatory solutions are currently coming out of states emerging from traumatic times and/or facing high threat, including revisionist powers (where trauma and/or threat may be more perceived than real, or rather, has been made real due to perceptions). This is particularly true for co-production, which leverages manpower to improve security through mobilizing more cognitive resources to either directly provide security, contribute otherwise unattainable resources to security forces, and/or help physically implement solutions to security problems. Co-production may be especially popular outside the West given it is less expensive to implement than many other solutions and can even reduce overall security expenditures once established. It can also compensate for lack of domestic expertise – which in less developed states may have been lost via brain drain (i.e. migration of skilled persons) – through integrating collective knowledge.

For instance, in its ongoing struggle against Russian-backed separatist forces in the Donbas[s] region of the country Ukraine has made use of modern tech-enabled participation in several ways. Firstly, on a simple crowdsourcing level, but for a contributing rather than controlling (as seen in Chapter 4) function, Ukraine has used websites and social media to organize the raising of resources, domestically and internationally, to support their armed forces, especially in the provision of basic supplies to irregular units (i.e. militias). One such effort, "Help the Army of Ukraine" based on Facebook (FB), claims to have raised $1.3 million from March to December 2014 (Patrikarakos 2014). Other sites serve information provision roles to counter alleged Russian misinformation (e.g. the page "Information Resistance," also on FB, for military news).

In a significant further step there are also Ukrainian efforts to implement an open intelligence system. Open intelligence is the active use of private persons to collect and/or analyze information to feed into decision and policy making; thus, it is distinct from open source intelligence, which uses public domain sources that can still be collected and analyzed by state agents. In Ukraine the focus is currently on collection, with a website having been established to report separatist activities (Gorenburg 2014). It divides these into categories – including such things as spies, bases, movements, and attacks – which are geotagged. As of 4 January 2017, participants had reported over 16,000 activities (Stop Terror 2017). To build on these early programs Ukraine's Ministry of Information Policy even called in 2015 for the establishment of an "Internet Army" (Yuriy Stets quoted in Chraibi 2015).

Such an organized Internet army builds on developments elsewhere. Under the condition of complex insecurity raised by the aforementioned cyberattacks in 2007, the Estonian government organized the all-volunteer *Küberkaitseliit*, or Cyber Defense League, as a new part of its larger citizen militia (Defense League) (Gjelten, 2011). This cyber militia allows private citizens to aid public efforts to defend the state and can be mobilized under the Ministry of Defence during emergencies (*Kaitseliit* 2016; Singer and Friedman 2014, 238). The group includes experts in a range of skills and, while providing a service to the state through a formalized transparent institution, does not entail the sacrifices of military life. Volunteers have found the work enjoyable, beneficial, and "cool" while also benefitting their personal development through skill development and networking. This formal militia has also been supplemented by a grassroots movement of so-called "elves" to counter information warfare by Russian "trolls" (Weiss 2016). These and related broader efforts, such as those seen in Chapter 4, have paid off. Brookings Institute national security expert P. W. Singer (2015) believes that while "Estonia may not have the same capabilities as the NSA and Cyber Command, [. . .] it does have deterrence by denial and an involved populace – giving it arguably better cybersecurity than the United States."

The Russian "patriotic hackers" who contributed to the Estonian innovation following the attacks of 2007 could also be considered a modern form of citizen participation in security (for a discussion, see Omand 2010, 71–72; Singer and Friedman 2014, 110–14). Though some of these hackers may be directly tied to the state (such as is the case for the Chinese PLA's Unit 61398 or indeed, the American NSA), there is no reason to outright dismiss Russian assertions that many are independent individuals acting for the Russian national cause. However, while the individuals and groups may be technically independent, the action is not. The relationship may be informal in a legal and bureaucratic sense, but it is still a rule-based, guided co-production of a task.

The actions of these groups are allowed, not investigated or punished, and a permissive environment is created including even through the sharing of tools and information. Through signalling in its rhetoric what actions they desire, the Russian government mobilizes these agents and then de-mobilizes them when their usefulness is past (Pomerantsev and Weiss, 2014). Other states are developing similar "cyber reserves," most notably China with possibly hundreds of thousands in volunteer cyber units (Singer and Friedman 2014, 112–14). The American response to their own patriotic hackers has been less receptive, despite leading security expert Audrey Cronin's (2006) call in a military journal for a cyber mobilization.

What makes this real co-production is that the hackers are not alone. Beyond the permissive environment, the Russian state supports the hackers' actions with a host of others: "manufactured fake think tanks, fly by night news websites, and an army of internet trolls" are used in conjunction as part of the doctrine of hybrid and, for now, mostly contactless war (see Chapter 3) (RFE/RL, 2015b). This is pure information warfare, in which all that matters is the story. It is not propaganda for war; it is not (typically) a prelude to invasion. It is the core of an invasion of another sort that seeks to strike deep into the enemy's will rather than destroy their capabilities, making it somewhat akin to 4GW (some ideas from Jasper 2009a, 12). In 2016 evidence emerged that this tactic was also being used against Western states, possibly effecting the outcome of the American election of that year and seeking next to topple the government of German chancellor Angela Merkel (Boffey 2016; Tucker 2016). Recently, several experts have called for the United States to adopt offensive tactics like those used by China and Russia in a proactive counter-messaging campaign against threats such as ISIS, a proposal exemplified in a cleverly titled article "The U.S. Government Should Pay Anonymous in Bitcoin to Fight ISIS" (Brooking 2015; see Leetaru 2015; Jesse Lehrke referenced in Ames 2015, 17; Pomerantsev 2014).

With these examples we again see that for many co-production tasks the citizen participants must have some specific technical skills. However, technology can make many even technical tasks more widely distributable. Firstly, on a relatively non-controversial front, co-production of a diffuse cyber defence would be relatively simple, and is indeed necessary since only one entry point – one person's computer – is needed to put the whole network at risk. Simply raising the general level of citizen awareness of the cyber-threat can contribute in a nontrivial way to increasing the general level of an entire nation's cyber infrastructure, as people patch their software, install antivirus systems, and protect their devices and accounts with sufficiently strong passwords (concurring, see Kori Schake in Foreign Policy 2015a). While the state should perhaps not intervene in the cybersecurity market, for instance by giving away free antivirus programs, they could incentivize their use, for instance through some form of gamification and/or by making investments in security-related goods and services tax deductible.

Escalating this defensive proposal to one embodying a more active OPSEC is not only possible; citizens have already engaged in Internet campaigns to such ends. As this book opened with, in the autumn of 2015, following the terrorist attacks in Paris, the city of Brussels was essentially on lockdown as the police engaged in a manhunt. In response to a police request that people not report on their movements in the ongoing operations, thereby alerting suspects, people began flooding the Internet with cat pictures tagged with the hashtag #BrusselsLockdown to bury any reports on police actions in "noise." China already operates a more organized effort in this vein, employing online commentators "to saturate the web with Beijing-friendly material" to drown out negative reports (Leetaru 2015). Russia takes another approach, giving heavy coverage to negative, even if false, reports about other countries, drowning out worries and stories about problems in Russia. As part of the proposed counter-messaging campaign against ISIS, Kelev Leetaru (2015) has advocated using noise to create "an environment where would-be Islamic State supporters and fighters could no longer distinguish between what was real and what was illusion, or who and what to trust." Identifying the real ISIS would be impossible. While we have spoken much of subjective insecurity in the West, its enemies can also be made to feel subjectively insecure.

More controversially, it is feasible to enable moderately technologically aware, but in no way specially trained, individuals to engage in offensive cyber operations. The Internet is even today awash with hacker toolkits that allow the curious or malevolent to design computer viruses or engage in other forms of penetration, seen currently in what are called "script kiddies." Given the implications of such activities it is of course something which would need to be carefully designed by experts, including civilians, and deployed only after high-level approval by the government and the community during a true emergency. Should this prove a step too far, the state could also opt for retaining more control over the process, perhaps organizing a "join a botnet for your country" initiative. In WWII people recycled their goods to become items for the war effort; today, you need only volunteer your computer's downtime.

There are also global civilian-led, yet security-related, solutions. Such private initiatives have a complicated relationship with states; they do not reinforce the legitimacy of the state, and may even undermine it somewhat as discussed in Chapter 4, though for some people such non-state solutions may be all that is possible. Regardless, these examples serve as useful proofs of concept, especially for a more active open intelligence. Currently, government open intelligence programs (if they even qualify as that) at best ask their citizens to become serendipitous intelligence collectors, passively observing in the off chance they see something. An example is the – allegedly little known – US DHS's "If you see something, say something" campaign to promote vigilance and reporting of suspicious activities (see http://www.dhs.gov/see-something-say-something). At worst these programs seek to turn people into informants in a manner inconsistent with their professional responsibilities, as some allege is the case for the UK's controversial PREVENT strategy to combat radicalization.

In more active open intelligence it seems even under-resourced NGOs are ahead of governments, not in gathering people's private information, but in accessing people's time and mental energies. The open-source platform "Ushahidi," developed after the violence in Kenya in 2007, is used for collecting individual reports from users through SMS, Web, and email (and more recently also voice) and provides tools for translating, classifying, and geotagging these reports, which are then made available on a map-based interface. The program has been widely acclaimed and seen use in Haiti (2010 earthquake), Afghanistan, Uganda, Malawi, and Zambia (Freifeld et al. 2010). More recently (2015), the International Bar Association and LexisNexis Legal Services deployed the "eyeWitness to Atrocities" app to establish a legally admissible way of reporting and gathering evidence of war crimes and crimes against humanity. The app stamps recordings with GPS coordinates, time and location, and other data which is encrypted and shows any editing. Similar apps have been trialled to monitor ceasefires in the Syrian civil war (Lynch 2016). When the ceasefires break down there are other networks that leverage the new tech-savvy communities borne from the Arab Spring to mobilize civil defence, for instance by warning of impending air strikes (Center for Civilians in Conflict 2016, 17–20). These apps, programs, and networks represent a human intelligence asset that current technology – whether drone, signal, or satellite based – cannot attain, and hopefully never will attain given the subjective implications of such a surveillance society. Moreover, many of them also represent the seizure of a controlling function: holding the state accountable for international law and agreements.

Upping the technological sophistication, and moving from collection to analysis, in 2010 several persons and groups came together to form the Satellite Sentinel Project (SSP), "the first sustained public effort to systematically monitor and report on potential hotspots and threats to human security in near real-time" by "fusing imagery, analysis, and advocacy" (SSP 2015). Reflecting the full transparency mission and linking the individual to a broader community, SSP adapts the motto: "The world is watching because you are watching." SSP seems to have learned the lessons of WikiLeaks and was designed with multiple partners each with their own task in the areas of development, collection, analysis, distribution, mobilization, and so on (Lacy 2014, 30). In a similar effort, a Digital Globe initiative crowdsourced the analysis of satellite imagery of Nepal following the 2015 earthquake to identify which transportation infrastructures were still operational, thereby helping the logistics of the rescue and relief operation. Within a lab setting this has been taken a step further towards full human-machine integration. By using EEGs (electroencephalograms) and algorithms researchers can capture fast human pattern recognition to identify and prioritize areas of interest in satellite images (e.g. a building), improving speed of satellite imagery analysis by 300 percent (*Horizons* 2012; Wang, Pohlmeyer, Hanna, Jiang, Sajda, Chang 2009).

Yet this technological sophistication does not necessarily imply higher value than simpler approaches. It is worth quoting the ever witty Russia and security expert Mark Galeotti at length on this point:

> It's all very well building a $1.7 billion NSA computer facility in Utah, or planning a $24 billion next generation spy satellite constellation – arguably you'd get vastly more bang for buck spending half as much on the best analysts around and giving them access to the huge amounts of open source information available. Predicting Russia's next move will come by sneaking into Putin's head; all the spy satellites will show is what he has decided as it starts to happen. (Galeotti 2015a)

Galeotti continues that "there is the scope to treat the outside analytic community – from journalists to academics to random bloggers – more often as analytic partners rather than just a passive resource" (Ibid.). In their landmark works on intelligence analysis and the direction it should take Wayne Michael Hall and Gary Citrenbaum are equally insistent on the need for the government intelligence sector to "work in an organized and disciplined way with subject matter experts (SMEs) from a virtual knowledge environment (VKE) [collaborative platforms]" if intelligence is to be anticipatory enough to meet current and future threats (2010, 5, 23–24). The argument being made here of course is that we are all experts in some area and that many of these areas could contribute to the co-production of intelligence analysis and security generally.

Indeed, we must qualify our earlier critique of the state's failure to open some analysis to the public. The US intelligence community has tried to do so, and moreover to make it anticipatory. In 2001 DARPA developed the Policy Analysis Market (PAM), which was to use market-based mechanisms the wisdom of the crowd combined with (very small) incentives to make predictions on the future of the Middle East (DARPA 2003). Due to poor marketing more than a poor idea, the program was cancelled in 2003 along with the whole Total Information Awareness (TIA) program. However, as is often the case, the innovation just moved; the Office of Incisive Analysis (OIA) at the Intelligence Advanced Research Projects Activity (IARPA) funded several similar programs, including through competitions, under the Aggregative Contingent Estimation (ACE) program from June 2010 until June 2015. These included the Decomposition-Based Aggregative (DAGGRE) (later SciCast) in 2011, which was to predict global crises (but avoided the market mechanisms given their controversy in PAM), and The Good Judgment Project (co-created by Philip E. Tetlock), harnessing a blend of statistics, psychology, training, and various degrees of interaction between individual forecasters (Mellers et al. 2014; for more, see Yeh 2007; Meirowitz and Tucker 2004).

The above examples illustrate the value of co-production primarily in areas such as logistic support, intelligence, and defence. The example of Russia, however, shows that co-production can be taken a step further, helping also in offensive operations, albeit currently limited to the area of non-kinetic cyber and information warfare, though it seems that the kinetic cyberattack boundary has now been crossed (in Ukraine, see Goodin 2016). The capabilities that co-production offers thus exceed deliberation and basic participation of the direct democratic sort, but to capture these capabilities also requires more information be released, while also raising some control and vetting issues (to ensure no participant is seeking to undermine the co-produced goods' value).

GAMES FOR RESILIENCE AND PROBLEM SOLVING

As introduced in the previous chapter, gamification is the application of principles of game design to solve complex problems, especially by making the problem-solving process "fun" and thereby increasing motivation for engagement and ensuring continuation in the process. Organizations gamifying a task hope to be able to capture part of the collective wisdom and creativity of the hundreds of millions of active gamers (estimated 700 million online, 1.2 billion total) worldwide and the billions of game-hours played per week (numbers from Kowert 2016 and Ivory 2016, respectively; see also and generally McGonigal 2011, 3–4, 6). While academically considered a distinct category, serious games will also be considered here. Serious games are exemplified by scenario and simulation exercises. They tend to be orientated on solving problems in practice, from strategy to tactics, allowing proactive solutions to be worked out in a virtual environment before being applied in the real world. Thus, they are usually modelled on at least possible real-world environments and situations. Compared to many gamified platforms, serious games are less about collective solutions, but still typically about the collective working together. Serious games in the military are usually called wargames, though due to their proliferation in the context of the same amount of resources, including experts (people), the quality of such intra-military games has recently been questioned (Pettyjohn and Shlapak 2016). The situation led to a 2015 memorandum by US Deputy Secretary of Defense Robert Work calling for "innovation" in wargaming (Work and Selva 2015; similar call in Hall and Citrenbaum 2010, 59–71).

Gamification of security issues has been, as with the other tools, more limited than in other economic sectors or policy fields. Nonetheless, one can see game elements – leaderboards, feedback, rewards, etc. – in many deliberation platforms. Some of the DARPA Challenges previously discussed come close to being gamified problem-solving solutions. The use of full games, in several ways, is somewhat more common. These games start in their most basic form as what are normal video games, ones modelled on a preferred vision of reality. These include privately developed games, typically first-person shooters such as the *Call of Duty* series, that are often nonetheless supported by elements of the traditional military establishment. The most popular state-developed game, with some eight million registered users (as of 2007), is a first-person team shooter game called *America's Army* developed by the US Department of the Army (2015). Yet Islamist extremists, including Hezbollah and ISIS, have their own such games (e.g. *Special Force*, *Ummah Defense*), another example of how in war and preparation for war innovation is emulated, with Michael Peck asking if we may soon see a "video games arms race" (2014; also Singer 2009, 269).

Yet these are essentially games for propaganda. Firstly, on an abstract yet nonetheless foundational level, they set the discourse for security by presenting threats, and the weapons to counter these, in a way that supports the military's preferred vision of war, specifically NCW, and thereby create a subtle consensus around future policy, budgetary, and investment decisions (Caldwell and Lenoir 2016). Secondly, such games serve as upgraded and interactive recruiting posters. Additionally, some have pointed out that these games can also act as a substitute for real control, allowing persons to work through modern security anxieties through escaping into a game where modern problems and solutions are more black and white (Power 2007, with references). While such a therapeutic function is good, as it can enhance subjective security, we would argue that it is not a permanent substitute for real control, for feeling more secure because you are helping create objective security. Unless control of threats is (re)established by somebody, the security situation will only get worse, thus undermining any therapy. However, control of modern threats can be attained only through distributed means. Thus, the control of the individual must be real, to enable objective security, so that (excessive) security failures do not undermine subjective security. These interactive feedback processes will be elaborated in the final two chapters.

If games can promote an idea like militarization, they are equally capable of promoting other ideas. Taking up this point, Derek Caelin (2016) has suggested trends in gamification could also be used to create games for peace, while Luke Caldwell and Tim Lenoir have highlighted that military wargames also need to be able to imagine peace as the end state; after all, that is a main goal of security (2016, 278). Currently, we see the goal of peace mostly integrated into the editorial games to raise awareness that were discussed in the last chapter. *Liyla and the Shadows of War* highlights the plight of children in the Gaza Strip (circa 2014); *Peacemaker* stays in the region and simulates the Israeli-Palestinian conflict to promote dialog and understanding. *A Force More Powerful* is more educational in its scope, aiming to teach how to resolve conflict using non-violent methods of direct action. The most famous, as in bestselling and award-winning, example is *This War of Mine*, in which the gamers play civilians caught up in a civil war and must help their group survive (for a discussion, see Kwiatkowski 2016). In many ways these games touch on the subjective security that is the theme of the next chapter. Through raising awareness of objective situations and problems with few (desirable or optimal) individual solutions, they seek to make the players feel insecure, thus encouraging them to support policies or arrive at group solutions that make the world objectively safer.

Video games are also used explicitly for training purposes, thereby improving task performance and thus objective security. These efforts build on older video game training tools such as VBS1 and VBS2, or the even older full simulators for pilots, tank crews, and numerous other weapons platforms (e.g. see Mead 2013). Some of the most advanced applications are being developed by the Air Force Research Laboratory (AFRL), 711th Human Performance Wing's Gaming Research Integration for Learning Lab (GRILL). However, while these efforts incorporate the science of games in a way beyond traditional simulators and engage civilians to help in their design, their end purpose is still primarily on using video games for internal training purposes (Eaton 2014). Such internal training platforms, while important, are slightly outside our area of interest. Falling more clearly into gamifying tasks are the efforts of the AFRL's "Gaming Lab," which is exploring applying gaming technology to modelling and simulation including for real-time analysis and situational awareness (US Department of the Air Force 2015). However, thus far this foundational research is also an internal military project only.

To find applications of games that seek, like DARPA, to reach beyond the traditional military community to solve problems, we must turn from the US Air Force to the US Navy. The US Office of Naval Research (ONR) has since 2011 operated the "Massive Multiplayer Online Wargame Leveraging the Internet" (MMOWGLI) program. MMOWGLI uses collective gaming to explore numerous strategic and policy issues, including piracy, capability and constraints, naval aviation, energy security, black swan events, cyberwarfare, and even how to engage millennials (i.e. young people). As a pilot program, the extent of participation in the MMOWGLIs has so far been limited, but not always highly restrictive (i.e. not always requiring a security clearance), and in principle the "massive multiplayer" aspect can and will be expanded.

Aside from these examples the full exploitation of gamification for security has yet to be realized, but (allowing ourselves some forward-looking vision here) there are some obvious candidates for strong variants of gamification. Risk analysis, point-of-failure identification, and mapping how events can cascade through a system could all be gamified as puzzles. Competitive games could be set up to encourage citizens to find confirmatory or contrary evidence of a given presumed "fact" through open sources. Searching for unexpected anomalies in data (financial records, call records, travel patterns) is another idea, while this data could be of the meta sort, and even (mathematically) transformed, to protect persons and collection methods.

Yet what about a technically hard problem, as in so-called NP-hard (nondeterministic polynomial-time hard), like the protein folding that was tackled by the *Foldit* game seen in the last chapter? Naturally, these problems must be identified by the relevant technical experts, and you and I are limited in our ability to help in designing these games since we do not know the problem structures. We can look here though at one clear example: the optimal patrol problem. This problem is the military equivalent of one of the hardest problems algorithms have yet to beat, the travelling salesman problem (also, vehicle routing problem): the most efficient way to cover a given area with set stops/checkpoints (on hardness, see Pasqualetti, Franchi, and Bullo 2012). As briefly mentioned in Chapter 3, scientists are studying the flower search and nectar recovery operations of bees to help solve this problem. In devising solutions for optimal patrols there is no current objective solution; currently mixed algorithmic methods are used while genetic algorithms are being explored (for example, Curtin, Hayslett-McCall, and Qiu 2007). Yet the solution here may be to take the mixed methods further and introduce not only bees but also humans into the equation.

There is also value in opening serious games, such as MMOWGLI, to participation by outside groups, especially to form opposition "red teams," which traditional security actors compete against. In their work Hall and Citrenbaum

(2010) emphasize the need for more such red teams in analytical wargaming, especially when states prepare for facing non-traditional (i.e. non-state) threats. The Estonian Cyber Defense League engages in just such red teaming exercises. The information the state must release for such games is high, but different in character than the information above. Game information can reveal the state's and its security agents' behavioural patterns, preferences, and likely course of action, and possibly also their capabilities. This information is possibly more valuable to an adversary than the classic data we worry most about protecting. However, this information could also (relatively) easily be protected, amongst other ways (see below), by simply ensuring the state's gaming strategy is experimental – not just testing preferred strategies. Currently, performance review and career incentives discourage such experiments given their higher risk of failure, despite their corresponding higher potential for learning (on career issues, see Foreign Policy 2015b and Kane 2011).

A potential area for advancement in serious games specifically aimed at citizens and which would be non-controversial are games for governments to learn about their citizens. A major problem for states today is that despite that citizens now constitute a dense and complex network of empowered individuals that are increasingly the object of security (and surveillance), governments know little about these persons' expected behaviour during crises. This was the logic of the game *World Without Oil*, aimed at learning how people would respond to this imagined (but feasible or even likely) world and thus better design policy in advance (McGonigal 2011, 302–11). Sir Omand (2010, 68) provides an excellent example of such failure to predict adaptive behaviour by citizens that undermined rationing during the UK's fuel shortage in September 2000. Even more ironically, nearly identical responses had been seen during WWII rationing, meaning the knowledge was out there if the state could capture it. Such games are equally valuable for faster-burning crises, for identifying citizen assets, assessing needs, and anticipating behavioural adaptations that can feed into disaster planning and recovery and crisis management. In this vein, Heather Rosoff and colleagues used a scenario game to test individuals' risk perception during a gradually escalating biological disaster (Rosoff, John, and Prager 2012). More than just feeding into government policy and plans though, experiments like Rosoff and her colleagues' are also intended to better our understanding of the underlying psychology during hazards (Breakwell 2014, 180). Thus, the information from such games can increase our scientific knowledge base, which can in turn be used to refine the security games as well as other forms of participation.

As introduced in the last chapter, there are also so-called alternate reality games (ARGs) that are played in both the virtual and physical world. Such games require real-world actions to progress in the virtual world. ARGs thus link gaming and co-production, here, of security provision. These games, often in the form of what one could call "challenges" or "missions," have been used to encourage positive social behaviours, such as energy saving and recycling, as well as to contribute to public information and safety, as seen in Chapter 4's discussion of the First Aid Corp game. Such games could contribute to intelligence collection, supplementing the intelligence analysis functions of other platforms (or combining the two, possibly as a team endeavour). To maximize game play when and where it is needed most, thus avoiding that people tire of the game (hedonistically adapt) before it has been able to contribute much, ARGs can be location-based games, activating a person's mobile device only when they are in the right place (e.g. an airport). To avoid ARGs turning us into a nation spying on each other, observe and report (e.g. suspicious activities) games should best be limited to moments of high need when push notifications can be issued (as is done even now with some alerts, an issue with rights implications that will be discussed in the conclusion). The focus during normal times should remain on environmental factors so that we can lead the normal lives security is intended to enable in the first place.

Lastly, a less participatory, and more controversial, aspect of games is the possible use of metadata gathered from the play of the game itself, meta-analysis of the participatory process.[7] Not all games need to be designed so that the user is consciously creating security; it can be the underlying processes in the games which are revealing information. Analysis of a game being played could, for example, reveal where information needs to go, and thus flag certain data to be forwarded to different organizations or give new behavioural insights on the players or on the avatars they play (e.g. a terrorist). A project by the IARPA, called Reynard, sought to do just this, to identify individual "real" world demographic and socio-political traits based on virtual game world behaviour (IARPA 2009). If terrorists are currently or start using video games for communications, training, or so on, such analytical ability could be of value, and the participation and analysis of normal citizens as the control group will be essential. From a security producer's perspective such meta-participation is advantageous since it would entail little or no release of real information. From a player's perspective games using this analytical approach could likely be made more fun. Since the data/information gathered is not personal (though it could include psychographics) the controversial aspect is somewhat mitigated. Nonetheless, in addition to privacy concerns, it may be unethical to engage people in constructing something which they have little or even no knowledge of and which they may or may not approve of. Moreover, oblivious participation would have little to no effect on subjective security, or even negative effects if it is discovered.[8]

In the sci-fi classic *Ender's Game* when the protagonist discovered his game was the war, one that had brought about friends' death and the genocide of the enemy, the emotional ramifications and withdrawal were severe and went on to transform society.

TRANSPARENCY AND INFORMATION

This discussion of OPS capabilities began with participation, in the belief that the action component is what matters first, that it is action that gives transparency meaning, that transparency is less important as a right (to the extent that it even is one) and more important because it facilitates participation, which itself consists of rights and responsibilities accrued over time to meet needs, including even the need to participate. In this light it makes no sense to condition participation on transparency, on whether someone is informed; the extent of viable, even necessary, participation instead determines the necessary transparency that must be provided. If this amount is unclear, create participation and the participants will soon tell you what information they need.

While some of the specific information requirements and possibilities for structuring the needed information were outlined above, it makes sense here to attempt to summarize what was discussed to see how these would fit into a general "information policy" that can replace our existing "classification policy." As we saw, the information that the state must release varies by the type of participation, though there is also considerable variation within each of the broad approaches outlined, especially the more advanced the form of participation. Very broadly speaking, the amount of information a state must release increases as one progresses from basic Participation 1.0 to deliberation to co-production to gamification. However, the extent to which the information must be clearly intelligible works the other way. Gamification and co-production require a good amount of information be released, but this information can also be more fragmented, compartmentalized based on a person's tasks/function, and/or provided in raw, degraded, aggregated, or even "meta" formats (thereby maintaining secrecy on certain capabilities, e.g. surveillance). This information can also be "hidden" until it is provided "just in time"; indeed, this style of release is used in game design, as it enhances engagement and task performance (Lerner 2014, 62–63 and 76–78). At the same time such an approach would leave our enemies with no data to mine or hints about our actions until the solution is already at hand or action is under way. For Participation 1.0 and deliberation the details matter less than providing a complete picture. The information for these approaches must be more comprehensive and context laden, including especially of the intent of a given policy, program, or actions. These approaches also benefit from information being released far in advance of any needed decision or action. The variation in the timing, depth, and amount of information released among the different tools leaves the state with many options to ensure sources and capabilities can still be obscured enough to prevent them from being compromised.

Failure to provide the right information in the right structure at the right time to any OPS platform can undermine its functioning, as the purpose of OPS is to fill in gaps in the state-provided information or services with citizen-generated information or services. Provide the wrong information, citizens will fill the gap with the wrong solution or fill the wrong gaps, and objective security will decline. Hereby, OPS builds transparency and participation into the "technical architecture" of the security system by making it, or rather demonstrating that it already was, essential to the performance of a critical state task: the provision of security (idea draws from Pasquale 2015, 157). In this way it can help secure what some call rights, or higher needs, by making clear how such rights are essential to our survival (to foundational needs). This is not to imply OPS does not also have subjective purposes, which will be covered in the next chapter. However, the state security actors are concerned foremost with its objective purpose, and its success or failure in this regard is what will determine whether the program is accepted and expanded.

Following from its gap-filling function, compared to older transparency-accountability systems shedding light on the inner workings of government, OPS requires specific targeted transparency. Targeted transparency requires the disclosure of specific information that is used to harness liberal democratic/market forces to reduce specific risks (Fung, Graham, and Weil 2007, xiii, 5). As it is intended to ensure informed action, the information must be proactively released before participation. Despite the burden of proactive release, that OPS requires only specific targeted transparency for seemingly functional purposes may for the moment lead to a sigh of relief from the security bureaucrats and professionals. Because targeted transparency is limited to some extent, the government can seemingly keep many of its secrets after all. Yet while the conclusion is correct, total relief on their part would be misplaced. Because it is meant to fill gaps, the information required for OPS is the very information that the government is not likely to want to share. This is true most obviously on a functional level as we seek to fill gaps in our tools, intelligence, and tactics, but also on the psychological level of information warfare. The existence of adaptive competitors seeking to beat you to air, and thus to dictate the anchor for people's perceptions (see Chapter 4), means release cannot be purely selective; it must consider also what could do the most damage, which is what competitors/enemies are most likely to release, and seek to proactively establish a counter-narrative before the competitor/enemy does. While resolving this dilemma will be challenging, it must be resolved by proactive government action and information, before the objective gaps become obvious during an attack or the subjective gaps are revealed in a leak or hack.

Moreover, our argument here for targeted transparency is intimately connected with the needs and structure of modern security making. Yet while security is a primary function of the state and need of society, there are other functions and needs in our lives, many which also feed back into security. These areas will require their own appropriate systems of transparency, which may or may not be targeted. Thus, targeted transparency can and should coexist with previous "generations'" transparency, forming part of "hybrid transparency systems" (Fung, Graham, and Weil 2007, 154). While targeted transparency is needed to feed specific a priori information into proactive, functionally oriented systems and processes, older transparency-accountability systems are still required to gather retrospective information that can be used for ex post accountability, including for institutions. Plenty of the past still needs to be unburied, not just for justice but because we (and OPS) depend on the past for evolution, learning, and progress. Traditional transparency, its citizen-driven pursuit reflecting needs perhaps unknown to the state, is the best way to unbury it without drowning us in government-released data.

CONCLUSION

What makes these and many other systems ideal for modern security in an age of distrust and austerity is that such participatory platforms can be progressively adaptive, self-improving, and self-structuring systems (e.g. Friman and Higgens 2009, 44). The apparently insurmountable demands of designing and moderating can be largely outsourced to the participatory community, even for such complex things as game design; user-generated content (including advanced "mods") is a core element of many modern games, such as *LittleBigPlanet*, *Spore*, and of course "sandbox" games like *Minecraft*. Yet the state must remain involved to maximize the contribution that the outputs of OPS make to real-world tasks, as well as if it is to capture the trust created within the network (see Chapter 6). It must release and structure the necessary information for developing solutions as well as structure how it will monitor, evaluate, select, and implement solutions. Equally critical, it must give feedback to the system and its participants – including both citizens and state security organizations – on their success to promote system and individual learning and create engagement loops that maintain participation over time.

As we would expect based on international relation and innovation theory as well as history, today it is also the *march* and revisionist states – replete with crises and threats – that have been the most willing to experiment with open participatory processes in their security structures and strategies. This is particularly true for co-production, which has the lowest financial intensity while offering vast capability enhancements. While co-production, and indeed all OPS approaches, have high reorganizational requirements, the *march* and revisionist states are less fearful of the social implications of new security solutions given they are already experiencing social strain and transition. Indeed, even more than objective capabilities these states may most desire to capture the subjective trust– and social cohesion–building capabilities of OPS discussed in the following chapter.

While the dominant status quo states have certainly developed the most cutting-edge technologies and capabilities, these for the most part have yet to be deployed beyond the experimental phase or pilot programs. The obsession of these states' security organizations with technology has led each individual bureaucratic actor to set up its own internal shop to develop new solutions, including those related to OPS, hoping that when the new technology is mature enough it will then be their organization that controls it or at least sets the standards (e.g. Rid and Hecker 2009, 212). Yet this very division has also allowed them to avoid reforms, to not even recognize when it is needed, as every organization tends to see any failure as not being their fault but that of another security or even political actor (Tom Ricks in Foreign Policy 2015c). Because of this organizational structure and mentality the new technological solutions being developed are focused on sustaining existing capabilities, particularly intra-organizational ones, which will make applying their solutions on a system level impractical, even dangerous. Yet on the positive side, these internal labs and other innovative elements in the existing government security apparatus mean there are numerous insider actors interested in new solutions. Linking these with partners in the political and civilian sectors who share this open and innovative spirit would form the cross-sectoral alliance with the correct configuration of resources that is necessary for gradual institutional reforms of a far-reaching nature.

The examples of modern participatory tools discussed in this chapter show not only their benefits for security, but also their possible non-monetary "costs." The Russian case is in this regard an exemplar. Just as the era of openness unleashed in the mid-1800s allowed some states to manipulate their societies, contributing to nationalism and war, there is today a "panic-inducing aspect of the transparent society" (Lacy 2014, 34) that can be used to either mobilize or normalize insecurity and induce apathy. Yet rather than being a reason not to adopt OPS, the costs are a reason OPS must be adopted by democratic status quo powers, for the revisionist states are already making use of these tools to undermine the trust Western societies have in information, their governments, and their entire liberal system. In any cost-benefit estimation one must consider also the cost of failure to adopt. As Robert Leonhard (1998, 13) has observed, "The ineffable power of doing nothing is a force often overlooked in the history of mankind. Inertia is a cold-blooded killer." While our current BiTS system can likely hold the barbarians at bay strategically for a bit longer, the aggregated tactical setbacks from other actors using illiberal variants of OPS are accumulating in the form of subjective insecurity, which inevitably feeds into objective security. While BiTS cannot restore subjective security, we will now turn to the way in which OPS can.

NOTES

1. In the Battle of Narva (1700) Swedish forces defeated a Russian force almost four times larger during the reign of Peter the Great.
2. Doctrine discussed in Chapter 3.
3. The question corresponding to this dilemma was raised in Chapter 3: Is it better to have a secret program you lose or a more public program you keep?
4. One could argue the initiatives examined are also about creating agreement and acceptance in one regard: they help solidify an institution's or community's position internally before they must take that position to an external actor, for instance in negotiations.
5. However, inclusion does not mean fully bringing into the fold (e.g. employing), even if this was possible, because, as mentioned in Chapter 3, this would alter the incentive *cum* motivation structure and thus reduce creative potential.
6. CLIQR Quest Challenge in 2012 was similar in nature but with less advance advertising and smaller targets (QR codes on posters), resulting in greater difficulty.
7. This differs from the "analytics" now used in video games, which are internally oriented for improvement of the game itself, whereas here the analysis is used to improve the external system of security.
8. It could still have some effect though, as all games, even those not designed for social purposes, influence the person and the knowledge of this effect is advancing enough that efforts to manipulate the effect could be built into games.

Chapter Six

Closing the Insecurity Gap

Open Participatory Security for Subjective Security

Objective security can make us feel safe, but it does not necessarily do so. Snipers on every roof, pervasive surveillance, walls on our borders, and sensors at every point of failure may provide near-perfect security, but the citizen enduring this world would likely not feel safe and may even experience more anxiety and fear. If the only way to protect ourselves is to turn our countries into prisons, then our enemies must be truly threatening. Progress, however defined, in such a condition would grind to a halt. Conversely, even in the face of high threat and routine security failures people may still feel relatively safe. This phenomenon of "normalization" is one factor that allowed a semblance of normal life to continue in places like Britain under the Blitz and later during the IRA bombing campaign, and which still does in Lebanon and Israel as well as modern Russia (though not without other psychological impacts) (on IRA, see Gearson 2012, 188, with reference on 191 to theories of Frank Furedi; on Russia, see Galeotti 2014a; on Lebanon, see Borell 2008).

As touched on throughout this book, our current system leans towards pursuing pure objective security and deterring our enemies and reassuring the public through the pervasive deployment of its tools. Yet the current dependence on objective, technology-driven security alone has ended up depriving our social order of the subjective sense of security that is essential for stable state-society relations and progress. The technology is not understood, or even known of, and there is less and less of a human element to relate to, with whom to bond and who in turn bonds us to the system. The secrecy and monopolization the technology enables, and is claimed to require, further entails a feeling of a loss of control, even in the context of democracies. This feeling is magnified when security fails, which it will inevitably do both because of gaps in the BiTS system and simply because perfect security is impossible.

The state's rhetoric of NCW and its promise of perfect security also transform these failures into a breach of trust.

While many adaptive adversaries target the gaps in our objective security system, for the majority this targeting has not been to reduce objective military capabilities (at least not yet), but to ultimately target subjective security and reduce it. From the perspective of 4GW, subjective security is especially important, as it is this subjective feeling of security that modern 4GW combatants seek to strike, to undermine the will of the enemy's people to support more offensive objective security measures (Rid and Hecker 2009, 127). Many of Russia's hybrid tactics are aimed not at undermining objective security first, but undermining subjective security and thereby weakening objective security capabilities (or shifting them in a direction that does not conflict with Russian interests). Even traditional third-generation force-on-force warfare relies heavily on subjective security at home and inducing just the right amount of subjective insecurity in enemies abroad. Anti-aircraft fire in WWII was often more a sign of defiance for the citizens than an effective defence (RAND study in Watson 1978, 219); the Doolittle Raid on Tokyo in 1942 had no effect on Japanese military capabilities, just on the island's feeling of invulnerability.

Because 4GW and hybrid warfare are population centric, not in the sense of trying to destroy the people but to undermine their will and thereby change their character and identity, the defence of the population must be visible to reinforce their will, as should be offensive operations of a preventive, or retaliatory, nature (Ibid.; similar ideas in Rid and Hecker 2009, e.g. 207). Moreover, the use of at least somewhat visible means to security need not undermine objective security. Keeping defences secret may help prevent an attack from succeeding once the attack is launched at you, but even if you stop an attack in progress it still disrupts your society and economy. On the other hand, deterrence prevents such attacks in the first place; but something secret cannot be a deterrent (General James Cartwright, USMC in Singer 2015, who [assumedly] unintentionally but ironically echoed wisdom from *Dr. Strangelove*). Equally, while secret offensive strikes destroy the target, public offensive operations have a greater disruptive effect because the visibility causes a cascade effect, as adversaries take protective measures that reduce their operational capability (Lehrke 2016). If the enemy is striking mainly at our subjective security, this is where we need to defend, and perhaps we need to target their subjective security as well. Put in Clausewitzian terms, the escalation of force as currently being tried by the existing objective security system needs to be matched, or we would argue preferably replaced when not in times of proper war, with an escalation of will through subjective security.

The following sections will show how citizen participation in security drives several psychological mechanisms, first seen in Chapter 2 and then in Chapter 4, that alter the individual and groups as well as the relationship between the two in a way that can bolster subjective security. The chapter also examines the close, mutually constituting relationship between subjective and objective security. In doing this the chapter begins to bring together much of the material covered thus far, thus serving as somewhat of a pre-conclusion. Structurally the chapter opens by recapping and elaborating on some material from earlier chapters on subjective insecurity in modern society and the "sparks" for participation. The core of the chapter then focuses on subjective security through three dimensions of trust: trust in self, in others (including groups and organizations), and in the system (the tools/processes *cum* state). Before concluding the chapter also returns to the issue of politics and rights, and explores some possible risks of OPS.

SUBJECTIVE SECURITY AS TRUST

Subjective security, as an internal psychological condition, is not as easily quantified (and thus also not as well studied) as objective security. Thus, even its conceptualization is less developed; what exactly does it mean to be subjectively secure? At its core, subjective security is about trust, in other actors and in outcomes, as seen in the definitions by Omand (2010) and Schneier (2012) from Chapter 1. As we have seen, historically a social contract between the state and society was to allow the formation of trust through state provision of security; thus, objective security typically came first, while subjective security was facilitated directly by this provision. It is this form of competence-based trust that the state still focuses upon. However, while objective security may be the first-order requirement and subjective security a welcome but ultimately second-order effect in states and societies living on the margins of survival, in societies that have already provided higher human needs, such as self-esteem and self-actualization, and which moreover are heterogeneous and not organized on traditional hierarchical lines, trust relationships and security are much more complex than a simple two-way exchange. In such contexts objective security alone is not just insufficient for subjective security, but can undermine it if it conflicts with other needs.

Trust itself is a complex concept and a whole field of study. As a starting point, Guido Möllering defines trust as an "ongoing process of building on reason, routine and reflexivity, suspending irreducible social vulnerability and uncertainty *as if* they were favourably [sic] resolved, and maintaining thereby a state of favourable [sic] expectations towards the actions and intentions of more or less specific others" (2006, 111 emphasis in original). In addition to the three pillars of reason, routine, and reflexivity, the key concept herein is suspension of what uncertainty remains. Such uncertainty is always present when we speak of trust, as if something is certain, trust is irrelevant; in security such uncertainty is always present because total security is impossible; thus, trust is always required in security relationships.

The key question then is what enables the final "leap of faith" to trust? Möllering's "quick answer" is agency, an individual's sense or capacity that they can think and act freely (2006, 125). While we are unable here to fully debate what exactly gives or constitutes agency, which like trust is an object of dense and pedantic discussion within numerous academic fields, for our purposes we can incorporate perspectives on agency from two extremes of the debate: that it is about knowledge and power (e.g. Giddens 1984) but also has unconscious sources (e.g. Willmott 1986). The unconscious sources were discussed in Chapters 2 and 4, these being the evolutionary socio-psychological mechanisms which demand and encourage the pursuit of knowledge and power in the first place, while these latter concepts then are used to fill the human needs that the unconscious mechanisms demand: from simple survival in an external context to self-actualization to the needs provided by an individual's group (for example, esteem [for how knowledgeable and powerful you are]).

This entire book is an argument for returning such agency to security making. Yet restoring trust, and subjective security, is not as easy as just providing individual agency (not to imply providing agency is itself easy). Sometimes people do not want agency; they want services provided in the background, what John R. Hibbing and Elizabeth Theiss-Morse (2002) have called "stealth democracy." The amount of agency that individuals see as desirable is variable, and trust in and the legitimacy of a socio-political arrangement is possible only when the amount of agency matches what individuals want; agency can neither be taken from nor thrust upon an unwilling agent (Meyer and Jepperson 2000). The extent of agency desired, and perceived as needed, is determined again by unconscious sources and existing knowledge and power structures: the former specifically being "interest" and the latter being the ideational and technological context upon which our world, and our view of it, is built.

The amount of agency required in a system is determined first by individual interest in agency for a given task, here security, as was first discussed in Chapter 4. Interest is determined by the extent that an issue demands the individual attention of a person in that a human need is not being provided for like manna from heaven or by another actor, whether person or group. Failure to fulfil a need or to protect a need from a hazard leads to anxiety and worry, which leads to a desire to control the factors that presently are uncontrolled (Myers, Henderson-King, and Henderson-King 1997). Thus, in much the same way as the state opens to innovation due to inability to provide a good, public interest in contributing to the production of a public good rises with the failure of the actual provision of that good (Ibid.; Bovaird, Loeffler, van Ryzin, and Parrado 2014, 123–24). Interest then kicks off seeking behaviour, specifically seeking to find a method of controlling the hazard that is threatening normal life (see Chapter 4; Dignan 2011, 2425; Panksepp 2004).

Yet interest in agency specifically, as in seeking an inner locus of control rather than interest in making somebody else deal with an issue, is influenced by the larger context. Within this context the organizational structure facilitating the desired amount of agency must be both technologically possible and ideologically conceivable; otherwise, it will not be desired, or if desired, will quickly fail (due to the technology not being there) and then no longer be desired. Thus, both perception of and actual capabilities are important. The extent of agency desired, and seen as necessary to restore control over an issue, is based on who an individual thinks can perform a task; nobody wants to do something they cannot do or do well, and nobody will assign a task to another actor they view as lacking competence.

In the modern era the ideal locus of control is seen as residing in the individual, and more recently in the network, while the state and other traditional hierarchical organizations are seen as having insufficient competence. As covered earlier (especially Chapter 3), by both design and accident, in modern liberal society individuals pursue their self-interest through self-help. Such self-actualization is the basis of the myths about how to make it in the modern world, myths based on fact, on a deeply ingrained biological need for self-actualization and the resulting creation of institutions reflecting this need, such as the market. Modern technologies were designed for and have furthered the individual, giving them to some extent the actual ability to provide for their own needs, empowering the individual with capabilities. Science and industry evolved also in this direction, devising new ways of knowing, producing, and problem solving based on the individual. Yet while rooted in the idea of the individual, these empowering technologies functioned because they embedded an individual in a network. While at first this network was intangible and unseen, once it became embedded in everyday life, coming even to constitute some persons' entire professional and social lives, it was recognized by individuals. This fact has led to the idea of individualism to gradually give way to the ideology of the network (Lanier 2010; Morozov 2014), itself based on our socio-biological roots of cooperation: Microsoft embraces the "power of the cloud," militaries acknowledge that "it takes networks to fight networks"

(Arquilla and Ronfeldt 2001, 15), politicians and marketers succeed based on their penetration of online social media.

This ideology does not provide the actual feeling of self-efficacy, but rather enables one to believe self-efficacy is possible. To determine if this belief results in action, in agency being activated for a task, requires consideration of whether there is an actual "viable self-protection plan that allows the control of both the danger and the fear" (Breakwell 2014, 156, referring to work of Girandola 2000). In one sense there is, and in another there is not. Technology has empowered the individual, as seen throughout this book. This has reinforced individual self-help tendencies, as it is increasingly possible for the individual to, if not directly fulfil their needs, then certainly reduce the number of middlemen in the process. While the faith some people have in technology may be exaggerated, if combined with a human element it does have the capability to provide many objective security needs. Because people know and believe in the capability of technology and more recently also in its social network component, people believe this power of the network is a viable plan to fulfil their needs. Thus, it may be able to also produce subjective security.

Yet this interest in security and belief in self-network solutions has not been mobilizing because, for the most part, there has been too much information poorly communicated and too little valuable information linked to actual capabilities that could enable action (see Chapter 3). Transparency may allow for awareness of a problem or threat, but for this awareness to be translated into something productive, not just fear or withdrawal, context needs to be provided (education allowing ranking and preference formation) as well as participatory mechanisms (even if "just" virtual). Yet even while individuals have gained increasing power and control over numerous aspects of their lives, political processes remain beyond their influence aside from irregular elections which themselves seem to offer little actual control over a security realm deemed so vital as to be "above politics." Thus a more active openness, a push not just of information but of mental tools is required, not only an input of data but an upgrading of the system with an action-oriented element. Participation using modern technological tools can offer more meaningful control, and evidence (feedback) of that control, and thereby create the trust needed for subjective security.

FACILITATING AGENCY

The modern individual is thus interested in security and desires agency to address current insecurity. It is the task of the state (if it wants to continue to exist) to facilitate the necessary agency to allow for trust, for subjective security. As shown in earlier chapters, the initial impulse for the state to open to allowing agency (participation) is not based on trust (in their citizens), an important fact if we are to break out of the current low-trust socio-political context (as well as not construct a circular argument). Rather, the state opens to such innovation based on how agency enabled by technology can contribute to objective security, the possibility for which was shown in Chapter 5. To create this possibility for objective security through OPS the state is required to disclose information, accept influence, and reduce control. The three factors are incidentally also what is required to promote trust, and thus subjective security, following from Dale E. Zand's spiral reinforcement model of trust (Zand 1972, 231). When the state engages in these three behaviours the citizens take it as a sign of the trustworthiness of the state, which increases their level of trust in the state and induces the citizens to reciprocate with similar behaviour: inducing them to share their specialized knowledge, accept the involvement and feedback from others, and recognize that control over their environment is possible only through shared control (more to follow). Thus, by surrendering control over the means, the state can gain more control over the desired end, that is, over real and felt security.

Because of the shifts towards ever more individualism and network centricism, no matter how much the state would like to rebuild a traditional state-society social contract it cannot use OPS in this way (or it would fail). Rather, it must be about building the individual's own trust in themselves as well as their trust in their fellow citizens (as a network). When all these are combined it allows trust to be given to the system that made trust between the individual nodes possible through its provision of security. To capture this network of trust required for sustainable subjective security we conceptualize it as having three elements: trust in self (to contribute to security), trust in others (to contribute their part), and trust in the tools and processes of security, which make up the state as a system of security (more trust in governance than government). If these all work together they allow also trust in current and future outcomes, which allows for continuation of normal life and the positive expectations that allow for risk taking and thus progress.

In the following we turn to these three areas of trust and how OPS can build them and thereby build subjective security. The chapter will then turn to how this subjective security directly contributes also to objective security. This discussion will involve drawing extensively on psychology, including both the traditional psychology of risk and new psychological research on the effects of technology. As a caveat, interventions to manage risk, to alter individual and group perceptions and behaviour, are not simple or straightforward. Studies occasionally, even routinely, conflict in their findings. However, the knowledge base is solid enough that "lower-level generalization that could feed into attempts to change risk responses" are available (Breakwell 2014, 308). The risks of such attempts to influence perceptions of subjective security will be turned to towards the end of the chapter, while the conclusion will turn again to the idea of evolutionary, iterative implementation to offset these and other objective security risks.

TRUST IN SELF

We turn first to examining how the process of participating in OPS changes the individual in ways that contribute to subjective security by building trust in self. When considering trust in one's self, the most relevant of Möllering's pillars to bear in mind is reflexivity, as such trust, despite being self-centred, always is related to or about external factors: other people and events (except perhaps for narcissists). This internal-yet-externally defined process of building one's trust in one's self is best captured in self-determination theory, an empirically robust approach often used in game studies which links action, internal perceptions, and external perceptions (Kazakova, Cauberghe, Pandelaere, and De Pelsmacker 2014). The core aspects of self-determination theory are competence, autonomy, and relatedness, as defined in Chapter 4. These aspects give an individual a feeling of control, or self-efficacy. In turn this control, when evidenced, contributes to intrinsic motivation to engage in an activity; that is, the changes in the person should be mirrored in changes in behaviour and actions.

COMPETENCE TO CONTROL

In addition to their problem-solving potential, interactive participatory approaches are an ideal way to increase awareness, to educate, and to improve an individual's system thinking, thereby inducing reflexive thinking and even behaviour change (in part, see Werbach 2014). While we saw in the last chapter how education and awareness help increase objective security, they have equally important psychological effects. Specifically, they increase an individual's opinion of their own competence, their ability regarding a specific task. The process of learning not only teaches specific things – a new language or how to ski – but increases confidence when dealing with those things – speaking to a foreigner or tackling a black diamond slope.

However, for belief in internal competence to be firmly established, it must be evidenced; one has to have reason to believe in their increased ability.

While for languages and sports feedback is provided almost immediately, for virtual activities the process can be somewhat more complicated. While simple feedback – such as points, awards, and other virtual pats on the back (e.g. "likes") – can suffice in the short term, to ensure continuation intention, to build motivation, longer-term feedback needs to come in the form of evidence of influence on one's environment. This evidence allows competence to translate into autonomy (which, to repeat, is *not* independence, see Chapter 4), a feeling that one has causal agency through making real choices that control an external environment. This control of one's environment, whether direct or through influence on others, allows a sense of relatedness that lets the agent know that they are contributing in a meaningful way to something larger and that their contribution, even mere interaction, matters: that they have the autonomous ability to make a difference.

This need for autonomy to be confirmed through feedback evidencing relatedness has been demonstrated in research on using computer systems to assist in decision making on ill-structured tasks, ones where there is no optimal solution (like in most policy decisions and many security decisions). Even when such computer systems improve objective outcomes, the user's confidence and commitment to those decisions does not increase unless they believe that they influenced the decision through their continuous involvement, and not that they were simply validating and verifying what the system (or its designers) already knew (Landsbergen, Coursey, Loveless, and Shangraw Jr. 1997). Nobody likes to feel as though they were merely a rubber stamp or were manipulated into approving or doing what others had already decided upon.

This competence *cum* control can be described as self-efficacy, which is the "person's belief in their capacity to perform in ways that give them control over events that affect their lives" (Breakwell 2014, 61; key work in this regard is Bandura 1997). Having self-efficacy is like the concept of having an internal (versus external) locus of control, which means the individual sees a causal relationship between their personal characteristics and behaviours, and their external experiences. Research on games especially has shown they can be effective at inducing such increases in self-efficacy. Increased self-efficacy contributes directly to more subjective security, in the same way that basic training contributes to soldiers' sense of control through an ability to influence their environment in a way that keeps them alive in combat even while contributing to mission success. This sense of control contributes also to what Marc Zimmerman (1990) calls "learned hopefulness," which limits the debilitating effects when we encounter problems in our lives. This feeling of optimism helps people maintain their normal life even in hard times, which is, recalling Sir Omand's definitions, the whole purpose of security.

Thus, even with no change in external threats, by increasing self-efficacy, participation in security can make an individual feel more secure. However, too much optimism can have negative effects, which will be discussed below, as well as how to mitigate these.

CONTROL TO BEHAVIOUR

The feeling of increased self-efficacy has a further internal effect that can also have external manifestations. This ability to transfer positive behaviour from the virtual to physical world, sometimes in counter-intuitive or incredibly simple ways, has been empirically established in several contexts, though is not something platform designers can take for granted; nothing is simply done when attempting to influence behaviour (see sources at Stanford University 2015; Yee, Bailenson, and Ducheneaut 2009). Here, we are concerned with one specific effect of virtual activity: its impact on real-world *risk* behaviour. When an individual has an internal locus of control, their risk perception, intention, and behaviour are altered, though the link between the three is rarely straightforward (Dahlstrom, Dudo, and Brossard 2012). In the standard model, when a person thinks that they can manage a threat, they find that threat less adverse, that is, less risky (Breakwell 2014, 61). Therefore, they will engage in activities that offer rewards even if they occur in the context of an objective threat or risk. The proficient skier who has seen their own competence on the slopes finds the black diamond run less risky and is eager to tackle it; the trained soldier fights the enemy willingly believing they will get through it okay.

In the context of security this has two impacts. One is passive, in that increased competence in providing security makes the threat seem less threatening. If we believe we can handle the terrorist threat, we are less worried about it. We can engage in the activities of normal life. The other impact is an increased willingness to actively engage in risky activities that we see ourselves and our security partners as competent in, such as war, operations just short of war (air strikes), or intelligence activities. While such proactive precautions still have real risks, those with an internal locus of control are willing to accept these risks since they believe they can be controlled, especially compared to longer-term risks (Breakwell 2014, 63). Thus, on the positive side, feelings of self-efficacy make it possible to take the risks that are necessary for survival and progress in a world and system where proactive solutions are required (as argued earlier). Nonetheless, there is an obvious negative side to this as well, one which will be turned to below.

Yet the above internal, psychological discussion does not imply there is no real effect, that the feelings of control are false, the risky behavioural shifts totally unjustified. Even putting aside OPS's direct educational effects, which are more important for objective security, games can help a player to "map" the world differently, to alter mental models variously called scripts, schema, or frames (Lacy 2014, 89; see also Breakwell 2014, 105; Kelley 1972; John Leach in Ruz 2015). Improved mental models can increase awareness and preparedness that can feed into security. In a project called Sirius, the US IARPA is examining ways to train people to overcome cognitive biases and thus make better decisions (IARPA 2011). The Heroic Imagination Project (HIP) (2015), founded by Dr. Philip Zimbardo (of Stanford prison experiment fame), has a similar goal, "to teach individuals the skills and awareness needed to make effective decisions in challenging situations." This includes mechanisms to overcome the bystander effect, to shift mind-set, combat social conformity, reduce stereotype threat, increase situational awareness, and combat prejudice. Thus, beyond teaching tangible skills OPS can teach its participants how to think, decide, and thus act more appropriately based on their environment (see below on resilience).

TRUST OF OTHERS: NODES IN THE NETWORK

Participation in OPS also enhances trust in the other components of the system, the other individual participants (in science speak, nodes) in the network, with which one cooperates and some of which an individual may bond to, as well as more generalized trust in the entire network of participants as a community. Trust today is now able to extend in novel ways, through virtual teams and networks (e.g. Coppola, Hiltz, and Rotter 2004; Iacono and Weisband 1997); today people are often distant to those physically close but close to others who are physically distant (same idea in Hammes 2006, 39; Lacy 2014, 72). Compared to the effects on individuals, there has been even more direct research on the positive effects that participation, including online participation, has on promoting trust within groups, amongst other effects (such as transfer to the real world, task engagement and success, etc.).

Inherent in the idea of reflexivity is that there are others in one's environment, persons who also contribute to the sense of relatedness that builds trust in the self (per self-determination theory). These other persons can come to form a community which a person considers themselves to be a part of, communities built on the socio-biological imperative to cooperate to survive. Traditionally, this sense of community was limited to smaller groups, but in modern times it is possible also to build such ideas of community on a larger scale through media which make people aware of their connections and commonalities with others. Historically, we saw this in the press and Reformation and radio and nationalism, but the means need not be so directly mobilizing; more passive participation can have similar effects. For example, while everyone was in their own living room to watch Walter Cronkite at 5:00 p.m. or the *Tagesschau* at 8:00 p.m., there was a feeling of relatedness in knowing others were doing the same (Ezrahi 2004). The psychology of this is so powerful it was even used as the basis for the recent surprise British television hit *Gogglebox*, which literally shows people watching television in their living room (*The Economist* 2016). Even by watching television you were participating in a social act that built a sense of community (some of the above draws also on Meyrowitz 1985).

Modern, non-political media have similar or greater community-building functions. Research on social networking sites (SNSs), the name alone which implies relatedness to others, has found that the "more time users spent interacting with other users [. . .], the closer they felt to other people," leading in turn to positive (internal) emotional states that would support the "trust-in-self" mechanisms (Neubaum and Krämer 2015). Research on gaming, ostensibly played by loners in basements, has also found that bonds of trust can form following the virtual activity of gaming together even while physically alone (Isbister 2016, 43–71; Lundmark 2015; McGonigal 2011, 89–90). This sense of community is reflected in the parallel support platforms (e.g. Wikis, called metagaming) developed by the gaming community that we discussed in Chapter 4. Even the ongoing culture war over misogyny and sexism that is dividing the gaming community indicates the community's importance: the definition and values of the identity of "gamer" is something worth struggling for.

These communities – even if formed purely for socializing or fun – can then lead to action in other areas, specifically to civic and political engagement and participation (Kahne, Lee, and Feezell 2013). This process of community mobilization looks something like the following: Shared interest in an object (a hobby, issue, etc.) sparks the formation of a social group. Over time the group's interactions progress from basic communication (chatting about) to other actions (doing together) for supporting the shared interest, which strengthens bonds and relationships until a generalized trust forms. The group could probably continue like this happily enough, but there is always an external world out there, and often this world does things which threaten the interests of the burgeoning community. These threats can then lead the community to mobilize for external action. For instance, telecommunications corporations could threaten equal Internet access and speeds, leading gamers (who rely on the Internet) to mobilize for net neutrality, seeking out also external allies to help in this effort (e.g. media companies). Moreover, under proper conditions this community can move to offline activities. Typically, we see this possibility expressed as a concern: of someone moving from reading radical jihadi forums to engaging in an actual external jihad (Rid and Hecker 2009, 137). However, it also has positive possibilities: it can lead a person from signing a petition online to holding a sign on the streets, or maybe from discussing security on a blog to taking steps to promote security in their community (on former, Vaccari, Valeriani, Barberá, Bonneau, Jost, Nagler, and Tucker 2015; Vissers and Stolle 2014; the latter of course refers to the potential of OPS). This process of levelling up community engagement in quality and scope will be an important part of the evolution of OPS as it moves from simple deliberation to higher forms of participation.

However, this relationship running from community formation to task performance, from social group to action, can work also the other way around: action can create the group as well as strengthen a pre-existing one. Participation in a task together can create a specific, functional trust. While this trust (specifically, confidence) is at first limited to trusting your teammates' ability to perform the task you came together for, it can and often does expand: first to other tasks as confidence grows in the nonspecific general competence of others, and then, as emotional responses to the task create emotional (affective) bonds between the team members, to more generalized forms of trust. The formation of trust in this manner is especially useful in places or times, such as here and now, where trust is low. Even in this context groups can and often do come together for a specific purpose, a shared interest, that requires cooperation due to a need for numbers or for diversity, and this can create communities over time. This phenomenon has been found to exist both in military/security settings (called task cohesion) and in online, as well as specifically OG, settings (see, respectively, King 2006, 2007 and Wojtczak and Morner 2015, 36).

Such bonds of course benefit from routine, as Möllering's definition highlights. However, the creation of "swift trust" is also possible. This is now a major area of research and activity not only in civilian realms but also in military affairs (Meyerson, Weick, and Kramer 1996; in military, see Ben-Shalom, Lehrer, and Ben-Ari 2005; Elron, Shamir, and Ben-Ari 1999; Bartone and Adler 1999). OPS meets many of the basic conditions for swift trust, such as early communication, involvement of team members in meaningful tasks, and reinforcement of predictable patterns (Coppola, Hiltz, and Rotter 2004, 103). Swift trust develops based on shared interest (in a task), which is evidenced the moment one is on an OPS platform; it can be enhanced by markers of reputation that can be built into participatory platforms (drawing from Kuo and Yu 2009) and be promoted by creating task interdependence in the teams constructed for a mission. Gamers do this in many of their virtual universes, selecting, for example, a fighter, a healer, a thief, and a wizard to be on their team. Shared interest, interdependence (due to distributed skills), and observable behaviour allow swift trust to contribute to task performance. Subsequently, this task-related trust contributing to successful performance can lead to more permanent bonds. This as well can be seen in the gamer community, with gamer teams sometimes moving as a group from the gaming platform where they met to another new game (Isbister 2016, 128–29; case study by Pearce and Artemesia 2009). Back in the physical world, veterans' associations are a long-established example.

Such rapid creation of social solidarity amongst socially dislocated individuals was evidenced in the Arab Spring and Occupy Wall Street movement (Lacy 2014, 75), while we can also identify similar phenomena of mobilization in post-9/11 America, Boston in 2013 (marathon bombing and manhunt), and France (and Europe generally) following the Charlie Hebdo and Paris attacks. Technology played a major role in all these events, sometimes constructive (allowing mobilization of peaceful protests in Egypt in 2013, or organizing places of refuge during the Paris attacks of 2015) and occasionally detrimental (e.g. interference in Boston bombing investigation including false attribution of guilt on specific individuals). However, only a shadow of the sense of community and swift trust seen in these events has been transferred into more permanent networks. Yet to an extent "permanent" and "network" are mutually exclusive, and while some of these networks disappeared (e.g. in Egypt) others simply transformed once the task changed. Occupy Wall Street moved on to "Feel the Bern" (that is, to supporting Bernie Sanders's bid for the Democratic party presidential nomination in the United States); once Syrian protests turned to civil war the network turned to civil defence, as seen in the last chapter, or defiance, exemplified by the underground citizen journalists of *Raqqa Is Being Slaughtered Silently*. Still other networks were captured by larger organizations, political parties, or even the state – something akin to what we are advocating here (albeit a more willing merger that maintains the network's structure and thus its advantages).

A key question that remains unexamined is how far this internal group trust and group efficacy can extend beyond the most active participants. It is unrealistic to expect every citizen to engage equally in OPS, and likely unhelpful to mandate such participation except to a limited extent, at the risk of crowding out motivation (see Chapter 3). However, through cascading (see Chapter 4) the effects of OPS can spill over from participants into the non-participant population. If they share the same end interests of the participants, non-participants can become supportive of the participants' effort, even if they do not find the time to directly engage in it. Moreover, in doing so they can share vicariously in the efficacy and trust created (also in Chapters 3 and 4). People can come to actively support their OPS team like they currently support their soldiers or football team, and can thereby share in their success, as well as help them recover in and from times of failure.

Regarding failure, the act of working together to produce security may have an additional positive effect: a reduction in the tendency to scapegoat or seek out others to blame when there is a security failure. This is because working together diffuses responsibility amongst all those involved. The role of diffusion of responsibility in military psychology is already well studied (Grossman 1996). The function of inducing complicity and shared responsibility through games has also been explored (Isbister 2016, 3, 8, 10). While these have negative aspects (see discussion of risks below), within a group they help to prevent recrimination and blame: if you succeed, you succeed together; if you fail, you failed together (a philosophy with which military service members, veterans, or fans of *Full Metal Jacket* will be familiar). Moreover, if we no longer need a scapegoat, people will not fear being made into one, and thus failure will be less likely to be covered up, which will allow the group to better learn from failure. Thomas Rid and Marc Hecker (2009, 223) have highlighted the need for just such a "culture of error tolerance" in the military in order to learn and improve security, but for them to adopt such a culture, their superiors – citizens and politicians – need to do the same.

TRUST IN THE SYSTEM: THE STATE AS A NETWORK

The state has traditionally relied mostly on objective security itself to gain trust, using this trust in turn to further bolster objective security measures. As defined elsewhere, the form of trust resulting is often called confidence, or specific trust relating to a specific task. If the state provides security, then we have *reason* to believe in its competence, which allows for confidence that there will be continued positive performance in this regard, which once confirmed through *routine* security gives us reason to trust the state. This trust could be considered shallow though, in that it does not encourage deeper bonding, making it especially vulnerable during difficult times. When security fails, we need another reason to trust the state and believe security will return.

To restore deeper and thus more sustainable trust the state must make more efforts to link itself and its task performance to the network. The state may have more difficulties than the people in accepting such new structures, which are so different from the structures the traditional state was built upon.

Yet active state engagement in OPS is critical to prevent the "emergence of incoherent parallel structures" discussed in Chapter 4, ones that compete for legitimacy and resources, a feudalization of the modern state (Gamper 2015, 83). The state can avoid this by becoming the channels through which the OPS network flows: the links (technically called "edges"), key nodes, and technology that make the system operate. This can form the basis of a "21st century networked sovereign" (Keen 2016 regarding Estonian President Toomas Hendrik Ilves) wherein what bonds us is a new system of governance in which the government is but one participant, albeit an important one.

If we return to the analogy of participant as a skier, the state would be the ski resort, giving the participant options of which run to take, providing the tools, guiding them, giving feedback, and giving them fulfilment when they reach their objective, making them want to mount the lift again and challenging them to advance to harder runs (and come back next season). Returning to OPS, the state provides the data and information that is fed into the system to enable participation, the mechanisms that translate the knowledge produced by participation into solutions, and the feedback on how an individual's actions contributed to collective action and subsequently to outcomes. By doing these things the state "encourages the public to feel a greater sense of control and this is translated into greater trust in the course that offers them control" (Heath and Palenchar 2000; for some confirming studies, see Breakwell 2014, 162; related ideas in Peters, Covello, and McCallum 1997; Wojtczak and Morner 2015, 38–39). When an OPS outcome requires a final executing action, it is often the state that must perform this action, and it must faithfully execute it in letter and spirit. Without actions following directly from the participants' inputs and feedback to the participants on the outcomes of these actions, the routine leg of trust cannot be built. Moreover, participants' interest will wane given lack of evidence of their autonomous influence on the environment.

However, a task-oriented trust in the state as a mere executor of popular knowledge and will as expressed through OPS would still be shallow. Fortunately, the state is not a monolithic entity; in the provision of security alone there are institutions, organizations, working groups, and numerous other entities which will be enabling and engaging in an OPS system. The state is thus also a collection of nodes scattered throughout the system, and OPS will empower not only the people but also these internal government entities. People's trust in these state actors will increase as it does with other individuals participating in the network, and the state can gain "reflected legitimacy" through the participation of their security agents in OPS. Here again, we see how OPS can use the very structure of BiTS, specifically the B(ureaucratic) part, in its own evolution.[1]

The state must also act as the router, not only in the sense of sending information where it needs to go, but in ensuring the proper nodes talk to each other. Particularly important is linking parts of the network together that normally would not be connected, preventing the echo chambers that Cass Sunstein (2007) and others speak of, which contribute to the polarization of many modern populaces (see Chapter 3). The state is needed to turn virtual teams and communities into citizens by linking interests and demonstrating clearly to participants how interests are linked, and how successfully attaining those interests is interdependent. This is essential not only to help build trust beyond small like-minded groups, but also to maximize the variation in the network, which is the key to maximizing its production of useful knowledge and the successful performance of tasks.

By participating in the process of making security the citizen participant also gains familiarity with and possibly even an understanding of how security is provided. Hereby, the participant can develop "reason" to trust in the tools, in the system and technology, of security, trust notably absent towards NSA surveillance and CIA drones. Trust in technology gained through experience with that technology can even enable the increased usage of automated technologies (David Bruemmer in Singer 2009, 134). If we personally trained the algorithms, and in the process learned about them and maybe even learned about ourselves, then they will no longer undermine subjective security (idea draws on Domingos 2015, 281). As the technology becomes more pervasive in our lives and we become more familiar with it, there will be a "societal normalization effect" (Lima, Barnett, and Vala 2005). Essentially, exposure to the technology increases the participants' self-efficacy specifically relating to the technology, their ability to control and use that technology for meaningful decisions in a way that produces meaningful outcomes. Thus, OPS can serve the same role the technologies of the RMA did for the US military in the 1980s and 1990s, shifting them from leaning towards anti-tech to being more trustful of their technology than of their own intuition (O'Grady 2016; Robinette, Li, Allen, Howard, and Wagner 2016; see also Chapter 3). However, since the human is built into the technical architecture of OPS this should prevent the citizen participants from becoming as enamoured with technology as some in military and security circles have.

Finally, the feedback aspect is perhaps most critical in the process. Firstly, as discussed above, this is needed to build individual and group efficacy and sustain their interest in participation. Secondly, in providing feedback the state communicates something essential for trust: that it shares the values of the participants including a high valuation of the individuals' contributions towards the shared goal of security and survival (idea derived from Wojtczak and Morner 2015, 38–39). It is consistency in values that most facilitates institutional trust, as well as allows this trust to persist even during security setbacks (Cvetkovich, Siegrist, Murray, and Tragesser 2002). It is perceived inconsistency between the values of citizens, and even the foundational (liberal) values of the state, and the (lack of) values in government policy following 9/11 that has undermined much public trust.

OPS AND POLITICS

As is evident from the above conversation, if the state does all these things, truly embraces OPS, as well as OG in other areas, this will go beyond an instrumental tool and will fundamentally alter politics. However, it will do so in a way which is consistent with the modern individual's views on how the world works and should work, how problems are appropriately addressed, views that hearken back to the liberal foundations of the current dominant world social order but which many governments seem not to reflect. While some, most popularly Evgeny Morozov (2014), criticize the ideology of the network and adjusting other systems and institutions to fit this ideology, the idea is too firmly rooted to overturn overnight. Where Morozov is right, though, is that the network is not permanent and unchanging. OPS is about changing this network, making it more human centric and linking it to governance. In doing so it will strengthen the political dimension of strategy, "perhaps" the only component that can be central to strategy, according to Colin Gray (2002, 280), and the component which when weak that has contributed to the defeat of numerous alternative systems even when they for a time had advantages in other dimensions (Ibid., 276). By ensuring a strong political dimension and linking it directly to the other strategic dimensions, including the hard military dimensions, it ensures these dimensions remain subservient to the political level and ends, and do not come to dominate strategy as has often happened in history. It will also ensure the political structure reflects actual power by distributing authority to those who hold power today: everyone. By making sure the object of security is also part of the means of security we ensure the ends of security provide for survival of the object of security: the individual citizen.

A specific political element that may change, and which this book has largely avoided getting too deeply into, is the idea of rights. As argued in the introduction, an expansion of participation has usually preceded an expansion of rights. Participation, by increasing competence and intrinsic motivation, contributes to continuation intention and behaviour, establishing a routine that bolsters trust. The upshot of this trust in combination with continuation intention is that withdrawal of the act which the individual intends to continue, here participatory security, then constitutes a violation of trust. In this sense, a social contract is forming, and in this light, perhaps rights are forming as well. Once participation is built into the technical architecture of the core tasks of the state, that of security to ensure the possibility of realizing fundamental human needs, participation may in turn become a fundamental right since the new "network state" – the new social contract – and even task performance (fulfilling needs) could not be maintained without the new participation (similar idea in Pasquale 2015, 157). The same would apply for transparency; since transparency is necessary for an OPS network to perform its essential task, withdrawal of transparency would constitute a threat to survival. Equally so, if the participants come to identify with the task, processes, and institutions that emerge from the act of participation, removal of participation would threaten their identity. Just as the technology of the (printing) press eventually was enshrined as a constitutional-level right and some are now pushing for Internet access to be a right (la Rue 2011), so may people demand OPS become a right. Since the state's own performance in security will depend on the people's participation, it may even beat the people to the punch and demand participation as a responsibility. This issue will be returned to, but not resolved, in the conclusion.

While not core to the argument herein nor to OPS, such a system may have an impact on the issue of privacy as well. Based on Zand's (1972) model of trust, if OPS builds trust, then all actors will increase their willingness to disclose information, accept influence, and reduce control. This applies not only to the state, which will loosen secrecy based on both trust and the objective need to feed information into OPS to realize its potential, but also to citizens. Once citizens are familiar with how security works and how the technology works, when they know who is doing what with their information, they will become less concerned with privacy (basic idea in Oulasvirta, Suomalainen, Hamari, Lampinen, and Karvonen 2014). Both the state and society may thus become increasingly transparent, a trend which should not surprise us when observing the online behaviour of younger generations who grew up with Web 2.0 technology.

TRUST IN OUTCOMES: SUBJECTIVE TO OBJECTIVE SECURITY

As seen in Chapter 4, participation can result in a sense of ownership regarding the resulting policy outcome or service provision/task performance. Closely intertwined with this sense of ownership, and indeed efficacy as well, is a high valuation of the "products" which people built "themselves," even if it is not as good as what an expert could have made (the IKEA effect of Norton, Mochon, and Ariely 2011). For OPS this means that the participants will have immediate respect for, that is, place trust in, the security system they helped to build. Vicarious group self-efficacy means this feeling can also spread to others not actively involved but who identify with and are supportive of the "team" effort, in the same way that any national (or community) effort and success contributes to feelings of national (or community) pride.

Nonetheless, after initial participation, competence must eventually be evidenced; one may admire their IKEA masterpiece but when it collapses before your eyes (or under your weight) your admiration of your product, and thus of your handcraft skills, quickly disappears. Subjective security can compensate for objective insecurity for only so long; continued breaches of objective security will undermine the competence pillar that is required for citizens' self-efficacy and intrinsic motivation and thus would break the participatory cycle. Similarly, it would undermine the reason pillar for trust in the other participants in the system – citizens and state organizations – as well as for placing trust in the system itself. Thus, it is important that participation also promote real objective security directly to create a sustainable and self-reinforcing cycle, to establish reason and routine that promotes trust (for a different approach [technology acceptance], but one that matches the trust perspective, see Al-Hujran, Al-Debei, Chatfield, and Migdadi 2015; Horst, Kuttschreuter, and Gutteling 2007). Moreover, while governments might not mind just subjective security, as it could be enough to win them elections, policy and security makers – with their functional mission and task orientation – need objective security if they are to be encouraged to continue investing in, supporting, and building an OPS system. All parties to OPS must have reason for maintaining positive expectations of the system's future usefulness to maintain trust in the system and its constituent participants and thus to favour continued usage of that system. OPS must show that threats are controllable or at least manageable.

While the required evidence of, and actual, objective security should be provided via the approaches discussed in Chapter 5, even if we put these aside (as a mental exercise, not because they do not exist), subjective security itself can directly create objective security through prevention, resilience, and deterrence. Subjective security is largely about risk perception (mediated by trust). Risk perceptions in turn influence risk behaviour, though the correlation between the two is neither perfect nor automatic. As discussed, participation leads to competence, which creates feelings (perceptions) of control. These feelings can alter behaviour, not only virtually, but in the real world. If coupled with OPS approaches to educate, increase awareness, redraw mental models, and/or aid in decision making – such as the Sirius project, HIP, and numerous games – this behaviour can also be objectively better, allowing persons to act or respond more appropriately to a given environment. Together, awareness leading to vigilance plus an idea of how to act when required allows citizens to co-produce security by reducing risks (fixing vulnerabilities) as well as responding to threats in real time. Thus, self-sufficiency can provide real objective security through prevention, that is, by stopping a threat either pre-emptively, such as by reporting suspicious activity, or by directly intervening in an event in progress.

Additionally, by helping individuals to feel and be more prepared the participatory tools can increase their resilience, which allows them to better weather, absorb, and recover from any security failure. They can take care of themselves (autonomy) and contribute to taking care of others (relatedness). This contributes to a feeling of subjective security even if there is a security failure. A failure may even enhance the sense of subjective security, as the act of responding to the failure produces evidence (feedback) of competence; this is why we often seem strongest in our darkest days. This has a real objective impact firstly in that it allows continuation of an individual's normal socio-economic routines and normal life, even given a threat or attack. Secondly, this resilience can increase objective security through deterrence. Resilience reduces the consequence (also called severity) and impact (measured as disruption and its duration) of an adverse event by allowing a quick response and then resumption of normal life. Provided our resilience is known to others, which it typically would be at least after it has been first demonstrated, then it can serve to deter the launching of an attack by an enemy; knowing that the consequences and impact of an attack would be less, adaptive competitors such as terrorists may seek to find another target or attack mode that promises a higher return on their investment (see Gearson 2012, e.g. 186, 191–92). Often, the new target will be in a different state, but even if the terrorists still seek to target the same state, the time and effort to make tactical adaptations provides time and leaves traces for authorities to detect and neutralize the threat (Lehrke 2016).

There is one additional way in which OPS, by increasing individuals' subjective security broadly and resilience specifically, can prevent threats from materializing. ISIS – and other extremists, whether left, right, or religious – radicalize by looking for insecure and threatened individuals with a need for some control over their own circumstances and a connection to something greater than themselves. By tying people to social networks and giving them purpose and self-esteem, OPS can offer an alternative. In this way OPS can also be an anti-/counter-radicalization program. It can offer the socially dislocated person identity and their actions, even life, meaning.

THE RISKS OF OPEN PARTICIPATORY SECURITY

Because subjective experiences, here subjective security, are rooted in the mind with all its biases, they are subject to manipulation. Any work with information technology is also an act of social engineering (Lanier 2011, 4), and humans – especially political leaders – have a history of being open to such engineering. Specifically, through OPS a state could increase the subjective security of the individual through manipulating the participant's experiences. We are concerned here less with simple manipulation of the design features of an interactive platform's user interface, which can increase trust levels in the system (Wang and Emurian 2005). Such minor nudges to increase trust in a system is desirable to promote system usage, especially at early stages; moreover, it would not interfere with the process by which OPS creates objective and subjective security. However, manipulation of initial information and the feedback provided are more serious concerns, in that they can alter the individual's trust in themselves and their co-producers and thus influence outcomes.

For example, people have hindsight bias, which is when they believe ex post that they have accurately predicted something which a priori they may not have so accurately foreseen. This "I knew that was going to happen" bias is adaptive; it gives an individual a greater sense of control over the future by making them feel they successfully predicted the past (Dekker 2004). On an OPS platform, metrics and feedback could show an OPS participant a skewed version of their past accuracy through creatively presenting the material and thus manipulate, specifically increase, the participants' self-efficacy (based on findings of Fischhoff, Gonzalez, Lerner, and Small 2005). This would increase their subjective security, which in turn would affect their risk tolerances going forward and the policies they will accept. Yet these feelings and policies would have no basis in reality, resulting in the means not matching the ends and thus making policy success unlikely.

Manipulation could also nudge people's participation to yield a preferred result, a subtle form of manipulation with many useful applications as elaborated most famously by Richard Thaler and Cass Sunstein (2008). Again, this would allow for subjective security increases since participants could be made to believe they still made autonomous meaningful choices. However, the resulting outcomes would then reflect the same outcomes of the current BiTS security system and its knowledge base, meaning the objective security advantages of Chapter 5 would not be realized. The only situation where such nudging could be beneficial without such implications for objective security is for those OPS platforms whose primary purpose is to educate, increase awareness, or improve decision-making ability, in others words, those aimed mainly at increasing societal precautions, response, and resilience, which are foremost subjective security issues (with objective follow-on effects). Ensuring there is no manipulation of information and feedback for short-term subjective purposes should be possible firstly by maintaining the traditional transparency mechanisms discussed in Chapter 5, thus providing an alternative source of verifying information's accuracy. Secondly, OPS tools should be primarily designed by non-political, technocratic, functional, task-oriented organizations with longer-term perspectives (much as current OPS manifestations are today).

RISK IN THE INDIVIDUAL

Risks can arise not only through intentional abuse, but also from the process itself, from the underlying psychological mechanisms that drive OPS. As mentioned, participation can lead participants to have an internal locus of control. While this has numerous positive effects that can make a person safer, it also can alter behaviour in a way that exposes them to greater risks, thus in aggregate making them possibly less safe. A person who believes they have more competence and can thus influence outcomes displays greater risk-taking propensity in their area of competence (Horswill and McKenna 1999; for qualification, see Trimpop 1994, 178; see Chapter 4). In short, the more the individual participates in an activity the less risky they see that activity as being (drawing on ideas first developed by Zuckerman 1979, albeit about other human activities). Thus, the more real OPS becomes, the more its virtual participation becomes a truly vicarious representation of reality, the riskier individual behaviour could become. This can translate into actions or support for actions that are inherently risky, such as personally apprehending a wanted suspect or supporting a war, in the belief that they are low risk or risk free. We are indeed already psychologically primed to see many of these activities as risk free given our exposure to the no-risk component in the rhetoric of NCW, which even while we shift to OPS, we will not be free of for a generation.

This is closely connected to a second psychological phenomenon: optimistic bias. Absence of control leads to unrealistic pessimism, such as we see across society today (Dolinski, Gromski, and Zawisza 1987; see also van der Velde, Hooykaas, and van der Pligt 1992). Conversely, when a risk is thought to be in the control of the individual it can result in unsubstantiated optimism (Heine and Lehman 1995; Klein and Helweg-Larsen 2002; Sparks, Shepherd, and Frewer 1994). Thus, persons with an enhanced feeling of control may not only engage in or support riskier activities; they do so in part based on the belief that the outcome will still be favourable regardless of actual probabilities. Put more directly in security terms, they may support risky security actions while being convinced only costless victory and success can result.

While attempts to mitigate this effect have so far been unsuccessful (Breakwell 2014, 95), other biases may offset optimistic bias, and methods promoting these could be built into an OPS platform. Humans tend to focus on the negative, something theorized to give an evolutionary advantage, enhancing survival by discouraging too much risk taking (Thompson 2014). It is not difficult to remind people *cum* participants of the negative risks of life; indeed life usually will do so by itself (see below on "failure"). Additionally, people also have a default zero-risk bias due to a preference for certainty, even if in accepting the status quo they are giving up on some possibilities in life. The resulting behaviour is usually, from an economic perspective, irrational. However, from a security perspective, if other factors encourage too much risk taking, people can be reset to their default by simply reminding them that things are good (not something media focuses on much today) and that they have a lot to lose from foolish risks.

RISK IN GROUPS

In addition to these shifts internal to individuals, which are additive in the way they contribute to larger group behaviour and outcomes, because OPS involves groups there are also emergent (that is, totally new, not merely additive) outcomes. The process of group decision making often results in what is called the "risky shift" (Stoner 1961; see also Breakwell 2014, 109–12). Studies have regularly found that group decisions made following discussion, even relatively little discussion, are riskier than individual decisions (Higbee 1972; Kogan and Wallach 1967). While the exact mechanism by which this occurs is still debated, the most common explanation is diffusion of responsibility, which we saw earlier also has positive benefits (Wallach, Kogan, and Bern 1962, 1964; later studied by Hashiguchi 1974; Vidmar and Burdeny 1971). Moreover, the effect is not only on the group decision; following participation in a group decision an individual's own risk decisions are altered in favour of taking more risks (Breakwell 2014, 110). As the effect's existence regarding significant decisions involving professional competence (in other words, experts) has been questioned, the importance of integrating security professionals into OPS processes is again highlighted (Higbee 1972).

Another danger of groups is that the individual may be subsumed into it, which can undermine the creative potential of OPS. Like all ICT platforms, OPS can "stimulate different potentials in human nature," from our "pack mentality" to "individual intelligence" (Lanier 2011, 5). Current technological design of most Web 2.0 platforms tends to promote the former. It is important that OPS be designed to encourage the latter, to sustain and enhance the individual. Firstly, this is consistent with liberal ideology, and thus supportive of a system based on a unified world view. Yet more practically and importantly, variation is essential to human evolution, and this also applies to ideas and the way we think: a "cognitively homogeneous population" would be vulnerable (Rosen 2005, 23; Schirrmacher 2009). OPS can arrive at objective security solutions only if those solutions can emerge from the maximum possible diversity of persons (for integrative solutions) and/or solutions (for selective solutions).

THE OFFENCE

Adding further to possible risks, Michael Colaresi (2014) has found that strengthening oversight institutions, which some aspects of OPS are (see Chapter 5), leads to an increase in public support for military actions. Robert Leonhard has observed increased citizen acceptance and/or active support for war with the current advance of precision weaponry, while the increased tempo of modern preparation for war implies also the potential to short-circuit debate and decisions (1998, 27, 29). If we reflect further on the observation that both technology and intelligence favour the offence, then – following from defensive realism (a theory of why wars start) – we can expect more wars of all sorts even if they will be fought in hybrid or contactless ways (doctrinal approaches which themselves also favour the offence) (related argument in Lieber 2005, 9, 24, and 156–57; on the offence, see, for example, Omand 2010, 133; Schneier 2003, 13, 89). Given that OPS will be an unknown technology, the risks of such contactless activities escalating due to misperceptions about capabilities also exists, though as a visible manifestation of national will, OPS should reduce misperceptions about a nation's intentions (on misperceptions and war, see Jervis 1988).

The cumulative effect of all these risks may be to promote risky, offensive state behaviour with wide popular support and participation in the belief that a costless victory is assured. Such an outcome would reflect the worst excesses of earlier eras of openness and participatory security systems as seen in Chapter 2. However, these risks would likely (and could purposely) be mitigated through offsetting mechanisms that de-link intention and behaviour as well as varying the levels of engagement and areas of activity of different citizens (which would be their preference anyway: to participate in what they are interested, for as much time as they like). OPS should not be, and the state should not encourage it to be, a system in which we all march in unison towards one task and objective; OPS is about swarming from many directions on many problems.

SELF-CORRECTING THROUGH FAILURE

More than the offsetting psychological mechanisms and state-led efforts to reduce the risks of OPS, these subjective effects on persons and groups should be self-correcting when OPS fails. The first point is that OPS will fail. It will fail in its outcomes because perfect security is not possible in a world of adaptive competitors. It will fail in its design because no system is perfect, because even with the crowd we cannot know everything and innovation entails risks. OPS will fail even by design, as by allowing failure, rather than covering it up or finding a scapegoat, it will be able to learn, thereby improving its design and outcomes.

Moreover, when OPS does fail, the failures will offset the psychological effects discussed above. It will reduce optimism bias and highlight the salience of uncontrollability, and by increasing anxiety, will lower risk tolerance. Provided the tools for self-efficacy are still provided, that OPS is not dismantled the day it fails, subjective security can be restored. People do not expect perfect security; research in London following a spate of bombings in the 1990s demonstrated that "the public did not expect the authorities to be able to guarantee to prevent every attack. Indeed, there was an element of fatalism in the attitudes of many respondents. The key demand was for well-coordinated and efficient recovery from any dislocations and as much information as could be shared" (Gearson 2012, 191). By building trust and subjective security through participation, OPS can provide the resilience needed when objective security fails, while these failures can prevent the excesses subjective security can entail.

Failure should also spark renewed interest in security and OPS, as too much objective security can lead to complacency and lower demands for participation (see Bovaird, Loeffler, van Ryzin, and Parrado 2014, 123–24; includes also further references). "[P]eriodic crises that concentrate users' interests" can help to sustain a system and promote its evolutionary reform over time (Fung, Graham, and Weil 2007, 17). The bottom line is that the state needs to willingly reveal failures and their causes, revelations it should fear less when OPS diffuses responsibility across the polity. Nonetheless, the task of managing failure will still be substantial, especially for certain demographic groups less familiar with failure (i.e. those who have had it good) or more vulnerable to failure (i.e. those who have it bad).

CONCLUSION

The subjective insecurity discussed in Chapter 3 is a result not only of objective security failures leading to reduced trust in the state and security institutions; indeed, while we have questioned their future performance, the current security system does not perform as badly as one would think based on viewing the nightly news or one's Facebook feeds. Rather, subjective insecurity has resulted due to individuals' lack of feelings of control over their own lives and security, and over the political institutions to which they have outsourced security tasks. The political apathy seen so often today is not a natural characteristic of the modern human; it is an outcome of current perceptions of an inability to make a difference. Our desire to contribute to security, even if not always directly by volunteering for military service, is evident: we buy war bonds and plant victory gardens; we keep calm and carry on; and when we can do nothing else we tie yellow ribbons around trees.

To restore a sense of security requires restoring a feeling of control as well as providing evidence of that control through feedback on actual outcomes. OPS has the potential to restore a more meaningful sense of individual control over security and the politics that direct it. It can increase individual and group efficacy and thereby trust in oneself and one's fellow participants. By providing the structure and tools for citizens to realize this control, and accepting this control, the state can position itself also in the resulting trust network. By allowing itself to be influenced, by loosening control and releasing information, the state gains influence over its citizens through trust. It thereby gains influence over the direction of the network, allowing it to mobilize its citizens as a means to security. The result will allow the state to increase control over the actual ends of interest, that is, over objective security outcomes. Yet in the process of creating this security, the state itself will alter, as it always does when participation in the state and security is expanded, coming in time to reflect the new realities of distributed power residing in individuals and networks.

NOTE

1. The first case, to recap, being how bureaucratic compartmentalization means there are many intra-state and intra-military/security institution actors that can partner with citizens and experiment with OPS.

Chapter Seven

Towards a Perpetual-Beta Open Participatory Security

> "Technological progress without an equivalent progress in human institutions can doom us."
>
> – US President Barack Obama, Hiroshima, Japan, 27 May 2016

This book opened by presenting the era in which we live as one in which technology shapes our security and insecurity. Embedded in our everyday technological existence we see a world of technological threats, seemingly capable of being countered only by technological solutions. Balancing the blessings and curses of modern technology is perhaps the defining task of our age. Technology is at times empowering, and at others, socially dislocating and disruptive; it creates freedom and facilitates oppression; it makes individuals the new sovereign, and as such makes them also the new object but also the target of security. In this light, this book has argued that the individual can also be the means to security.

After the attacks of 9/11 in the United States, people wanted to do something more than "go shopping" as then President George W. Bush famously advised, but not everyone could join the military. In a quite different call to action, following the 2016 terrorist attack in Nice, France, Interior Minister Bernard Cazeneuve urged all patriotic French citizens to join the reserves. Yet as the military and the threats we face are structured, it is unclear how this could help. Would a mass army really help in fighting a diffuse, often hidden enemy? Yet aside from taking on the full sacrifices of military service, it seems that there is little positive contributions that citizens can make to security, only negative ones, sacrificing rights and privacy, not questioning the ethics of policy and tactics. Our security institutions were not, and still are not, open to outside talent or contribution.

Yet while his choice of words may have been poor, President Bush's advice was rooted in an accurate assessment of the situation: the country needed the people to carry on with their normal lives. In trying to encourage such routine behaviour, the state sought to provide security in the background more than ever before: secrecy would preserve normality even while protecting our soldiers and in turn our nations. There would be no (or at least less) footage of smart bombs, only second-hand accounts of drone strikes; public trials would be forgone for extraordinary rendition, CIA black sites, and Gitmo; the state would quietly listen in and gather information while the citizens went about their business, their very normality providing the control against which algorithms could identify deviance. Yet while in previous eras such provision in the background may have been preferred or even demanded, the people have changed along with their technology. With these changes people would not accept claims of effectiveness without evidence, and what was functionally effective was no longer automatically legitimate. The state secrecy deemed so necessary to keep people calm while providing security against vague or even secret threats – unlike the specific and visible enemies of the past – undermined the people's ability to perceive effectiveness. While security successes remained classified, security failures – real and speculative – were and continue to be ever present in the media. Failures were made even more unacceptable since the system was seen as pervasive, even invasive; if even "total information awareness" supported by dollars and data and sacrifices of rights could not be effective, then something must be wrong with the entire system itself.

Indeed, something was wrong with the system. Built up during the age of industrialization and great power politics, and legitimated by its credited success in the World and Cold Wars, it was designed for the security of a different era. Security is not static; as technology changes it alters the threats to the socio-political-economic system by introducing new vulnerabilities to our lives while also creating new capabilities that enable new attackers. What worked yesterday may not work tomorrow and may even make you weaker. Security in our era is more complex, fast-moving, nonlinear, and interdependent than it was in the past century. Threats are more than ever unpredictable "black swans" that our technology cannot address, the "unknown unknowns" of (Donald) Rumsfeld-ian fame. Even while objectively we (arguably) may be safer today than in any previous era, largely thanks to technology, that very technology has led to complex interdependence that makes our overall system brittle, vulnerable to cascading or catastrophic failures with little resilience to help us quickly bounce back, but with severe political backlashes including some which run counter to the ideological basis of liberal democracy. Even as the world gets more complex, and threats diffuse, modern security forces can do less and less even if they do their well-defined tasks incredibly well; they can utilize and counter indirect fire (e.g. artillery, missile) but cannot defend against distributed attacks. The traditional means to security are unable to match their solutions to the structures of our current problems, while also being increasingly at odds with both modern economic needs (e.g. encryption, austerity) and social preferences, and in turn with the liberal ideas and modern technology that helps shape them.

The current security gap has emerged not because power has disappeared, but because it has diffused, while insecurity arises when the people nonetheless feel powerless. In its chosen means and ways to security, the state had underestimated the power and creativity of the people – whether object or target of security – and their will for information and drive for action when issues of relevance to survival of lives, but also dignity, are at stake. Technology makes the state, despite its best efforts, and world transparent and gives the people new power, the means to their own survival. If the state does not recognize this fact and enable the citizens' participation, then the state will be seen as not necessary to the people's survival, and they will look for other sources of belonging.

In this sense the French call may be on the right track, though only time will tell if they make the necessary organizational changes to allow these reservists to contribute in an effective way, not to simply be another set of eyes standing in uniform on the corner. A model is there for how to facilitate such contributions, as seen in Estonia but also in the numerous other small programs distributed globally among many different types of actors (e.g. NGOs, firms, states, proto-states). Rather than venerate technology and seek to remove the person, a source of errors and leaks, from the system, these approaches seek to integrate technology and its human users to maximize the potential of both for meeting human needs, both objective and subjective. Yet most states have been unable to adopt a more appropriate system and build a basis for a new social contract with citizens who have been greatly altered by technology. Path dependencies, institutional resistance, status quo bias, group think, and technological "lock-in" are amongst a host of factors that have conspired together to ensure modern technological solutions have been adapted for – or even just strapped onto – old platforms, organizations, and tactics. The barriers to open participatory security seem insurmountable; thus, its adoption may be delayed until tragedy sweeps away these barriers and crisis drives us to innovate.

CRISIS: HOW FAR GONE ARE WE?

Despite the assessment above, itself based on arguments made in earlier chapters, how bad can it really be? Maybe the reason change is so slow is that it is not necessary. As was pointed out, the current security system is – despite its weaknesses – holding up well, even if a lot of collateral damage and/or sacrifices come with the bargain. Perhaps instead of speaking of crisis we should borrow a term from an earlier but not so distant era of global change. In the 1980s Mikhail Gorbachev used the term "pre-crisis" to describe what his country, the USSR, was then experiencing (Lehrke 2013, 27). Despite arguably noble attempts though, the Soviet Union's political institutions were unable to reform enough to counter the social change and economic stagnation afflicting the country as it sought to adjust to changing technological realities. In a relatively short time, historically speaking, the USSR went from the height of its power (circa 1978) through pre-crisis and into crisis on its way to total collapse in 1991. Today, the Western liberal democratic model and liberal world order is under similar pressure from similar causes: technological progress, economic transformation, social dislocation, and political stagnation. The crisis of liberal democracy was once a topic of interest only to political theorists; now its manifestations appear on the streets and on our ballots.

This political and social pre-crisis then feeds into security provision (just as security feeds into the political and social realms). While a functional, means-centric security policy is certainly capable of holding the flood of threats at bay for a time – technocratic governments in general can do quite well in the short term – a politically and socially disconnected security system is in the medium term a recipe for insecurity and strategic defeat. Without faith and trust in the underlying political institutions, proper political guidance of the security system becomes increasingly impossible. The political level is needed to connect the means of war/security to political ends that are in the interest of the larger socio-political unit/community. Moreover, without political and ultimately social support, our security institutions will be unable to reform. Indeed, considering the current feeling of low trust and high insecurity, they will likely find themselves slowly starved even of the resources needed just to maintain existing tools and approaches. Unable to keep up with adaptive adversaries that are more able to maximize their capabilities through modern technology and the globalized world, objective security will begin to break down. Because of non-linearity and interdependence, even a minor event could become existential.

As was the conclusion (and title) of an Editor's Roundtable podcast of *Foreign Policy* (*FP*) magazine "It's Time the U.S. Military Reinvented Itself to Operate in the Information Age" (Foreign Policy 2015b). Yet in that and previous podcasts there was a sense of doom, of impending disaster, and more than a bit of pessimism about the prospects for reforming our security system (Ibid.; Foreign Policy 2015a). Nonetheless, *FP*'s experts (here especially David Rothkopf, Rosa Brooks, Kori Schake, and Tom Ricks) also were adamant that we have solutions elsewhere in the economy, that as a people we are good at many things even if our governments are not.[1] Rosa Brooks even saw one way out of having to wait to learn from catastrophe, specifically through a new universal national service, a view echoed even more recently by (retired) General Stanley A. McChrystal (2016). OPS can be such a service.

Even if full-blown crisis is not yet upon us, we should not ignore its warning signs. We cannot wait for the market to self-correct, a new election to bring fresh leadership, our enemies to tire, or technology to solve human problems. Yet neither must we wait for trauma and tragedy to induce learning and transformation. We – as individuals, nations, and a species – have enough incremental failure under our belt to learn from and skills to apply to the thereby developed solutions. This book is itself part of an effort seeking to change old overarching ideas of security and how it is organized and implemented before tragedy forces change. In place of the old we seek to promote the idea of openness, participatory organization, and a human-machine technological system capable of addressing real and felt security.

A MODEL OF OPEN PARTICIPATORY SECURITY

A non-linear security context requires a non-linear security system; diffuse threats against almost any citizen or sector calls for diffuse mobilization of citizens from all walks of life (similar proposals in Arquilla and Ronfeldt 2001; Cronin 2006; Pomerantsev 2014). The contemporary context, the condition of pre-crisis, necessitates new adaptive structures that introduce more agency into security making, for a perpetual beta system that is self-reinforcing, -structuring, and -improving even while it meets current needs (related see Friman and Higgens 2009, 44). Such mobilization and structures must use and maximize the current technology *and* its underlying ways of knowing and solving problems. The system that emerges will require that the entirety of Clausewitz's Trinity – government, army, and people – work together, each contributing their own capabilities, and in the process coming together in a modern networked social contract (following the ideas of former Estonian President Toomas Hendrik Ilves for a "21st century networked sovereign"; see Keen 2016).

A key advantage of open participatory security is its promise to be sustainable, even in the face of a degree of (citizen) apathy and (state) austerity, through the creation of feedback mechanisms that reinforce and promote the expansion of the system. Governments like success, and they like objective security. Provision of security fulfils one of their main tasks, if not *the* main task. Successful task fulfilment ensures power, however one conceptualizes it (re-election, control, a means for other ends, etc.). Once participation proves to be effective at ensuring objective security, the government will have more trust in participation as an approach. This in turn will lead it to find more ways to encourage, even mandate, meaningful participation. Such new approaches will in turn require that more information be released, as the system depends on transparency for its success.

From the perspective of citizens, participation leads to feelings of empowerment and self-actualization; it can give self-efficacy and even a measure of self-sufficiency while simultaneously repairing social bonds by giving individuals a sense of relatedness when working with or in relation to others on a task. These positive feelings of competence create a feedback loop, reinforcing and increasing motivation to engage in the behaviour which led to the "reward" of increased ability; in other words, they maintain and even increase their interest in open participatory security. Thus, once participation in security is established, it will become demanded, and over time will be demanded in ever higher forms.

This can all be brought together in a model (Figure 7.1) which illustrates the cycle of insecurity, participation, security, and trust. The model and the process it illustrates have two perspectives, that of the state (policy maker, including those making security) and that of society (individuals). Both desire security. However, the state is somewhat conservative in this policy area and hesitant to experiment. Society on the other hand has delegated this task to its representatives and must generally get on with the business of living life, contributing to building state power in the process. If these actors are to be mobilized to try a new approach, a catalyst is needed. Such a catalyst is the complex insecurity that characterizes the contemporary world and which cannot be addressed with current solutions (i.e. with current security instruments [means] or strategy [ways]). For society this insecurity leads to lack of specific confidence and general trust in the state, to subjective insecurity. Yet as security is essential for survival (and accumulation/progress) its absence inspires interest in the issue. This interest translates into increased demands for state provision and/or efforts at self-provision.

As the state cannot provide security with the existing system (or there would be no insecurity), the insecurity leads the state to be more open to innovation. Historically, such innovation requires the inclusion and integration of new actors, ideas, and tools combined in such a way as to maximize the

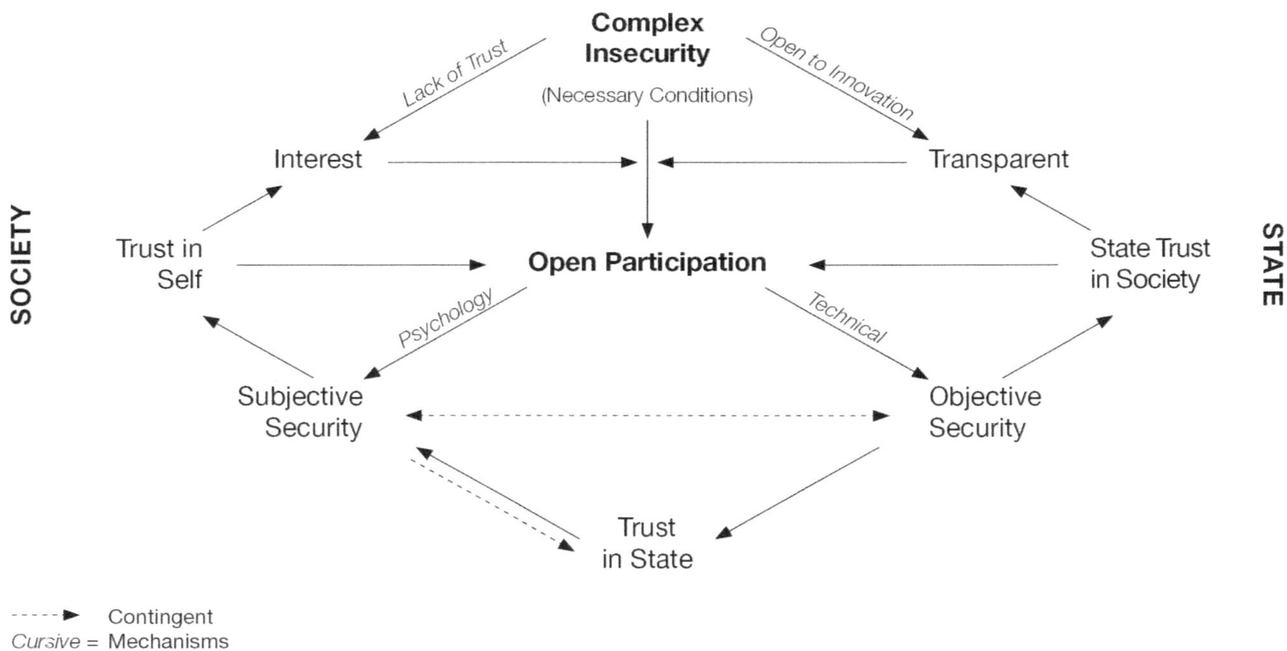

Figure 7.1. A Model of Open Participatory Security

system's potential. Only by being transparent can the state capture the self-provision instinct of an anxious society and transform it into something more beneficial to the group and able to provide collective goods (security). The information that transparency releases is necessary for the mobilization of the people and for the development of appropriate innovations (i.e. ones directed at weaknesses in the system). This puts in place all the necessary conditions to lead an engaged society and transparent state to come together and explore open participatory security to resolve complex insecurity.

Such open participation can address the complexity of (contemporary) security by providing both subjective security, through psychological mechanisms that facilitate self-actualization and -efficacy, and objective security, through the technical effectiveness of open approaches for solving complex problems. Increased objective security then leads, on the one side, to an increase in the state's trust in society, more specifically leading government actors to trust that social participation is a good thing for security making. Once it has such confidence in OPS, the state will support further participation, which will require more transparency to facilitate new participatory initiatives, creating the model's first feedback loop. On the other side, objective security also leads society to have more confidence in the state. Both objective security and the resulting trust in the state also feed into subjective security, where they bolster the direct psychological mechanisms promoting feelings of security through participation (with this possibly then feeding back into trust in the state, depending on individual perceptions of who gets the most credit). Subjective security then in turn feeds back again into objective security, in that it allows for deterrence, prevention, and resilience. Simultaneously subjective security leads society to have more trust in itself due to self-actualization leading to feelings of control and autonomy.[2] Increased trust in one's self and one's own competence leads to increased interest (motivation) for continued or even increased participation, as well as more interest in the area in which you have proven your ability (here security), thus creating the second feedback loop. Importantly, because the task performance was embedded in a larger group, the conception of self comes to overlap with the others in the group, contributing to trust in a self that is networked to others.

While models are nice for the academic part of us and offer a vision of what we should strive for, they illustrate a perfect process that in reality will encounter friction from within the system modelled, but also from outside the model (Berlin 1998, 30). Thus, we must also ask how will this all likely look in reality? How do we get there? Is OPS for everyone? How will the military and security forces that have integrated OPS into their tools and tactics look? Correspondingly, will civilians and society also change? What are the limits of OPS's capabilities and what should its political limits be? While a typical approach to exploring such questions would be going step-by-step through the process of design, implementation, application, and outcome, such a linear problem-solution approach is, as has been covered, based on old forms of knowledge and technology. Conversely, OPS is emerging and will (and should) further develop in an iterative and evolutionary way; so we must start from there.

AN EVOLUTIONARY APPROACH TO REALIZING OPS

Evolutionary approaches – rather than pre-planned and directed design, implementation, and application (and hopefully outcomes) – are now widely practiced for developing/implementing new structures and processes. Their current favour arises from several reasons. Firstly, technology has enabled such iterative processes also to be possible in the first place for larger-scale projects. Second, and tied to this, iterative development can lower the investment risk; start-up investment can be smaller and scaled up as needed, while if a project is not producing a high enough return, it can be redirected. Third, and again tied to the prior point, the project can be improved over time using what was learned in earlier iterations. When complex organizations engage in reforming their structures and processes, they often take such an evolutionary approach. Frameworks for defence transformation call for similar approaches. Another example appropriate here is agile software development, such as Scrum and eXtreme Programming, given that OPS is in some ways the software for our kinetic security hardware. Wikipedia was also developed in such a manner; leading adopters built the platform enabling early adopters to expand and redirect it to facilitate eventual mass adoption (Karpf 2011). Such lead adopters are, obviously, essential, and fortunately two structural characteristics of bureaucracy, compartmentalization and competition between units for resources, mean there are actors which will be open to innovation. These are seen today in security institution's military labs, research institutes, special forces, and certain specialized units (e.g. information warfare units). The military is not the monolithic unitary actor many imagine it to be, or that it sometimes seeks to be.

Yet OPS it is not just about the system's organization and technical platforms. A key component that needs to evolve to advance OPS is the participants, the people. The state needs its citizens to expand and deepen, in quality if not quantity, their participation to address increasingly difficult security problems, as well as to keep the people feeling subjectively secure through their contributions to objective security. Yet OPS is something to which people will likely hedonistically adapt: they will get used to it and get bored.

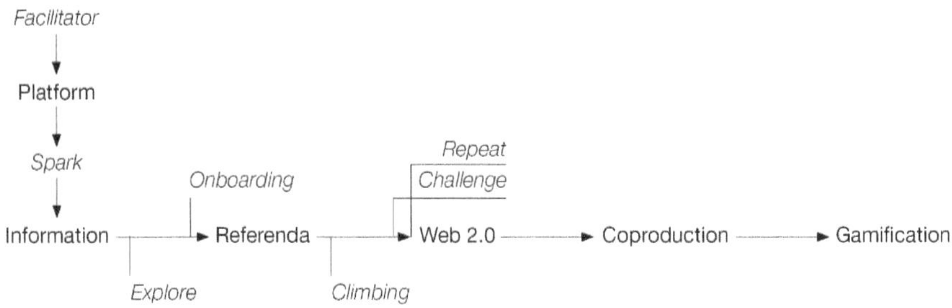

Figure 7.2. The Evolution/Levelling Up of OPS

Thus, there needs to be opportunities for the participants to level up once they have gotten used to the first participatory opportunities. Fortunately, the same evolutionary development and deployment taken for internal institutional reasons and outcome improvement can be used to structure citizens' participation with opportunities to level up over time. As a new OPS platform is developed it can be rolled out and simultaneously tested, applied, and improved by the citizen users. For citizens this evolutionary design would be experienced as it is in games: as they progress from task to task they would encounter opportunities to onboard, explore and learn, climb and confront challenges, and then to rest and receive feedback (Figure 7.2). Subsequently they could level up to the next platform for new and more interesting challenges. While this illustration of levelling up ends where our categories of open approaches end, both technological development and the strategic adaptations of our enemies will ensure there are always new tasks/levels to introduce to solve new problems, thereby keeping the people engaged and system evolving.

VARIATION IN TASKS, PLATFORMS, AND LEVELS

While it is easy to lose sight of, especially given the attention the media, politicians, and scholars shine upon it, terrorism is neither the only nor for many people the biggest threat we face. Nor is a rising China, an aggrieved and intransigent Russia, or, from another perspective, a declining imperial America or overreaching undemocratic European Union. Most of the security threats to our countries and systems come from within, within our borders or, even from a broader perspective, within our liberal, yet imperfectly so, world order. Discontent, crime, riots, and police abuse are increasingly not only problems confined to the Parisian *banlieues*, Rio's *favelas*, or south-central Los Angeles. As the social dislocation of the modern information *cum* economic revolution spreads, so do these and other manifestations of insecurity, as does the backlash against our system. While peaceful movements like Black Lives

Matter can be forces for positive change, the sniper attack of 8 July 2016 in Dallas, Texas, shows the violence that current insecurity and lack of faith in the agents of our security can engender domestically. Repressive regimes have been the first to experience the most dramatic consequences of mistrust in the authorities and technologically enabled backlash (e.g. in the Arab Spring), but the West is not immune. Naval patrols on the seas and walls on our borders, gates around privileged communities and firewalled (or even air-gapped) IT systems, cannot forever hold back what Robert D. Kaplan once called "the coming anarchy" (1994), and it may be that Peter Pomerantsev (2014) is right: "The future might just belong to the raiders."[3] The issues of violent crime and white collar crimes; of migrants, refugees, and nativist backlashes; of even poverty and education, are those which ultimately make us insecure and which must be addressed proactively. OPS can play a role also in these security issues by addressing them objectively while also giving people subjective meaning and purpose, thereby countering radicalization whether right, left, or religious.

This observation draws attention to two points: one on the design of OPS, and the other on where OPS is needed. First, because of variations in problems and people, OPS is not a single platform (perhaps an obvious point, but worth highlighting). Different platforms will be required for different people, who have different areas of security that most affect their interests and needs. Platforms will also need to vary in the approach they use, not only because problem-solution structures differ and thus require different approaches, but also because people have different time resources, skills, and privacy and platform preferences (on this in practice, see Jagoda, Gilliam, McDonald, and Russell 2015, 91). Some people are gamers, others are trolls (put more positively, provocateurs for disruptive thinking), and still others would prefer minimal participation via apps activated only intermittently. Nonetheless, platforms should be designed to promote cross-fertilization of people with different values and backgrounds to reach the best outcomes: variation in platforms, variation in participants.

These problems highlight also that OPS is not a system for only the national level. Indeed, just as it is the labs and small organizational units currently experimenting with open approaches within security and military institutions, any governmental forays into leveraging openness for security is likely to happen first at the local level. What's more, our large cities, with their complex and independent social relations and technological systems, with the numerous resulting problems and vulnerabilities, are those places most in need of OPS. Conveniently, they are also the most suited for adopting OPS given their high density of possible participants, their variation, and (when required) supporting technical systems that would be more financially and organizationally manageable. Lower administrative levels make excellent testing grounds for innovation, after which the best solutions can be scaled up (Kössler 2015). However, this does not imply that once a "best" solution is found at some local level it should be universally adopted (or enforced); variation will remain vital for system effectiveness (and redundancies), though the systems must be able to talk to each other to ensure sharing and cooperation between levels and their citizens.

Yet even if we look at the state level, there is much variation in the tasks that different states need to perform for security and in the societies that they have available for participation in these tasks, on top of differences in their political and economic systems. Thus, the designs of different state-level OPS platforms will vary based not only on task but assets and cultural preferences. The resulting differences in OPS systems will represent also another pool of variation to draw upon. Because OPS has no socio-economic prerequisites, as many of the examples seen in Chapter 5 demonstrate, it is suitable for many different states. While OPS can have a large technological component, much of the technology is inexpensive and widely available or easily developed using domestic talent. Thus, the financial burdens of implementation can be low enough that even transitioning and developing states can deploy OPS. Moreover, such states, which often have unstable state-society relations, could be those that would most benefit from the community, trust, and legitimacy-building functions of OPS. Nonetheless, much of the knowledge that must be built into OPS is currently in the West. Some OPS systems will require sophisticated design, requiring input from scientists and security experts, for instance to build their knowledge into algorithms, structure the platform appropriately for the problem, present and structure the needed information, and guide the participatory process to build iterative knowledge. Thus, we can expect status quo powers to accrue more power as well, provided they can overcome their status quo preferences.

Moreover, as pointed out in the introduction, there is nothing inherently democratic about openness, neither in its transparency nor participation dimensions. Nonetheless, democratic states would benefit most from OPS given their openness in other social, economic, and political areas. Because of this openness, OPS is more consistent with the other sectors, and foundational values, of democratic states than it is in more authoritarian regimes. By allowing for a more unified social, political, and technological security system – one in which ideas, organizations, and technology of security are internally as well as externally consistent – OPS is more stable and sustainable in liberal democracies and thus better able to ensure attainment of medium-term policy goals. Conversely, in authoritarian states the use of OPS could unleash forces of social and political revolution; attempts to put a cap on these forces could artificially truncate the OPS process, leading its solution to be invalid and dangerous if put into practice, resulting in strategic defeat in the medium term even if the short-term tactical victories seem impressive (e.g. Putin's Russia).

THE INDIVIDUAL PARTICIPANTS AND THE LIMITS OF PARTICIPATION

At its heart OPS is not about the states that participate, but about bringing together the two defining actors of the state: the people and the government. Yet just as the government faces challenges and resistance to creating the right type and amount of openness (targeted information and opportunities), so are their challenges to ensure OPS creates the right type and amount of participation. OPS has to ensure both "vetting and voice," that bad apples are weeded out, but all apples are represented (Bean 2011, 123). Active government efforts to engage the common citizen are required to ensure that participatory processes are not dominated by a small number of self-selected individuals with their own agendas. Some argue that such self-selected participation is inevitable, but we should not surrender to the assumption that the average citizen is uninterested, uninformed, or even apathetic. Current citizen disengagement is a contingent outcome of the current context created by numerous aspects of modern life, not a biological human trait or a structural condition of our socio-political system. Yet equally so, the state cannot buy into the "if you build it, they will come" fallacy; the platform is the facilitator of action, but the information is needed as a spark for that action.

Just as selective openness and participation is not desirable, mass undifferentiated openness is an equally unwise approach. Starting with the transparency, Alasdair Roberts points out that many arguments for secrecy and against openness are based on the claim that it would imply an "untrammeled right to riffle through the file cabinets" (Roberts 2004, 72). Yet even in the so-called "mass dump" made by WikiLeaks during Cablegate, there was no such unreflexive treatment; all documents were redacted by staff at *The Guardian* for sensitive points, and WikiLeaks accepted these redactions in their entirety (Leigh and Harding 2011, 6, 112–13). Moreover, WikiLeaks's earlier attempts to dump unstructured data showed that demand for information has its limits, which are determined by the people's time and energy, which in turn are a function of their interest. This limit to the individual and collective ability to contribute to a participatory initiative is called the participation bandwidth (McGonigal 2011, 226). This bandwidth limitation highlights the need to spread participation and distribute tasks as widely as possible. This in turn requires the state to spark the interest of possible participants by releasing targeted information that enables specific action, rather than releasing a deluge that creates anxiety or a backlash through alternative mechanisms (extremism, crime, or a fully stocked cabin in the woods). The initial release through targeted transparency can then be followed with just-in-time information, which is not only more effective for learning and task performance, but also is more engaging for the participants, creating a sense of exploration and discovery along with a quick sense that the information learned is useful for performing a task (as seen in game design; see Chapters 4 and 5).

The bandwidth issue in turn highlights the importance that also the participation aspect not be an undifferentiated mass assault on the people's time, energy, and senses. Because of the hedonistic adaptation covered in parts of this book, even if at first people like the idea of participation and if it is made fun through gamification, too much and too routine participation will cause the internal rewards to level off. The literature on games is most developed in this regard, warning of "ubiquitous gaming" that will lead to what Jesse Schell calls the "Gamepocalypse" (Dignan 2011, especially Chapter 6).[4] This concern is so tangible that it has even begun appearing in our fiction, for example, in the dystopian British sci-fi anthology *Black Mirror* (2011). There needs to be space for the government to create new forms of participation to re-engage people's interest, opportunities for the citizen to level up, and opportunities and encouragement for them to unplug so they can carry their virtual lessons and behaviour into the physical world, and vice versa. Despite the positive connotations associated with the words, and the demands of some political activists, there is such a thing as too much information and too much participation.

Determining where the limits of openness should be drawn is challenging; exactly how far can we take OPS? There is a tendency to err on the side of caution, especially in security institutions, which tend to be conservative and risk averse in their mind-set. In discussing journalistic reporting, Alan Campen once pointed out that it and the information it provides "is relevant to the function of democracy only when the people can influence the activity reported" (referenced in Leonhard 1998, 24). If you have no influence, you need no information. As we saw in Chapter 4 this road can quickly lead also to the withdrawal of other rights. Moreover, your lack of participation implies that giving you information may even be dangerous; we do not want armchair generals who are not facing the risk and possible sacrifices of battle to interfere. Yet, as discussed throughout this book, many of today's battles are not fought on foreign fields, but at home, where the people are sacrificing their normal lives, and as the target of our enemies, even their physical lives. On these and many other modern battlefields wider citizen participation is a requirement for effective action given the empowerment of the individual, the influence they can have on their environment. Thus Campen's logic can be reversed: because of the people's influence (power) they need to participate, and they thus need the information to ensure that participation leads to the best outcomes. Proactive transparency is required to facilitate the participation needed for security, rather than just ex post transparency needed for accountability (or more often for recrimination and blame). The viable limits of participation determine the degree of transparency, not the reverse. The task to be done, but which currently cannot be done, sets where targeted transparency and defence procurement to create participatory opportunities are required.

Yet given all the tasks to do, the constraints of bandwidth limits, the undesirability of mass openness, and the need for evolutionary deployment, where should we start? What should be selected for our first tasks? Firstly, of course this needs to be determined by the people's interests so that there is demand for participation. Yet the state can influence demand, often simply by releasing the proper information to spark interest. This is where it gets hard for the state, as the information that needs to be released often will be exactly what the current system wants to hide, but thus exactly what our enemies (as well as hackers and whistle-blowers) will target, especially in their operations seeking to increase our subjective insecurity. The information cannot be an advertising or recruiting campaign by the state and military; interest is not sparked by telling the people how well we are doing. Only by releasing the not-so-good information will the action enabled – and which the state must enable – address the weaknesses and problems that need to be fixed. This said, from a political marketing perspective it would also be wise to begin with (divisible) problems best suited for crowdsourced solutions and easily made interesting, as some clear early successes would be good for the longer-term prospects of OPS. Starting with a task for which the supporting subsystems are already in place would also be desirable, so new networked technologies would not have to be invested in until the platform has proven itself and public and political support has accrued.

WHERE WILL ALL THE SOLDIERS GO? THE ROLE OF EXPERTS

Our current system is based on experts in the management of violence having a monopoly on (legitimate) violence: we leave war to the soldiers. In many regards this arrangement has merit; security requires expertise (reason) in many areas, as well as some commitment to the cause (passion), which enables willingness to tackle difficult and dangerous tasks. Just because we now rightly recognize a good idea can come from anyone does not mean all ideas are equal and expertise irrelevant; just because we all have interest does not mean we all have the passion required for the sacrifices, whether simply time or our lives. The performance of OPS in successfully tackling objective security problems and tasks will require the traditional experts contribute as well. Even when diffuse technology enables participation, guidance and leadership is required to attain strategic (rather than just tactical) objectives and thus policy goals. Experts are required to structure (in advance) and integrate (ex post) the diffuse knowledge created or tasks performed and direct them towards a problem or objective, and when needed the experts are the boots on the ground who will implement our solutions.

Yet despite our (generally) patriotic support of individual soldiers, we also currently see a lack of trust by the people in many security experts. Even military leaders know the high esteem in which they are held can quickly fade following a Vietnam, Afghanistan, or Dreyfus Affair, or once they too are drawn into the polarized politics of our age as some worry is happening even now in the United States (for cross-sectoral concerns on this, see Dempsey 2016; Schake 2016; Feaver 2016). Expertise has little value if the people do not trust it. The best idea and advice in the world may well have never existed if they are not accepted and followed or supported. Here too, OPS can help. The interaction and coordinated action taken while performing a task together as part of OPS can help to bridge the gap between professionals and laypersons by creating trust, and thus subjective security (Möllering 2006, 73, drawing on ideas of Talcott Parsons). By sacrificing their monopoly on violence, their control of the entire process of security making, security experts can increase the trust people have in them, thereby actually bolstering their influence and acceptance of their contributions to solutions. OPS would not mean the end of expertise, but its restoration. It would return experts to positions of leadership that may not be as authoritative and blindly accepted as before, but which by being more democratic and open are far more realizable, sustainable, and effective, enabling the experts to turn their knowledge into actual policy and successful policy outcomes that in turn enhance their legitimacy.

This is not to imply that the security and military institutions and their individual members will not change. On the contrary, they will look totally different as will their underlying ideas and ethics. Yet the break from our current force structure and its organizational identity will be no different than any other transformation that has preceded it. Armed forces specifically, and the means to security, are not static just as security is not static; history has seen numerous different forms of security provision, and it will see many more. The next system will be much more integrated with society and broader in scope (a necessary connection, as broader scope [i.e. more citizen-created security] with an isolated military is a short path to tyranny) (concurring, see

Rosa Brooks and Tom Ricks in Foreign Policy 2015b). Institutions and ideas will be less functionally structured, the natural further evolution of combined arms, AirLand, and AirSea doctrines. The nature of command will change. The tactical independence of smaller teams will take on a new form which may change how we conceptualize the separation of strategy, operations, and tactics. Swarms and stigmergy will simultaneously give such units more independence of manoeuver yet also constrain them. Their actions will be channelled in the direction determined by the people/units that preceded them and surround their flanks and rear, including the diffuse OPS participants who act as subject matter experts, bridgeheads, deep penetration special ops, or stay-behind forces. Military leaders will have a big job on their hands for this reorganization; luckily they will have the people to help them in this task.

OPS BEYOND THE STATE

The question that will come to the more critical- and libertarian-leaning readers will be whether OPS could work without the state. This book contained numerous examples of open participatory security solutions adopted by NGOs and groups of private citizens. Likewise, the structure and tactics of some of our non-state enemies resemble an open approach to security. Yet these examples highlight the first problem: while citizen militias sound empowering, their existence often reflects a negative security environment, a necessity to defend small diffuse groups against raiders, pirates, bandits, or even the remnants of a state that has succumbed to the anarchical forces diffuse power can unleash. This is OPS out of desperation in anarchy, not out of necessity to prevent a coming anarchy. Moreover, if non-state OPS initiatives occur within the context of a state, but without that state's involvement, the results will be limited in scope, including in such a way as to be detrimental to overall stability. Subjectively, non-state OPS solutions will not build social trust among larger communities within states. Yet the smaller communities formed around non-state participatory security would still exist within a larger state wherein there will be other communities that are not included in their newly formed non-state community of trust, and which may thus even become competitors. Thus, non-state participatory security within states could aggravate current social fragmentation and, while hastening the end of the state, not offer a viable alternative until it first passes through a dark age from which a "winner" eventually emerges. On the other side of security, objective security, some of the tools to maximize OPS still require more traditional security instruments – for example, satellites – that require the resources of large actors. These need not be states, but the other existing alternatives, such as corporations, seem no more desirable, while waiting for costs to decline further is not viable.

While this book does not argue against the longer-term broader emancipating transformation of the state towards a new form of socio-political unit, it would humbly advise the libertarian or anarchist readers that they should fear the state less in the medium term (though the state's short-term power, and its misuse of that power, gives many plenty of reasons for immediate concern). States are not unchanging, and are far less in control of the forces of change (including their own change) than they would like to be, want us to think, or as some fear. States are victims of their own necessity to survive, which requires their evolution. The citizen can play a role in this evolution if they so choose. Nonetheless, the citizens' ability to transform the state, ideally peacefully, varies over time. The state is much more likely to open outward to ideas and be open to innovation when the security threat is high, current capabilities are failing, resources (including voluntary participation) are needed, (social and economic) power is diffuse, and technology is conducive to or even requires wider release. The same also applies to the state's security agents' openness to innovation. Citizens will often even find them to be more open than their political representatives. There is an old line by Leon Trotsky – one ironically later widely seen in the Western military sociology literature – that goes "the Army is a copy of society and suffers from all its diseases, usually at a higher temperature." There are and will be security experts who are open and pushing for reform, and there will be a conservative old guard; there will be liberals and extremists. We can best change the security sector (from the bottom up) by changing society and then linking up citizen innovators (from the top down) with the security elites that are open to the needed reforms. We are at an ideal moment for such change.

When we think "beyond" the state, we could also be thinking not temporally – awaiting the post-state age – but geographically, that is, thinking globally. If OPS can best be maximized by drawing on the largest pool of skills, creativity, and variation, and moreover can build positive social relations of trust and community, then the larger the population participating, the better for both objective and subjective outcomes. Yet how can states draw on participants beyond their borders, and what would be the social and political implications of casting such a wide participatory net? Certainly if a state does reach beyond its borders there is a risk of enemy agents signing up to OPS and attempting to either glean information from it or to undermine it. However, both these tasks would be difficult provided OPS was properly designed (which to get its own citizens and security actors to engage in, it would need to be). The most sensitive information would be distributed in such a way that piecing it back together again would not be a simple task; it would be easier for enemy agents to just (continue to) hack the departments and ministries that have all the information consolidated in one place. Trying to game the system, and thereby undermine the solutions produced, would likely just lead an algorithm or the community to flag you for investigation, and then possible exploitation as you're fed false information and given false tasks. Beyond these risks the benefits, as shown, would be substantial.

These benefits in turn raise a final point: if foreign persons are contributing to another state's security, that state and its citizens will come to recognize those foreigners' importance and assistance, perhaps realizing even that the task could not be done without them. Given that the state cannot be permanently insulated from the security system and its effects, opening the security system to those beyond the borders may lead the political system to also open. This is not to say non-citizens will overnight receive rights to vote in those countries they contribute to defending, but new and unfamiliar political arrangements reflecting their contribution, sacrifice, importance, trust, and power will emerge. Otherwise the participation will cease, or more accurately, be transferred to a more open country. Thus, this point could be a positive one, leading to a transnational system that could do much for the cause of international relations and peace, the construction of a global community/identity, or even eventually, evolutionarily, a post-state era.

CONCLUSION

While our world may be fragmented, these fragments are not isolated. Our world and our socio-economic system, and every individual therein, are interconnected. Yet we still treat security in a compartmentalized and sectoralized manner. Our problems require adaptability, and yet we still cling to principles and pillars. We fail to maximize the variation that our past policies and technologies have created, instead turning variation into the enemy. Open participatory security can capture the benefits of variation, balancing and integrating the technological and the human, the professional insider and expert outsider, service members and civilians, transparency and secrecy, rights and responsibilities. In this way OPS puts into practice the *Star Trek* canon: "Infinite Diversity in Infinite Combinations" (IDIC).

While OPS seeks the return of the human to a prominent place in security, this does not imply human command over technology. OPS is not simply the mirror image reversal of BiTS. The control that will lead to subjective security does not come about by controlling technology, but by controlling outcomes. To control those outcomes requires the integration of technology and its human users in a symbiotic relationship. Consider the example from Chapter 5 wherein electroencephalograms are used to connect the human and the machine for the rapid analysis of satellite imagery. Or take another example: as disappointing as it will be to some, it is unlikely private individuals will be getting their own personal armed drone any time soon, or even a simple surveillance drone (beyond the private ones available online now). While individuals have many skills, the individual still has limitations, ones which will be reflected and enhanced by the technology of the drone (to continue the example). Some of these limitations may simply result in errors, but other people's limitations (to call them that) may lead to mischievous or even malevolent actions. Drones are like any system in OPS; to maximize this technology requires integrating the variation of numerous human users into its decisions and actions. Hundreds or thousands of OPS contributors would be feeding into a single robot's actions, in real time or over time (asynchronously). Any automated actions resulting will then be both more appropriate and more trusted.

Yet just because our technology requires participation and the way of problem solving and security requires openness along many dimensions does not mean experts and organization have no role to play in our future security. Open participatory security does not imply anarchy; indeed the participation aspect of openness is needed precisely to ward off the anarchy that current technology and ideas could unleash. Conversely, structure need not imply domination (or bureaucracy), and indeed lack of structure can reinforce traditional and informal hierarchies and power (drawing on Jo Freeman's [(1970) 2017] classic essay "The Tyranny of Structurelessness"; applied to games, see Lerner 2014, 61). OPS can be open and participatory while still being structured and including (metaphorically) old soldiers. Moreover, OPS cannot be the only pillar of security given adaptive adversaries and varied threats. Rather, OPS will be an essential part of a hybrid security that includes also our current instruments and experts (e.g. Galeotti 2015b; Gray 2002, 93–94; Horowitz 2010, 215). Organization and structure will still be required, but the nature of authority within these will change to reflect actual knowledge and power.

Once authority and power change, who needs to know changes; those with the knowledge need the information (the data) to be able to apply their knowledge to solving a problem. Thus, rights to and necessity for transparency merge. Nonetheless, the full transparency envisioned by some shall for the foreseeable future, but maybe not forever, be confined to fiction (for examples, see Eggers 2013; Farley 2003). Secrecy currently has its place in every state, including democratic ones, at least until full transparency can be enforced on all states or even all actors, down to the individual (as envisioned by Brin 1999). Yet while secrets will still exist, secrecy will not be a guiding principle, and with its end one reason for bureaucracy also ends. The high level of secrecy seen recently and that some still advocate is consigned to the history books, no longer possible, justifiable, or desirable (Aldrich and Moran in Johnson 2014, 795; Don Burke in Bean 2011, 2). Meaningful openness is necessary not just for democracy but for security, and this must be done in a controlled and useful way rather than through uncontrolled leaks, self-selected releases, or serendipitous discovery.

Participation and information are required for security because of the current technology, organization, and ideas that make up the world and its problems. They are necessities, required to fill a need (security). Does this make them rights or responsibilities? In many ways they are positive rights that the state must provide, and increasingly provide in greater quantity and quality, though they are offset by negative rights that limit what the state can do: you are rarely required today to be informed or to participate. Yet (other) people have a positive right to security, to survival, and if (your) participation is necessary for this (as we argue it is), then it is your responsibility, not the state's, to provide that positive right. Take, for example, the push notification system (Wireless Emergency Alerts) that exists for AMBER alerts about missing children and other emergencies. Currently, phone settings allow almost all these to be turned off. Does the (negative) right to privacy mean not only that the state cannot dig into your private information but that it also cannot force information upon you? Do you have a right to be left alone even if your negative "right to ignore" information impinges on the survival of others? Don't you have a positive obligation towards others to inform yourself and act if you can? While this book eschewed legal or normative arguments for a positivist security and strategic line of reasoning, if the arguments for OPS made herein are accepted, then these questions highlight the need for more legal and philosophical research to go along with our technological advances and new security arrangements. Yet this research, and resulting legal developments, should follow from the policy of OPS so that it is the increasing demands for information and participation as people level up that drives the law, rather than the law compelling people's participation, which could very well offset the objective and subjective security benefits that participation offers.

The need for such examinations is because of the need to find a balance between rights and responsibilities. However, this isn't the only balance OPS seeks to attain; it seeks to balance objective security and subjective security, risk taking for progress and preference (and protection) for the status quo, and seeking to win while also accepting failure. To find these balances requires accepting, encouraging, and maximizing variation and that we all learn from each other and integrate learning and lessons learned into our system. These two aspects – variation and learning – highlight an important consideration. If variation is the key, then we must stop the homogenizing effects of globalization and maintain or even encourage the fragmentation we see now as a threat. Yet while this is true, social fragmentation need not imply anarchy. Fragmentation does of course threaten the unified state-society that most governments have pursued over the ages through education, conscription, and other means; yet there is no reason to assume the traditional state-society organization is better or worth fighting to maintain. Fragmented yet orderly social systems have existed, in the Greek city-states, feudal Europe, federal systems, and, on another level but a highly relevant one, within the fractal structure of our militaries. Multiple identities are fine, provided they are overlapping and are not mutually exclusive; they can even be a good if they are self-supporting. We are not advocating a return to a feudal order of course; humanity has progressed beyond that. However, governments need to seriously consider if we have also progressed beyond the traditional state-society social contract and now need a new network social contract to bond the individual to others, one which could be built on the new exchanges within open participatory security. Such bonds are what make a strong social order, not cohesion through homogeneity.

Despite the evolutionary movement towards an OPS system to match the security environment, resistance to the idea remains strong. The innovators, products of individualized technological society, are made into threats by status quo securocrats, ostracized and excluded from contributing to a society that often remains conservative even at its most liberal. Citizens and securocrats alike resist change and new forms of participation, which once institutionalized, they ironically often then cling to, as seen in the formation of militias, its transformation to conscription, and the subsequent transformation to professional contracted soldiers. While an opening now exists for a necessary transformation, a receptive citizenry and soldiery needs to be matched with political will and visionary leadership, for the reactionary path is there as well, but leads only to our own Jena.

Yet while an evolutionary path to OPS is the best way forward, evolution does not imply we can take it slow (evolution itself has been found to often be faster than we once thought). The environment has changed and will continue to do so, threatening our needs and ultimately even our survival. The advocates and forces of reform cannot wait, as the conservative forces of the status quo and reaction are already in place. As this chapter's opening acknowledged, simultaneous to the emergence of all the new possibilities of the information age a wave of creative destruction is transforming the economy, perhaps permanently destroying jobs that can now be done by computers or automated machines (Schwab 2016; World Economic Forum 2016; see also Cave 2000; Cookson 2016). The impact of the social dislocation engendered promises to be as great as any of the economic or agricultural revolutions of the past, perhaps greater given the empowering, yet inexpensive, technologies available to even the dislocated, down and out, and desperate modern *sans-culottes*. There is thus a risk that the "new technologies [. . .] will actually create more losers, more anger, and more conflict" (Richard Clarke in Singer 2009, 293).

Yet in this context, as we go through this transformation and search for a new social contract, we may find new sources of occupation and meaningfulness. When we consider the vulnerabilities of all these new systems, which will only grow as they expand and interconnect to create greater complexity, there is a clear, new area in which humans will be needed: securing our system (and securing their faith in that system at the same time) (similar ideas in Arkin 2015, 283, and Domingos 2015, 280). With a system like OPS enabling and empowering individuals by providing information, guidance, and tasks, and facilitating learning, self-efficacy, and trust, it may be that in the future every citizen – regardless and indeed because of variations in their backgrounds and capabilities – is truly an agent of our security in a new and more active form of participation.

NOTES

1. The contributors were speaking of the United States, but we have taken the liberty of generalizing their statement.
2. As mentioned in Chapter 4, autonomy is causal agency through control over meaningful choices that have consequences and is not the same as independence.
3. For those paying attention, yes, your author liked this quote so much that it was used twice in this book.
4. Which was the title of Schell's speech at the D.I.C.E. (Design, Innovate, Communicate, Entertain) Summit for video game executives in 2010.

Bibliography

Adams, David. 1995. "Internal Military Interventions in the United States." *Journal of Peace Research* 32 (2): 197–211.

Agar, Jon. 2013. *Science in the 20th Century and Beyond*. Cambridge, UK: Polity Press.

Albrecht, Hans-Jörg. 2008. "Terrorism, Risk, and Legislation." *Journal of National Defense Studies* (6): 13–49.

Al-Hujran, Omar, Mutaz M. Al-Debei, Akemi Chatfield, and Mahmoud Migdadi. 2015. "The Imperative of Influencing Citizen Attitude Toward E-Government Adoption and Use." *Computers in Human Behavior* 53 (December): 189–203.

Altschuller, Shoshana, and Raquel Benbunan-Fich. 2010. "Trust, Performance, and the Communication Process in Ad Hoc Decision-Making Virtual Teams." *Journal of Computer-Mediated Communication* 16 (1): 27–47.

Ames, Paul, ed. 2015. *Spring 2015 Security Jam Report: Reappraising Global Security*. Brussels: Friends of Europe. www.friendsofeurope.org/media/uploads/2015/02/SecurityJamReport2014-finalLR.pdf.

Amsterdam Uncertainty Lab. 2017. *Coping with Perceived Threats*. www.uncertaintylab.nl/our-research-program/coping-with-perceived-threats/.

Arce, Daniel G., Rachel T. A. Croson, and Catherine C. Eckel. 2011. "Terrorism Experiments." *Journal of Peace Research* 48 (3): 373–82.

Arendt, Hannah. 1963. *On Revolution*. London and New York: Penguin Books.

Arkin, William M. 2015. *Unmanned: Drones, Data, and the Illusion of Perfect Warfare*. New York: Little, Brown and Company.

Arquilla, John. 2007. "Introduction: Thinking about Information Strategy." In *Information Strategy and Warfare: A Guide to Theory and Practice*, edited by John Arquilla and Douglas A. Borer, 1–15. New York and Abingdon, UK: Routledge.

Arquilla, John, and David Ronfeldt. 2001. *Networks and Netwars: The Future of Terror, Crime, and Militancy*. Santa Monica, CA: RAND Corporation. www.rand.org/pubs/monograph_reports/MR1382.

Axe, David. 2009. "Debating the Navy's 'Plug-and-Play' Warship." *Wired*, 26 August. www.wired.com/2009/08/debating-the-navys-modular-warship/.

Bainbridge, Lisanne. 1983. "The Ironies of Automation." *Automatica* 9 (6): 775–79.

Baker, William H., H. Lon Addams, and Brian Davis. 2010. "Critical Factors for Enhancing Municipal Public Hearings." In *Transparency and Secrecy: A Reader Linking Literature and Contemporary Debate*, edited by Suzanne J. Piotrowski, 119–32. Lanham, MD: Lexington Books.

Bandura, Albert. 1997. *Self-Efficacy: The Exercise of Control*. New York: Freeman.

Bartone, Paul, and Amy Adler. 1999. "Cohesion Over Time in a Peacekeeping Medical Task Force." *Military Psychology* 11 (1): 85–107.

BBC News, Business. 2016. "How Blockchain Tech Could Change the Way We Do Business." *BBC News*, 22 January. www.bbc.com/news/business-35370304.

BBC News, Technology. 2016. "Pentagon Invites Hackers in and Backs Encryption." *BBC News*, 2 March. www.bbc.com/news/technology-35706988.

Bean, Hamilton. 2011. *No More Secrets: Open Source Information and the Reshaping of U.S. Intelligence*. Santa Barbara, CA: Praeger.

Beckhusen, Robert. 2016. "The U.S. Navy's New 'Frigate': A Complete (And Obsolete) Mess?" *The National Interest*, 12 June. http://nationalinterest.org/blog/the-buzz/the-us-navys-new-frigate-complete-obsolete-mess-16563.

Ben-Shalom, Uzi, Zeev Lehrer, and Eyal Ben-Ari. 2005. "Cohesion During Military Operations: A Field Study on Combat Units in the Al-Aqsa Intifada." *Armed Forces & Society* 32 (1): 63–79.

Bergen, Peter, David Sterman, Emily Schneider, and Bailey Cahall. 2014. *Do NSA's Bulk Surveillance Programs Stop Terrorists?* Washington, DC: New America Foundation. http://www.newamerica.net/publications/policy/do_nsas_bulk_surveillance_programs_stop_terrorists.

Berggruen, Nicolas, and Nathan Gardels. 2013. *Intelligent Governance for the 21st Century: A Middle Way between West and East*. Cambridge, UK, and Malden, MA: Polity Press.

Berlin, Isaiah. 1998. *The Proper Study of Mankind: An Anthology of Essays*. London: Pimlico.

Bershidsky, Leonid. 2015. "Envying Estonia's Digital Government." *BloombergView*, 4 March. www.bloombergview.com/articles/2015-03-04/envying-estonia-s-digital-government.

Black Mirror. 2011. Season 1, episode 2, "Fifteen Million Merits," first broadcast 11 December by Channel Four Television Corporation. Directed by Euros Lyn, written by Charlie Brooker and Konnie (Kanak) Huq.

Blanton, Thomas S. 2003. "National Security and Open Government in the United States: Beyond the Balancing Test." In *National Security and Open Government: Striking the Right Balance*, 33–73. Syracuse, NY: Campbell Public Affairs Institute. www.maxwell.syr.edu/uploadedFiles/campbell/events/NSOG.pdf.

Blomgren Amsler, Lisa, and Susanna Foxworthy. 2014. "Collaborative Governance and Collaborating Online: The Open Government Initiative in the United States." In *Public Administration and the Modern State: Assessing Trends and Impact*, edited by Jos Raadschelders, Eberhard Bohne, and John Graham with Jesse Lehrke, 189–202. Basingstoke, UK: Palgrave Macmillan.

Boedeltje, Mijke, and Juul Cornips. 2004. "Input and Output Legitimacy in Interactive Governance." Working Paper No. NIG2-01. Netherlands Institute for Government. NIG Annual Work Conference 2004, Rotterdam, Netherlands, 19 October. http://repub.eur.nl/pub/1750/NIG2-01.pdf.

Boffey, Daniel. 2016. "Russia 'Stoking Refugee Unrest in Germany to Topple Angela Merkel.'" *The Guardian*, 5 March. www.theguardian.com/world/2016/mar/05/russia-refugee-germany-angela-merkel-migration-vladimir-putin?CMP=share_btn_fb.

Bohne, Eberhard, John Graham, Jos Raadschelders, and Jesse P. Lehrke, eds. 2014. *Public Administration and the Modern State: Assessing Trends and Impact*. Basingstoke, UK: Palgrave Macmillan.

Borell, Klas. 2008. "Terrorism and Everyday Life in Beirut 2005: Mental Reconstructions, Precautions and Normalization." *Acta Sociologica* 51 (1): 55–70.

Borer, Douglas A. 2007. "Conclusion: Why Is Information Strategy Difficult?" In *Information Strategy and Warfare: A Guide to Theory and Practice*, edited by John Arquilla and Douglas A. Borer, 233–40. New York and Abingdon, UK: Routledge.

Bousquet, Antoine. 2009. *Scientific Way of Warfare: Order and Chaos on the Battlefields of Modernity*. London: Hurst & Company.

Bovaird, Tony. 2007. "Beyond Engagement and Participation: User and Community Coproduction of Public Services." *Public Administration Review* 67 (5): 846–60.

Bovaird, Tony, Elke Loeffler, Gregg G. van Ryzin, and Salvador Parrado. 2014. "User and Community Coproduction of Public Services: What Influences Citizens to Coproduce." In *Public Administration and the Modern State: Assessing Trends and Impact*, edited by Jos Raadschelders, Eberhard Bohne, and John Graham with Jesse Lehrke, 109–24. Basingstoke, UK: Palgrave Macmillan.

Brannen, Kate. 2015. "#Disrupt the Pentagon." *FP*, 10 February. http://foreignpolicy.com/2015/02/10/ashton-carter-pentagon-silicon-valley/.

Breakwell, Glynis M. 2014. *The Psychology of Risk*, 2nd edition. Cambridge, UK: Cambridge University Press.

Brickman, Philip, and Donald T. Campbell. 1971. "Hedonic Relativism and Planning the Good Society." In *Adaptation-Level Theory: A Symposium*, edited by Mortimer H. Appley, 287–302. New York: Academic Press.

Brin, David. 1999. *The Transparent Society: Will Technology Force Us to Choose Between Privacy and Freedom*? Cambridge, MA: Perseus Books.

Brooking, Emerson. 2015. "The U.S. Government Should Pay Anonymous in Bitcoin to Fight ISIS." *FP*, 3 March. http://foreignpolicy.com/2015/03/03/the-u-s-government-should-pay-anonymous-in-bitcoin-to-fight-isis.

Brooks, Rosa. 2015. "The Threat Is Already Inside." *FP*, 20 November. http://foreignpolicy.com/2015/11/20/the-threat-is-already-inside-uncomfortable-truths-terrorism-isis/.

Burby, R. J. 2003. "Making Plans That Matter: Citizen Involvement and Government Action." *Journal of the American Planning Association*, 69: 33–49.

Burke, Brian. 2014. *Gamify: How Gamification Motivates People to Do Extraordinary Things*. Brookline, MA: Bibliomotion.

Buzan, Barry, Ole Waever, and Jaap de Wilde. 1998. *Security: A New Framework for Analysis*. Boulder: Lynne Rienner Publishers.

Caelin, Derek. 2016. "Can Your PlayStation Stop a War?" *FP*, 8 February. http://foreignpolicy.com/2016/02/08/can-your-playstation-stop-a-war-videogames-peace/.

Caldwell, Luke, and Tim Lenoir. 2016. "Wargaming Futures: Naturalizing the New American Way of War." In *Zones of Control: Perspectives on Wargaming*, edited by Pat Harrigan and Matthew G. Kirschenbaum, 253–79. Cambridge, MA: MIT Press.

Carr, Nicholas. 2015. *The Glass Cage: Automation and Us*. New York and London: W.W. Norton & Company.

Cavafy, Constantine P. (1904) 1975. "Waiting for the Barbarians." In *C. P. Cavafy: Collected Poems*, translated by Edmund Keeley and Philip Sherrard. Princeton, NJ: Princeton University Press.

Cave, Damien. 2000. "Artificial Stupidity." *Salon*, 4 October. www.salon.com/2000/10/04/lanier/.

Cebrowski, A. K., and J. J. Garstka. 1998. "Network-Centric Warfare: Its Origin and Future." *Proceedings of the U.S. Naval Institute* 124 (1): 28–35.

Center for Civilians in Conflict. 2016. *Waiting for No One: Civilian Survival Strategies in Syria*. Washington, DC: Center for Civilians in Conflict. http://civiliansinconflict.org/uploads/files/publications/Syria_Civilian_Survival_Strategies.pdf.

Chadwick, Andrew. 2011. "Explaining the Failure of an Online Citizen Engagement Initiative: The Role of Internal Institutional Variables." *Journal of Information Technology & Politics* 8 (1): 21–40.

Chraibi, Christine, trans. 2015. "Yuriy Stets, Minister of Information Policy Wants to Create 'Internet Army.'" *EuroMaidan Press*, 28 January. http://euromaidanpress.com/2015/01/28/yuriy-stets-minister-of-information-policy-wants-to-create-internet-army/.

Clark, Christopher. 2007. *Iron Kingdom: The Rise and Downfall of Prussia 1600–1947*. London: Penguin Books.

Colaresi, Michael P. 2014. *Democracy Declassified: The Secrecy Dilemma in National Security*. Oxford: Oxford University Press.

Cookson, Clive. 2016. "AI and Robots Threaten to Unleash Mass Unemployment, Scientists Warn." *Financial Times*, 14 February. www.ft.com/cms/s/0/063c1176-d29a-11e5-969e-9d801cf5e15b.html.

Cooper, Seth, Firas Khatib, Adrien Treuille, Janos Barbero, Jeehyung Lee, Michael Beenen, Andrew Leaver-Fay, David Baker, Zoran Popović, and Foldit Players. 2010. "Predicting Protein Structures with a Multiplayer Online Game." *Nature* 466 (7307): 756–60. www.nature.com/nature/journal/v466/n7307/full/nature09304.html.

Coppola, Nancy W., Starr Roxanne Hiltz, and Naomi G. Rotter. 2004. "Building Trust in Virtual Teams." *IEEE Transactions on Professional Communication* 47 (2): 95–104.

Costello, Carol. 2015. "America: Too Fat to Fight." *CNN*, 21 April. http://edition.cnn.com/2015/04/21/opinions/costello-america-fat/.

Coulson, Mark, and Christopher J. Ferguson. 2016. "The Influence of Digital Games on Aggression and Violent Crime." In *The Video Game Debate: Unravelling the*

Physical, Social, and Psychological Effects of Digital Games, edited by Rachel Kowert and Thorsten Quandt, 54–73. New York: Routledge.

Cowen, Nick. 2016. "Inside *Eve: Online*'s Propaganda Machine—from Photoshop to DDoS." *Ars Technica*, 7 September. http://arstechnica.com/gaming/2016/09/eve-online-propaganda-machine-imperium-mbc/.

Cronin, Audrey K. 2006. "Cyber-Mobilization: The New Levée en Masse." *Parameters* XXXVI (2): 77–87.

Csikszentmihalyi, Mihaly. 1975. *Beyond Boredom and Anxiety*. San Francisco, Washington, London: Jossey-Bass Publishers.

Csikszentmihalyi, Mihaly. 1990. *Flow: The Psychology of Optimal Experience*. New York: HarperCollins Publishers.

Curtin, Kevin M., Karen Hayslett-McCall, and Fang Qiu. 2007. "Determining Optimal Police Patrol Areas with Maximal Covering and Backup Covering Location Models." *Networks and Spatial Economics* 10 (1): 125–45.

Cvetkovich, George, Michael Siegrist, Rachel Murray, and Sarah Tragesser. 2002. "New Information and Social Trust: Asymmetry and Perseverance of Attributions about Hazard Managers." *Risk Analysis* 22 (2): 359–67.

Dahlstrom, Michael F., Anthony Dudo, and Dominique Brossard. 2012. "Precision of Information, Sensational Information, and Self-Efficacy Information as Message-Level Variables Affecting Risk Perceptions." *Risk Analysis* 32 (1): 155–66.

Dale, Gillian, and C. Shawn Green. 2016. "Video Games and Cognitive Performance." In *The Video Game Debate: Unravelling the Physical, Social, and Psychological Effects of Digital Games*, edited by Rachel Kowert and Thorsten Quandt, 131–52. New York: Routledge.

Darby, Michael R., and Lynne G. Zucker. 2003. "Growing by Leaps and Inches: Creative Destruction, Real Cost Reduction, and Inching Up." *Economic Inquiry* 41 (1): 1–19.

DARPA (Defense Advanced Research Projects Agency). 2003. "Report to Congress Regarding the Terrorism Information Awareness Program: In Response to Consolidated Appropriations Resolution." Pub. L. No. 108-7, Division M, Subsection 111(b), 20 May. https://www.hsdl.org/?abstract&did=3479.

DARPA (Defense Advanced Research Projects Agency). 2009. "MIT Red Balloon Team Wins DARPA Network Challenge." *DARPA, News Release*, 5 December. http://archive.darpa.mil/networkchallenge/darpanetworkchallengewinner2009.pdf.

DARPA (Defense Advanced Research Projects Agency). 2011. "DARPA's Shredder Challenge Solved." *DARPA News*, 2 December. http://archive.darpa.mil/shredderchallenge/.

DARPA (Defense Advanced Research Projects Agency). 2014. "The DARPA Grand Challenge: Ten Years Later." *DARPA News*, 13 March. http://www.darpa.mil/news-events/2014-03-13.

Dekker, Sidney W. A. 2004. "The Hindsight Bias Is Not a Bias and Not about History." *Human Factors and Aerospace Safety* 4 (2): 87–99.

De Luce, Dan. 2015a. "Did Centcom Cook the Books in the War Against the Islamic State?" *FP*, 11 September. http://foreignpolicy.com/2015/09/11/did-centcom-cook-the-books-in-the-war-against-the-islamic-state/.

De Luce, Dan. 2015b. "Did the Pentagon Cook the Books on Its Afghanistan Intel?" *FP*, 19 November. http://foreignpolicy.com/2015/11/19/did-the-pentagon-cook-the-books-on-its-afghanistan-intel/.

Dempsey, Martin E. 2016. "Letters to the Editor: Military Leaders Do Not Belong at Political Conventions." *Washington Post*, 30 July. www.washingtonpost.com/opinions/military-leaders-do-not-belong-at-political-conventions/2016/07/30/0e06fc16-568b-11e6-b652-315ae5d4d4dd_story.html?utm_term=.7534f1b4a9f6.

Dennett, Daniel C. 2013. "The Normal Well-Tempered Mind." In *Thinking: The New Science of Decision-Making, Problem-Solving, and Prediction*, edited by John Brockman, 1–17. New York: Harper Perennial.

Diamond, Jared. 1992. *The Third Chimpanzee: The Evolution and Future of the Human Animal*. New York: HarperCollins Publishers.

Diamond, Jared. 1999. *Guns, Germs, and Steel: The Fates of Human Societies*. New York and London: W.W. Norton & Company.

Dignan, Aaron. 2011. *Game Frame: Using Games as a Strategy for Success*. New York, London, Toronto, Sydney: Free Press.

Dixon, Brian E. 2010. "Towards E-Government 2.0: An Assessment of Where E-Government 2.0 Is and Where It Is Headed." *Public Administration & Management* 15 (2): 418–54.

Dolinski, Dariusz, Wojciech Gromski, and Ewa Zawisza. 1987. "Unrealistic Pessimism." *Journal of Social Psychology* 127 (5): 87–99.

Domingos, Pedro. 2015. *The Master Algorithm: How the Quest for the Ultimate Learning Machine Will Remake Our World*. New York: Basic Books.

Dunbar, R. I. M. 1992. "Neocortex Size as a Constraint on Group Size in Primates." *Journal of Human Evolution* 22 (6): 469–93.

Eaton, Michele. 2014. "AFRL Gaming Lab Provides Real-World Training." 15 August. *Wright-Patterson Air Force Base*. www.wpafb.af.mil/News/Article-Display/Article/819103/afrl-gaming-lab-provides-real-world-training.

Eggers, Dave. 2013. *The Circle*. New York: Random House.

Eichenbaum, Adam, Daphne Bavelier, and C. Shawn Green. 2014. "Video Games: Play That Can Do Serious Good." *American Journal of Play* 7 (1): 50–72.

Ellis, Michael J. 1998. "Play and the Origin of the Species." In *Readings from Play as a Medium for Learning and Development*, edited by Doris Bergen, 29–31. Olney, MD: Association for Childhood Education International.

Elron, Efrat, Boas Shamir, and Eyal Ben-Ari. 1999. "Why Don't They Fight Each Other? Cultural Diversity and Operational Unity in Multinational Forces." *Armed Forces & Society* 26 (1): 73–98.

Ezrahi, Yaron. 2004. "Science and the Political Imagination in Contemporary Democracies." In *States of Knowledge: The Co-Production of Science and the Social Order*, edited by Sheila Jasanoff, 254–73. London and New York: Routledge.

Farley, Patrick. 2003. "The Spiders: A Graphic Novel." *Electic Sheep Comix*. www.electricsheepcomix.com/spiders/.

Fazal, Tanisha M. 2014. "Dead Wrong? Battle Deaths, Military Medicine, and Exaggerated Reports of War's Demise." *International Security* 39 (1): 95–125.

Feaver, Peter. 2016. "We Don't Need Generals to Become Cheerleaders at Political Conventions." *FP*, 29 July. http://foreignpolicy.com/2016/07/29/we-dont-need-generals-to-become-cheerleaders-at-political-conventions/.

Fischhoff, Baruch, Roxana M. Gonzalez, Jennifer S. Lerner, and Deborah A. Small. 2005. "Evolving Judgments of Terror Risks: Foresight, Hindsight, and Emotion." *Journal of Experimental Psychology: Applied* 11 (2): 124–39.

Foreign Policy. 2015a. "The E.R.: Cyberoffense, Deterrence, and the Dawn of a New Era of War." *Foreign Policy Podcast*, 13 October. http://foreignpolicy.com/2015/10/12/the-e-r-cyberoffense-deterrence-and-the-dawn-of-a-new-era-of-war/.

Foreign Policy. 2015b. "The E.R.: It's Time the U.S. Military Reinvented Itself to Operate in the Information Age." *Foreign Policy Podcast*, 26 October. http://foreignpolicy.com/2015/10/26/the-e-r-its-time-the-us-military-reinvented-itself-in-the-age-of-information/.

Foreign Policy. 2015c. "The E.R.: 'We Fail Better' Should Not Be the Motto of the U.S. Military." *Foreign Policy Podcast*, 19 October. http://foreignpolicy.com/2015/10/19/the-e-r-we-fail-better-should-not-be-the-motto-of-the-u-s-military/.

Fraenkel-Haeberle, Cristina, Sabine Kropp, Francesco Palermo, and Karl-Peter Sommermann, eds. 2015. *Citizen Participation in Multi-Level Democracies*. Leiden and Boston: Brill Nijhoff.

Franzoni, Chiara, and Henry Sauermann. 2014. "Crowd Science: The Organization of Scientific Research in Open Collaborative Projects." *Research Policy* 43 (1): 1–20.

Freedman, Lawrence. 2014. *Strategy: A History*. Oxford: Oxford University Press.

Freeman, Jo. (1970) 2017. "The Tyranny of Structurelessness." Jo Freeman.com. www.jofreeman.com/joreen/tyranny.htm.

Freifeld, Clark, Rumi Chunara, Sumiko R. Mekaru, Emily H. Chan, Taha Kass-Hout, Anahi Ayala Iacucci, and John S. Brownstein. 2010. "Participatory Epidemiology: Use of Mobile Phones for Community-Based Health Reporting." *PLoS Med* 7 (12). http://journals.plos.org/plosmedicine/article?id=10.1371/journal.pmed.1000376.

Frewer, Lynn J., Chaya Howard, Duncan Hedderley, and Richard Shepherd. 1996. "What Determines Trust in Information About Food-Related Risks? Underlying Psychological Constructs." *Risk Analysis* 16 (4): 473–86.

Friman, Henrik, and Susan Higgens. 2009. "The Influence of the Information Age." In *Transforming Defense Capabilities: New Approaches for International Security*, edited by Scott Jasper, 41–55. Boulder, CO: Lynne Rienner Publishers Inc.

Fung, Archon, Mary Graham, and David Weil. 2007. *Full Disclosure: The Perils and Promise of Transparency*. New York: Cambridge University Press.

Galeotti, Mark. 2014a. "'Keep Calm and Carry On': Russians and Terrorism." *Russia!* 13 January. https://inmoscowsshadows.wordpress.com/2014/01/14/keep-calm-and-carry-on/.

Galeotti, Mark. 2014b. "The 'Gerasimov Doctrine' and Russian Non-Linear War." *In Moscow's Shadows*, 6 July. https://inmoscowsshadows.wordpress.com/2014/07/06/the-gerasimov-doctrine-and-russian-non-linear-war/.

Galeotti, Mark. 2015a. "If US Intelligence on Russia Is Broken (A Bit), What Can Be Done to Help Fix It?" *In Moscow's Shadows*, 2 November. https://inmoscowsshadows.wordpress.com/2015/11/02/if-us-intelligence-on-russia-is-broken-a-bit-what-can-be-done-to-help-fix-it/.

Galeotti, Mark. 2015b. "Time to Think About 'Hybrid Defense.'" *War on the Rocks*, 30 July. http://warontherocks.com/2015/07/time-to-think-about-hybrid-defense/.

Gallagher, Sean. 2015a. "Bus Pass: Civic Hackers Open Transit Data MTA Said Would Cost Too Much to Share." *Ars Technica*, 25 February. http://arstechnica.com/information-technology/2015/02/bus-pass-civic-hackers-open-transit-data mta-said-would-cost-too-much-to-share/.

Gallagher, Sean. 2015b. "How Tech Fails Led to Air Force Strike on MSF's Kunduz Hospital." *Ars Technica*, 30 November. http://arstechnica.com/information-technology/2015/11/how-tech-fails-led-to-air-force-strike-on-msfs-kunduz-hospital/.

Gallagher, Sean. 2015c. "WarGames for Real: How One 1983 Exercise Nearly Triggered WWIII." *Ars Technica*, 25 November. http://arstechnica.com/information-technology/2015/11/wargames-for-real-how-one-1983-exercise-nearly-triggered-wwiii/.

Gallup. 2016. *Confidence in Institutions*. www.gallup.com/poll/1597/confidence%ADinstitutions.aspx.

Gamper, Anna. 2015. "Forms of Democratic Participation in Multi-Level Systems." In *Citizen Participation in Multi-Level Democracies*, edited by Cristina Fraenkel-Haeberle, Sabine Kropp, Francesco Palermo, and Karl-Peter Sommermann, 67–84. Leiden and Boston: Brill Nijhoff.

Garfinkel, Michelle R. 2004. "Global Threats and the Domestic Struggle for Power." *European Journal of Political Economy* 20 (2): 495–508.

Garstka, John J. 2009. "Patterns in Innovation." In *Transforming Defense Capabilities: New Approaches for International Security*, edited by Scott Jasper, 57–78. Boulder, CO: Lynne Rienner Publishers Inc.

Gat, Azar. 2006. *War in Human Civilization*. Oxford: Oxford University Press.

Gearson, John. 2012. "Deterring Conventional Terrorism: From Punishment to Denial and Resilience" *Contemporary Security Policy* 33(1): 171–98.

Giddens, Anthony. 1984. *The Constitution of Society: Outline of the Theory of Structuration*. Berkeley and Los Angeles: University of California Press.

Gilbert, Daniel. 2013. "Affective Forecasting . . . or . . . The Big Wombassa: What You Think You're Going to Get, and What You Don't Get, When You Get What You Want." In *Thinking: The New Science of Decision-Making, Problem-Solving, and Prediction*, edited by John Brockman, 55–68. New York: Harper Perennial.

GIMPS (Great Internet Mersenne Prime Search). 2016. *Great Internet Mersenne Prime Search: Finding World Record Primes Since 1996*. www.mersenne.org/.

Girandola, Fabien. 2000. "Peur et persuasion: présentations des recherché (1953–1998) et d'une nouvelle lecture [Fear and persuasion: Review and re-analysis of the literature (1953–1998)]." *Annee Psychologique* 100 (2): 333–76.

Gjelten, Tom. 2011. "Volunteer Cyber Army Emerges in Estonia." *NPR*, 4 January. www.npr.org/2011/01/04/132634099/in-estonia-volunteer-cyber-army-defends-nation.

Goodin, Dan. 2016. "First Known Hacker-Caused Power Outage Signals Troubling Escalation." *Ars Technica*, 4 January. http://arstechnica.com/security/2016/01/first-known-hacker-caused-power-outage-signals-troubling-escalation/.

Goodwins, Rupert. 2015. "Debunking the Biggest Myths about Artificial Intelligence." *Ars Technica*, 25 December. http://arstechnica.com/information-technology/2015/12/demystifying-artificial-intelligence-no-the-singularity-is-not-just-around-the-corner/.

Gorenburg, Dmitry. 2014. "Ukrainian Military Capabilities." *Russian Military Reform*, 22 December. http://russiamil.wordpress.com/2014/12/22/ukrainian-military-capabilities/.

Gray, Colin S. 2002. *Strategy for Chaos: Revolutions in Military Affairs and the Evidence of History*. London and Portland, OR: Frank Cass.

Gray, John. 2003. *Al Qaeda and What It Means to Be Modern*. London: Faber and Faber.

Gray, John. 2015. "John Gray: Steven Pinker Is Wrong about Violence and War." *The Guardian*, 13 March. https://www.theguardian.com/books/2015/mar/13/john-gray-steven-pinker-wrong-violence-war-declining.

Gray, Peter. 2009. "Play as a Foundation for Hunter-Gatherer Social Existence." *American Journal of Play* 1 (4): 476–521.

Green, C. Shawn, and Daphne Bavelier. 2003. "Action Video Game Modifies Visual Selective Attention." *Nature* 423 (6939): 534–37.

Grizzard, Matthew, Ron Tamborini, Robert J. Lewis, Lu Wang, and Sujay Prabhu. 2014. "Being Bad in a Video Game Can Make Us Morally Sensitive." *Cyberpsychology, Behavior, and Social Networking* 17 (8): 499–504.

Groll, Elias. 2016. "Turns Out You Can't Trust Russian Hackers Anymore." *FP*, 22 August. http://foreignpolicy.com/2016/08/22/turns-out-you-cant-trust-russian-hackers-anymore/.

Grossman, Dave. 1996. *On Killing: The Psychological Cost of Learning to Kill in War and Society*. New York: Open Road, Integrated Media.

Hackers Wanted. 2009. Unreleased documentary. Directed and written by Sam Bozzo, produced by Dana Brunetti and Kevin Spacey.

Hall, Wayne Michael, and Gary Citrenbaum. 2010. *Intelligence Analysis: How to Think in Complex Environments*. Santa Barbara, CA: Praeger.

Hammes, Thomas X. 2006. *The Sling and the Stone: On War in the 21st Century*. Saint Paul, MN: Zenith Press.

Hans, T. 2000. "A Meta-Analysis of the Effects of Adventure Programming on Locus of Control." *Journal of Contemporary Psychotherapy* 30 (1): 33–60.

Hashiguchi, Katsuhisa. 1974. "The Number of Decision Makers and the Level of Risk-Tasking Within a Group." *Japanese Journal of Experimental Social Psychology* 14 (2): 123–31.

Heath, Robert L., and Michaek Palenchar. 2000. "Community Relations and Risk Communication: A Longitudinal Study of the Impact of Emergency Response Messages." *Journal of Public Relations Research* 12 (2): 131–61.

Heine, Steven J., and Darrin R. Lehman. 1995. "Cultural Variation in Unrealistic Optimism: Does the West Feel More Invulnerable than the East?" *Journal of Personality and Social Psychology* 68 (4): 595–607.

Henricks, Thomas S. 2014. "Play as Self-Realization: Toward a General Theory of Play." *American Journal of Play* 6 (2): 190–213.

Heroic Imagination Project. 2015. *The Heroic Imagination Project*. http://heroic imagination.org/.

Herridge, Catherine. 2015. "FBI Using Elite Surveillance Teams to Track at Least 48 High-Risk ISIS Suspects." *Fox News*, 27 November. www.foxnews .com/politics/2015/11/26/fbi-using-elite-surveillance-teams-to-track-at-least-48-high-risk-isis-suspects.html.

Hibbing, John R., and Elizabeth Theiss-Morse. 2002. *Stealth Democracy: Americans' Beliefs About How Government Should Work*. Cambridge, UK: Cambridge University Press.

Higbee, Kenneth L. 1972. "Group Risk Taking in Military Decisions." *Journal of Social Psychology* 88 (1): 55–64.

Hobbes, Thomas. (1651) 2010. *Leviathan: Or the Matter, Forme and Power of a Common-Wealth Ecclesiastical and Civil*. New Haven, CT, and London: Yale University Press. http://studymore.org.uk/xhobint.htm.

Hobsbawm, Eric. 1997. *On History*. London: Abacus.

Hoffman, Frank G. 2007. *Conflict in the 21st Century: The Rise of Hybrid Wars*. Arlington, VA: Potomac Institute for Policy Studies.

Horizons. 2012. Episode "Out of Control?" first broadcast 13 March by BBC 2. Directed and written by Ben Lawrie.

Horowitz, Michael C. 2010. *The Diffusion of Military Power: Causes and Consequences for International Politics*. Princeton, NJ: Princeton University Press.

Horst, Mark, Margôt Kuttschreuter, and Jan M. Gutteling. 2007. "Perceived Usefulness, Personal Experiences, Risk Perception and Trust as Determinants of Adoption of E-Government Services in The Netherlands." *Computers in Human Behavior* 23 (4): 1838–52.

Horswill, Mark S., and Frank P. McKenna. 1999. "The Effect of Perceived Control on Risk Taking." *Journal of Applied Social Psychology* 29 (2): 377–91.

Huizinga, Johan. 1949. *Homo Ludens: A Study of the Play-Element in Culture*. London: Routledge & Kegan Paul.

Huntington, Samuel P. (1957) 1972. *The Soldier and the State: The Theory and Politics of Civil-Military Relations*. Cambridge, MA: The Belknap Press of Harvard University Press.

Iacono, C. Suzanne, and Suzanne Weisband. 1997. "Developing Trust in Virtual Teams." *Proceedings of the 30th Hawaii International Conference on System Sciences: Information Systems Track-Collaboration Systems and Technology* 2: 412–20.

IARPA (Intelligence Advanced Research Projects Activity). 2009. *Reynard*. Office of the Director of National Intelligence. www.iarpa.gov/index.php/research-programs/reynard.

IARPA (Intelligence Advanced Research Projects Activity). 2011. *Sirius*. Office of the Director of National Intelligence. www.iarpa.gov/index.php/research -programs/sirius.

ICBL (International Campaign to Ban Landmines). 2016. *Treaty Status*. http://www .icbl.org/en-gb/the-treaty/treaty-status.aspx.

Indridason, Indridi H. 2008. "Does Terrorism Influence Domestic Politics? Coalition Formation and Terrorist Incidents." *Journal of Peace Research* 45 (2): 241–59.
Isbister, Katherine. 2016. *How Games Move Us: Emotion by Design*. Cambridge, MA, and London: The MIT Press.
Ivory, James D. 2016. "History of Video Games." In *The Video Game Debate: Unravelling the Physical, Social, and Psychological Effects of Digital Games*, edited by Rachel Kowert and Thorsten Quandt, 1–21. New York: Routledge.
Jagoda, Patrick, Melissa Gilliam, Peter McDonald, and Christopher Russell. 2015. "Worlding through Play: Alternate Reality Games, Large-Scale Learning, and 'The Source.'" *American Journal of Play* 8 (1): 74–100.
Janowitz, Morris. 1960. *The Professional Soldier: A Social and Political Portrait*. Glencoe: Free Press.
Jansson, Gabriella, and Gissur Ó Erlingsson. 2014. "More E-Government, Less Street-Level Bureaucracy? On Legitimacy and the Human Side of Public Administration." *Journal of Information Technology & Politics*, 11 (3): 291–308.
Jasanoff, Sheila. 2004. "Ordering Knowledge, Ordering Society." In *States of Knowledge: The Co-Production of Science and the Social Order*, edited by Shiela Jasanoff, 13–45. London and New York: Routledge.
Jasper, Scott. 2009a. "The Capabilities-Based Approach." In *Transforming Defense Capabilities: New Approaches for International Security*, edited by Scott Jasper, 1–22. Boulder, CO: Lynne Rienner Publishers Inc.
Jasper, Scott, ed. 2009b. *Transforming Defense Capabilities: New Approaches for International Security*. Boulder, CO: Lynne Rienner Publishers Inc.
Jervis, Robert. 1978. "Cooperation under the Security Dilemma." *World Politics* 30 (2): 167–214.
Jervis, Robert. 1988. "War and Misperception." *The Journal of Interdisciplinary History* 18 (4): 675–700.
Johnson, Loch K., ed. 2014. "An INS Special Forum: Implications of the Snowden Leaks." *Intelligence and National Security* 29 (6): 793–810.
Johnson, Steven. 2006. *Everything Bad Is Good for You: How Today's Popular Culture Is Actually Making Us Smarter*. New York: Riverhead Books.
Kagan, Donald, and Gregory F. Viggiano. 2015. *Men of Bronze: Hoplite Warfare in Ancient Greece*. Princeton, NJ: Princeton University Press.
Kahne, Joseph, Man-Jin Lee, and Jessica T. Feezell. 2013. "The Civic and Political Significance of Online Participatory Cultures among Youth Transitioning to Adulthood." *Journal of Information Technology & Politics* 10 (1): 1–20.
Kaitseliit. 2016. *Estonian Defence League's Cyber Unit*. www.kaitseliit.ee/en/cyber-unit.
Kane, Tim. 2011. "Why Our Best Officers Are Leaving." *The Atlantic*, January/February. www.theatlantic.com/magazine/archive/2011/01/why-our-best-officers-are-leaving/308346/.
Kaplan, Robert D. 1994. "The Coming Anarchy." *The Atlantic*, February. www.theatlantic.com/magazine/archive/1994/02/the-coming-anarchy/304670/.
Karpf, David. 2011. "Open Source Political Community Development: A Five-Stage Adoption Process." *Journal of Information Technology & Politics* 8 (3): 323–45.

Kathlene, Lyn, and John A. Martin. 1991. "Enhancing Citizen Participation: Panel Designs, Perspectives, and Policy Formation." *Journal of Policy Analysis and Management* 10 (1): 46–63.

Kazakova, Snezhanka, Veroline Cauberghe, Mario Pandelaere, and Patrick De Pelsmacker. 2014. "Players' Expertise and Competition with Others Shape the Satisfaction of Competence Needs, Gaming Gratifications, and Contingent Self-Esteem in a Gaming Context." *Cyberpsychology, Behavior, and Social Networking* 17 (1): 26–32.

Keen, Andrew. 2016. "E-stonia: The Country Using Tech to Rebrand Itself as the Anti-Russia." *The Guardian*, 21 April. http://www.theguardian.com/world/2016/apr/21/e-stonia-country-using-technology-to-rebrand-itself-as-the-anti-russia.

Kelley, Harold H. 1972. "Causal Schemata and the Attribution Process." In *Attribution: Perceiving the Causes of Behaviour*, edited by Edward E. Jones, David E. Kanouse, Harold H. Kelley, Richard E. Nisbett, Stuart Valins, and Bernard Weiner, 151–74. Morristown, NJ: General Learning Press.

Kennedy, Pagan. 2016. *Inventology: How We Dream Up Things That Change the World*. New York: Eamon Dolan/Houghton Mifflin Harcourt.

King, Anthony. 2006. "The Word of Command: Communication and Cohesion in the Military." *Armed Forces & Society* 32 (4): 493–512.

King, Anthony. 2007. "The Existence of Group Cohesion in the Armed Forces: A Response to Guy Siebold." *Armed Forces & Society* 33 (4): 638–45.

Kissinger, Henry. 2014. *World Order: Reflections on the Character of Nations and the Course of History*. London: Allen Lane.

Kittilson, Miki Caul, and Russell J. Dalton. 2011. "Virtual Civil Society: The New Frontier of Social Capital? *Political Behavior* 33 (4): 625–44.

Klein, Cynthia T. F., and Marie Helweg-Larsen. 2002. "Perceived Control and the Optimistic Bias: A Meta-Analytic Review." *Psychology and Health* 17 (4): 437–46.

Klein, Gary. 2013. "Insight." In *Thinking: The New Science of Decision-Making, Problem-Solving, and Prediction*, edited by John Brockman, 193–214. New York: Harper Perennial.

Knox, MacGregor, and Williamson Murray, eds. 2001. *The Dynamics of Military Revolution, 1300-2050*. Cambridge: Cambridge University Press.

Kogan, Nathan, and Michael A. Wallach. 1967. "Risky-Shift Phenomenon in Small Decision-Making Groups: A Test of the Information-Exchange Hypothesis." *Journal of Experimental Social Psychology* 3 (1): 75–82.

Kössler, Karl. 2015. "Laboratories of Democratic Innovation? Direct, Participatory, and Deliberative Democracy in Canadian Provinces and Municipalities." In *Citizen Participation in Multi-Level Democracies*, edited by Cristina Fraenkel-Haeberle, Sabine Kropp, Francesco Palermo, and Karl-Peter Sommermann, 286–308. Leiden and Boston: Brill Nijhoff.

Kowert, Rachel. 2016. "Social Outcomes: Online Game Play, Social Currency, and Social Ability." In *The Video Game Debate: Unravelling the Physical, Social, and Psychological Effects of Digital Games*, edited by Rachel Kowert and Thorsten Quandt, 94–115. New York: Routledge.

Krepinevich, Andrew F. 1994. "Cavalry to Computer: The Pattern of Military Revolutions." *The National Interest* 37 (fall): 30–42.

Krug, Etienne G., Linda L. Dahlberg, James A. Mercy, Anthony B. Zwi, and Rafael Lozano, eds. 2002. *World Report on Violence and Health*. Geneva: World Health Organization. www.who.int/violence_injury_prevention/violence/world_report/en/.

Krugman, Paul. 1994. "Europe Jobless, America Penniless?" *Foreign Policy* 95 (summer): 19–34.

Kuo, Feng-Yang, and Chia-Ping Yu. 2009. "An Exploratory Study of Trust Dynamics in Work-Oriented Virtual Teams." *Journal of Computer-Mediated Communications* 14 (4): 823–54.

Kwiatkowski, Kacper. 2016. "Civilian Casualties: Shifting Perspectives in 'This War of Mine.'" In *Zones of Control: Perspectives on Wargaming*, edited by Pat Harrigan and Matthew G. Kirschenbaum, 691–702. Cambridge, MA: MIT Press.

Lacy, Mark. 2014. *Security, Technology and Global Politics: Thinking with Virilio*. London and New York: Routledge.

Lakoff, Andrew. 2007. "From Population to Vital System: National Security and the Changing Object of Public Health." ARC Working Paper, No. 7. Anthropology of the Contemporary Research Collaboratory. http://anthropos-lab.net/wp/publications/2007/08/workingpaperno7.pdf.

Landsbergen, David, David H. Coursey, Stephen Loveless, and R. F. Shangraw, Jr. 1997. "Decision Quality, Confidence, and Commitment with Expert Systems: An Experimental Study." *Journal of Public Administration Research and Theory* 7 (1): 131–57.

Lange, Siri. 2008. "The Depoliticisation of Development and the Democratisation of Politics in Tanzania: Parallel Structures as Obstacles to Delivering Services to the Poor." *Journal of Development Studies* 44 (8): 1122–44.

Lanier, Jaron. 2010. *You Are Not a Gadget: A Manifesto*. London and New York: Penguin.

Laqueur, Walter. 1999. *The New Terrorism: Fanaticism and the Arms of Mass Destruction*. New York: Oxford University Press.

Larsson, Anders Olof. 2013. "'Rejected Bits of Program Code': Why Notions of 'Politics 2.0' Remain (Mostly) Unfulfilled." *Journal of Information Technology & Politics* 10 (1): 72–85.

La Rue, Frank. 2011. *Report of the Special Rapporteur on the Promotion and Protection of the Right to Freedom of Opinion and Expression, Frank la Rue*. United Nations, General Assembly, Human Rights Council, 17th session, agenda item 3. Doc A/HRC/17/27. www2.ohchr.org/english/bodies/hrcouncil/docs/17session/A.HRC.17.27_en.pdf.

Lee, Yu-Hao. 2015. "Does Digital Game Interactivity Always Promote Self-Efficacy?" *Cyberpsychology, Behavior, and Social Networking* 18 (11): 669–73.

Leetaru, Kalev. 2015. "A Few Good Twitter Trolls." *FP*, 14 July. http://foreignpolicy.com/2015/07/14/islamic-state-twitter-recruiting/.

Lehrke, Jesse P. 2013. *The Transition to National Armies in the Former Soviet Republics, 1988-2005*. Abingdon, UK: Routledge.

Lehrke, Jesse P. 2016. "Terrorism Alerts and Target Transference: Evidence and Implications from the 2010 Europe-Wide Terrorism Alert." *European Security* 25 (1): 3–27.

Leigh, David, and Luke Harding. 2011. *Wikileaks: Inside Julian Assange's War on Secrecy.* London: Guardian Books.

Leonhard, Robert R. 1998. *The Principles of War for the Information Age*. New York: Ballantine Books.

Lerner, Jennifer S., and Dacher Keltner. 2000. "Beyond Valence: Toward a Model of Emotion-Specific Influences on Judgment and Choice." *Cognition and Emotion* 14 (4): 473–93.

Lerner, Josh A. 2014. *Making Democracy Fun: How Game Design Can Empower Citizens and Transform Politics*. Cambridge, MA: MIT Press.

Lévy, Bernard-Henri. 2015. "Thinking the Unthinkable: This Is War." *The Globe and Mail*, 16 November. www.theglobeandmail.com/globedebate/thinkingtheunthinkablethisiswar/article27284617/.

Liang, Qiao, and Wang Xiangsui. 1999. *Unrestricted Warfare*. Beijing: PLA Literature and Arts Publishing House. http://www.c4i.org/unrestricted.pdf.

Lieber, Keir A. 2005. *War and the Engineers: The Primacy of Politics Over Technology*. Ithaca, NY: Cornell University Press.

Lima, M. L., J. Barnett, and J. Vala. 2005. "Risk Perception and Technological Development at a Societal Level." *Risk Analysis* 25 (5): 1229–39.

Linn, Allison. 2016. "Project Malmo: Using Minecraft to Build More Intelligent Technology." *The Official Microsoft Blog*, 13 March. http://blogs.microsoft.com/next/2016/03/13/project-malmo-using-minecraft-build-intelligent-technology/#74gs1o0ppsuLtZz3.99.

Lipschutz, Ronnie D. 2000. *After Authority: War, Peace, and Global Politics in the 21st Century.* Albany, NY: State University of New York Press.

Lobel, Adam, Isabela Granic, and Rutger Engels. 2014. "Stressful Gaming, Interoceptive Awareness, and Emotion Regulation Tendencies: A Novel Approach." *Cyberpsychology, Behavior, and Social Networking* 17 (4): 222–27.

Lundmark, Sebastian. 2015. "Gaming Together: When an Imaginary World Affects Generalized Trust." *Journal of Information Technology & Politics* 12 (1): 54–73.

Lynch, Colum. 2016. "How to Crowdsource the Syrian Cease-Fire." *FP*, 23 March. http://foreignpolicy.com/2016/03/23/how-to-crowdsource-the-syrian-cease-fire/.

Lynn, William J. III. 2014. "The End of the Military-Industrial Complex." *Foreign Affairs* 93 (6): 104–10. http://www.foreignaffairs.com/articles/142199/william-j-lynn-iii/the-end-of-the-military-industrial-complex.

Marshall, Jessica, and *Nature* Magazine. 2012. "Online Gamers Achieve First Crowd-Sourced Redesign of Protein." *Scientific American*, 22 January. http://www.scientificamerican.com/article/victory-for-crowdsourced-biomolecule2/.

Maslow, Abraham. 1943. "A Theory of Human Motivation." *Psychological Review* 50 (4): 370–96.

Maslow, Abraham. 1954. *Motivation and Personality*. New York: Harper.

May, Ernest R. 2000. *Strange Victory: Hitler's Conquest of France*. New York: Hill and Wang.

McChrystal, Stanley A. 2016. "You Don't Have to Wear a Military Uniform to Serve Your Country." *The Atlantic*, 20 July. www.theatlantic.com/politics/archive/2016/07/you-dont-have-to-wear-a-military-uniform-to-serve-your-country/491765/.

McClure, Matthew. 2014. "FoW (No. 21): To Succeed, We Need to Act Less Like Dinosaurs and More Like Bacteria." *FP*, 21 March. http://foreignpolicy.com/2014/03/25/fow-no-21-to-succeed-we-need-to-act-less-like-dinosaurs-and-more-like-bacteria/.

McGonigal, Jane. 2008. "The New Game Plan." *SEED, Special Issue: The Universe in 2008* 14 (January/February): 55–56. www.avantgame.com/SEED%20Gaming%20Article_JanFeb08.pdf.

McGonigal, Jane. 2011. *Reality Is Broken: Why Games Make Us Better and How They Can Change the World.* New York: Penguin Books.

McNeill, William H. 1982. *The Pursuit of Power: Technology, Armed Force, and Society since A.D. 1000*. Chicago: University of Chicago Press.

Mead, Corey. 2013. *War Play: Video Games and the Future of Armed Conflict*. New York: Eamon Dolan/Houghton Mifflin Harcourt.

Meirowitz, Adam, and Joshua A. Tucker. 2004. "Learning from Terrorism Markets." *Perspectives on Politics* 2 (2): 331–36.

Mellers, Barbara, Lyle Ungar, Jonathan Baron, Jaime Ramos, Burcu Gurcay, Katrina Fincher, Sydney E. Scott, Don Moore, Pavel Atanasov, Samuel A. Swift, et al. 2014. "Psychological Strategies for Winning a Geopolitical Forecasting Tournament." *Psychological Science* 25 (5): 1106–15.

Meyer, John W., and Ronald L. Jepperson. 2000. "The 'Actors' of Modern Society: The Cultural Construction of Social Agency." *Sociological Theory* 18 (1): 100–20.

Meyerson, D., K. Weick, and R. Kramer. 1996. "Swift Trust and Temporary Groups." In *Trust in Organizations: Frontiers of Theory and Research*, edited by Roderick Kramer and Tom Tyler, 166–96. Thousand Oaks, CA: SAGE Publications.

Meyrowitz, Joshua. 1985. *No Sense of Place: The Impact of Electronic Media on Social Behaviour*. New York and Oxford: Oxford University Press.

Michels, Robert. (1911) 1915. *Political Parties: A Sociological Study of the Oligarchical Tendencies of Modern Democracy.* Translated by Eden Paul and Cedar Paul. New York: The Free Press.

Micklethwait, John, and Adrian Woolridge. 2014. *The Fourth Revolution: The Global Race to Reinvent the State.* New York: The Penguin Press.

Min, Seong-Jae. 2010. "From the Digital Divide to the Democratic Divide: Internet Skills, Political Interest, and the Second-Level Digital Divide in Political Internet Use." *Journal of Information Technology & Politics* 7 (1): 22–35.

Mindell, David A. 2015. *Our Robots, Ourselves: Robotics and the Myths of Autonomy*. New York: Viking.

Möllering, Guido. 2006. *Trust: Reason, Routine, Reflexivity*. Amsterdam: Elsevier.

Moore, Barrington Jr. 1978. *Injustice: The Social Bases of Obedience and Revolt*. London: Palgrave Macmillan.

Mora, Nicolás Medina, and Mike Hayes. 2015. "The Big (Imaginary) Black Friday Bombing." *BuzzFeed News*, 16 November. www.buzzfeed.com/nicolasmedinamora/did-the-fbi-transform-this-teenager-into-a-terrorist#.mp94Dj9OQ.

Moran, Daniel. 2009. "On Military Revolution." In *Transforming Defense Capabilities: New Approaches for International Security*, edited by Scott Jasper, 25–40. Boulder, CO: Lynne Rienner Publishers.

Mordvintsev, Alexander, Christopher Olah, and Mike Tyka. 2015. "Inceptionism: Going Deeper into Neural Networks." *Google Research Blog*, 17 June. http://googleresearch.blogspot.de/2015/06/inceptionism-going-deeper-into-neural.html.

Morgan, Timothy Prickett. 2015. "Google Sees Long, Expensive Road Ahead for Quantum Computing." *The Next Platform*, 22 July. www.nextplatform.com/2015/07/22/google-sees-long-expensive-road-ahead-for-quantum-computing/.

Morozov, Evgeny. 2014. *To Save Everything, Click Here: The Folly of Technological Solutionism*. New York: PublicAffairs.

Morris, Desmond. 1962. *The Biology of Art: A Study of the Picture-Making Behaviour of the Great Apes and Its Relationship to Human Art*. London: Methuen.

Morris, Ian. 2014. *War: What Is It Good For? The Role of Conflict in Civilization, from Primates to Robots.* London: Profile Books.

Mueller, John, and Mark Stewart. 2015. *Chasing Ghosts: The Policing of Terrorism*. New York: Oxford University Press.

Myers, Judith R., Donna H. Henderson-King, and Eaaron I. Henderson-King. 1997. "Facing Technological Risks: The Importance of Individual Differences." *Journal of Research in Personality* 31 (1): 1–20.

Nacos, Brigitte. 1994. *Terrorism and the Media*. New York: Columbia University Press.

Nakatsu, Robbie T., Elissa B. Grossman, and Charalambos L. Iacovou. 2014. "A Taxonomy of Crowdsourcing Based on Task Complexity." *Journal of Information Science* 40 (6): 823–34.

Nakayachi, Kazuya. 2013. "The Unintended Effects of Risk-Refuting Information on Anxiety." *Risk Analysis* 33 (1): 80–91.

National Commission on Terrorist Attacks Upon the United States (9/11 Commission). 2004. *The 9/11 Commission Report: Final Report of the National Commission on Terrorist Attacks Upon the United States*. https://9-11commission.gov/report/911Report.pdf.

Neubaum, German, and Nicole C. Krämer. 2015. "My Friends Right Next to Me: A Laboratory Investigation on Predictors and Consequences of Experiencing Social Closeness on Social Networking Sites." *Cyberpsychology, Behavior, and Social Networking* 18 (8): 443–49.

Nguyen, Anh, Jason Yosinski, and Jeff Clune. 2015. "Deep Neural Networks Are Easily Fooled: High Confidence Predictions for Unrecognizable Images." *Computer Vision and Pattern Recognition* CVPR '15, IEEE: 427–36.

North, Douglass C. 1990. *Institutions, Institutional Change and Economic Performance*. Cambridge, UK: Cambridge University Press.

North, Douglass C. 1995. "The New Institutional Economics and Third World Development." In *The New Institutional Economics and Third World Development*, edited by John Harriss, Janet Hunter, and Colin M. Lewis, 17–26. London and New York: Routledge.

North, Douglass C., John Joseph Wallis, and Barry R. Weingast. 2013. *Violence and Social Order: A Conceptual Framework for Interpreting Recorded Human History*. Cambridge, UK: Cambridge University Press.

Norton, Michael I., Daniel Mochon, and Dan Ariely. 2011. "The 'IKEA' Effect: When Labor Leads to Love." Working Paper No. 11-091. Harvard Business School Marketing Unit, 4 March. http://papers.ssrn.com/sol3/papers.cfm?abstract_id=1777100.

Oehmichen, Anna. 2008. "Incommunicado Detention in Germany: An Example of Reactive Anti-Terror Legislation and Long-Term Consequences." *German Law Journal* 9 (7): 855–88.

O'Grady, Cathleen. 2016. "We May All Happily Follow Our Robot Overlords to Disaster." *Ars Technica*, 8 March. http://arstechnica.com/science/2016/03/we-may-all-happily-follow-our-robot-overlords-to-disaster/.

Omand, David. 2010. *Securing the State*. Oxford: Oxford University Press.

Open Government Partnership. 2015. *Open Government Partnership*. www.opengovpartnership.org/.

Oreskes, Naomi, and John Krige, eds. 2014. *Science and Technology in the Global Cold War*. Cambridge, MA: MIT Press.

Oulasvirta, Antti, Tiia Suomalainen, Juho Hamari, Airi Lampinen, and Kristiina Karvonen. 2014. "Transparency of Intentions Decreases Privacy Concerns in Ubiquitous Surveillance." *Cyberpsychology, Behavior, and Social Networking* 17 (10): 633–38.

Panksepp, Jaak. 2004. *Affective Neuroscience: The Foundations of Human and Animal Emotions*. Oxford and New York: Oxford University Press.

Pariser, Eli. 2011. *The Filter Bubble*. New York: Penguin.

Pasquale, Frank. 2015. *The Black Box Society: The Secret Algorithms That Control Money and Information*. Cambridge, MA: Harvard University Press.

Pasqualetti, Fabio, Antonio Franchi, and Francesco Bullo. 2012. "On Cooperative Patrolling: Optimal Trajectories, Complexity Analysis, and Approximation Algorithms." *IEEE Transaction on Robotics* 28 (3): 592–606. https://arxiv.org/pdf/1101.3973.pdf.

Patrikarakos, David. 2014. "Ukraine's Facebook Warriors." *New York Times*, 29 December. http://www.nytimes.com/2014/12/30/opinion/ukraines-facebook-warriors.html.

Pearce, Celia, and Artemesia. 2009. *Communities of Play: Emergent Cultures in Multiplayer Games and Virtual Worlds*. Cambridge, MA: MIT Press.

Peck, Michael. 2014. "Congratulations, You Have Been Martyred!" *FP*, 28 March. http://foreignpolicy.com/2014/03/28/congratulations-you-have-been-martyred/.

Peled, Alon. 2014a. "Erecting the Public Sector Information Exchange." In *Public Administration and the Modern State: Assessing Trends and Impact*, edited by Jos Raadschelders, Eberhard Bohne, and John Graham with Jesse Lehrke, 163–75. Basingstoke, UK: Palgrave Macmillan.

Peled, Alon. 2014b. *Traversing Digital Babel: Information, E-Government, and Exchange*. Cambridge, MA: The MIT Press.

Pellis, Sergio, and Vivien Pellis. 2009. *The Playful Brain: Venturing to the Limits of Neuroscience*. Oxford, UK: Oneworld Publications.

Pereira, Anthony W. 2003. "Armed Forces, Coercive Monopolies, and Changing Patterns of State Formation and Violence." In *Irregular Armed Forces and Their Role in Politics and State Formation*, edited by Diane E. Davis and Anthony W. Pereira, 387–407. Cambridge, UK: Cambridge University Press.

Perrow, Charles. 1984. *Normal Accidents: Living with High-Risk Technologies*. Princeton, NJ: Princeton University Press.

Peters, Richard G., Vincent T. Covello, and David B. McCallum. 1997. "The Determinants of Trust and Credibility in Environmental Risk Communication: An Empirical Study." *Risk Analysis* 17 (1): 43–54.

Pettyjohn, Stacie L., and David A. Shlapak. 2016. "Gaming the System: Obstacles to Reinvigorating Defense Wargaming." *War on the Rocks*, 18 February. http://warontherocks.com/2016/02/gaming-the-system-obstacles-to-reinvigorating-defense-wargaming/.

Pinker, Steven. 2011. *The Better Angels of Our Nature: Why Violence Has Declined*. New York: Viking.

Piotrowski, Suzanne J., ed. 2010. *Transparency and Secrecy: A Reader Linking Literature and Contemporary Debate*. Lanham, MD: Lexington Books.

Polyani, Karl. (1944) 2001. *The Great Transformation: The Political and Economic Origins of Our Time*. Boston: Beacon Press.

Pomerantsev, Peter. 2014. "How Putin Is Reinventing Warfare." *FP*, 5 May. http://foreignpolicy.com/2014/05/05/how-putin-is-reinventing-warfare/.

Pomerantsev, Peter, and Michael Weiss. 2014. *The Menace of Unreality: How the Kremlin Weaponizes Information, Culture and Money*. New York: The Institute of Modern Russia, Inc. www.interpretermag.com/wp-content/uploads/2014/11/The_Menace_of_Unreality_Final.pdf.

Posen, Barry. R. 1984. *The Sources of Military Doctrine: France, Britain, and Germany between the World Wars*. Ithaca, NY: Cornell University Press.

Power, Marcus. 2007. "Digitized Virtuosity: Video War Games and Post-9/11 Cyber-Deterrence." *Security Dialogue* 38 (2): 271–88.

Praetorius, Dean. 2011. "Gamers Decode AIDS Protein That Stumped Researchers for 15 Years in Just 3 Weeks." *The Huffington Post*, 19 September. www.huffingtonpost.com/2011/09/19/aids-protein-decoded-gamers_n_970113.html.

Pratkanis, Anthony R. 2007. "Winning Hearts and Minds: A Social Influence Analysis." In *Information Strategy and Warfare: A Guide to Theory and Practice*, edited by John Arquilla and Douglas A. Borer, 56–85. New York and Abingdon, UK: Routledge.

Przybylski, Andrew K., C. Scott Rigby, and Richard M. Ryan. 2010. "A Motivational Model of Video Game Engagement." *Review of General Psychology* 14 (2): 154–66.

Rahwan, Iyad, Sohan Dsouza, Alex Rutherford, Victor Naroditskiy, James McInerney, Matteo Venanzi, Nicholas R. Jennings, and Manuel Cebrian. 2013. "Global Manhunt Pushes the Limits of Social Mobilization." *Computer* 46 (4): 68–75. http://web.media.mit.edu/~cebrian/IEEEmanhunt.pdf.

Radio Free Europe/Radio Liberty (RFE/RL). 2015a. "Head Games." *The Power Vertical* (Podcast), 6 February. www.rferl.org/content/podcast-head-games/26834076.html.

Radio Free Europe/Radio Liberty (RFE/RL). 2015b. "Putin's Hybrid War – In Europe." *The Power Vertical, The Daily Vertical* (Video), 17 February. www.rferl.org/content/daily-vertical-putin-new-hybrid-war/27241129.html.

Radio Free Europe/Radio Liberty (RFE/RL). 2015c. "Talking Security in Warsaw." *The Power Vertical* (Podcast), 6 November. www.rferl.org/content/podcast-talking-security-in-warsaw/27348791.html.

Reeves, Byron, and J. Leighton Read. 2009. *Total Engagement: Using Games and Virtual Worlds to Change the Way People Work and Businesses Compete*. Boston: Harvard Business Press.

Rid, Thomas, and Marc Hecker. 2009. *War 2.0: Irregular Warfare in the Information Age*. Westport, CT, and London: Praeger Security International.

Ries, Tomas. 2012. "Insecurity in the Post-Liberal Age: Key Security Challenges of the Early 21st Century." In *The European Union and Emerging Powers in the 21st Century: How Europe Can Shape a New Global Order*, edited by Sven Biscop and Thomas Renard, 21–40. Abingdon, UK: Routledge.

Rimal, R. N., and K. Real. 2003. "Perceived Risk and Efficacy Beliefs as Motivators of Change." *Human Communication Research* 29 (3): 370–99.

Roberts, Alasdair. 2004. "National Security and Open Government." *The Georgetown Public Policy Review* 9 (2): 69–86.

Roberts, Alasdair. 2017. *Four Crises of Democracy: Representation, Mastery, Discipline, Anticipation*. Oxford and New York: Oxford University Press.

Robinette, Paul, Wenchen Li, Robert Allen, Ayanna M. Howard, and Alan R. Wagner. 2016. "Overtrust of Robots in Emergency Evacuation Scenarios." Paper presented at 2016 ACM/IEEE International Conference on Human-Robot Interaction (HRI 2016), Christchurch, New Zealand, 7–10 March. http://ieeexplore.ieee.org/document/7451740/.

Robinson, Glenn E. 2007. "Jihadi Information Strategy." In *Information Strategy and Warfare: A Guide to Theory and Practice*, edited by John Arquilla and Douglas A. Borer, 86–112. New York and Abingdon, UK: Routledge.

Rosen, Stephen Peter. 2005. *War and Human Nature*. Princeton, NJ: Princeton University Press.

Rosoff, Heather, Richard S. John, and Fynnwin Prager. 2012. "Flu, Risks, and Videotape: Escalating Fear and Avoidance." *Risk Analysis* 32 (4): 729–43.

Rothkopf, David. 2014. *National Insecurity: American Leadership in an Age of Fear*. New York: PublicAffairs.

Runkle, Benjamin. 2015. "Is the Islamic State a Cyber Threat?" *War on the Rocks*, 9 September. warontherocks.com/2015/09/is-the-islamic-state-a-cyber-threat/.

Ruz, Camila. 2015. "What Should You Do in an Attack?" *BBC News Magazine*, 18 November. www.bbc.com/news/magazine-34844518.

Sagar, Rahul. 2013. *Secrets and Leaks: The Dilemma of State Secrecy*. Princeton, NJ: Princeton University Press.

Sageman, Marc. 2014. "The Stagnation in Terrorism Research." *Terrorism and Political Violence* 26 (4): 565–80.

Said, Edward W. 1978. *Orientalism*. New York and Toronto: Vintage Books.

Sandoval-Almazan, Rodrigo, and J. Ramon Gil-Garcia. 2012. "Are Government Internet Portals Evolving Towards More Interaction, Participation, and Collaboration? Revisiting the Rhetoric of E-Government among Municipalities." *Government Information Quarterly* 29 (Supplement 1), S72–81.

Satellite Sentinel Project (SSP). 2015. *Satellite Sentinel Project: The World Is Watching Because You are Watching*. http://www.satsentinel.org.

Scales, John, Brig. Gen. (Ret.). 2016. "Thoughts as I Watch My Army Walk Away from Counterinsurgency Once Again." *FP*, 11 February. http://foreignpolicy.com/2016/02/11/thoughts-as-i-watch-my-army-walk-away-from-counterinsurgency-once-again/.

Schake, Kori. 2016. "Why Donald Trump's Endorsement by 88 Generals Is So Dangerous." *FP*, 6 September. http://foreignpolicy.com/2016/09/06/why-donald-trumps-endorsement-by-88-generals-is-so-dangerous-civilian-military-relations/.

Schirrmacher, Frank. 2009. "The Age of the Informavore." *Edge.org*, 25 October. http://edge.org/conversation/frank_schirrmacher-the-age-of-the-informavore.

Schneier, Bruce. 2003. *Beyond Fear: Thinking Sensibly about Security in an Uncertain World.* New York: Copernicus Books.

Schneier, Bruce. 2012. *Liars & Outliers: Enabling the Trust That Society Needs to Thrive*. Indianapolis: John Wiley and Sons.

Schwab, Klaus. 2016. *The Fourth Industrial Revolution*. Cologne and Geneva: World Economic Forum.

Singer, P. W. 2009. *Wired for War: The Robotics Revolution and Conflict in the 21st Century*. London: Penguin Books.

Singer, P. W. 2015. "How the United States Can Win the Cyberwar of the Future." *FP*, 18 December. http://foreignpolicy.com/2015/12/18/how-the-united-states-can-win-the-cyberwar-of-the-future-deterrence-theory-security/.

Singer, P. W., and August Cole. 2015. *Ghost Fleet: A Novel of the Next World War*. New York: Houghton Mifflin Harcourt Publishing.

Singer, P. W., and Allan Friedman. 2014. *Cybersecurity and Cyberwar: What Everyone Needs to Know*. Oxford and New York: Oxford University Press.

Sjöberg, Lennart, and Elisabeth Engelberg. 2010. "Risk Perception and Movies: A Study of Availability as a Factor in Risk Perception." *Risk Analysis* 30 (1): 95–106.

Slayton, Rebecca. 2013. *Arguments That Count: Physics, Computing, and Missile Defense, 1949-2012.* Cambridge, MA: MIT University Press.

Smith, Richard. 2002. "10 Things You Should Know about Security, Privacy and Encryption." *Edge.org*, 21 October. www.edge.org/conversation/richard_smith-10-things-you-should-know-about-security-privacy-and-encryption.

Sommermann, Karl-Peter. 2015. "Citizen Participation in Multi-Level Democracies: An Introduction." In *Citizen Participation in Multi-Level Democracies*, edited by Cristina Fraenkel-Haeberle, Sabine Kropp, Francesco Palermo, and Karl-Peter Sommermann, 1–12. Leiden and Boston: Brill Nijhoff.

Sparks, Paul, Richard Shepherd, and Lynn J. Frewer. 1994. "Gene Technology, Food Production and Public Opinion: A UK Study." *Agriculture and Human Values* 11 (1): 19–28.

Spina, Alessandro. 2014. "Open Government, Behavior Control, and the Privacy Risk of Digital Government." In *Public Administration and the Modern State: Assessing Trends and Impact*, edited by Jos Raadschelders, Eberhard Bohne, and John Graham with Jesse Lehrke, 176–88. Basingstoke, UK: Palgrave Macmillan.

Stanford University. 2015. *Virtual Human Interaction Lab*. http://vhil.stanford.edu/.

Stanhope, Philip Henry, Fifth Earl of. (1886) 2001. *Notes of Conversations with the Duke of Wellington, 1831-1851*. New York: Adamant Media Corporation.

Steinkuehler Squire, Constance. 2011. "Games for Grand Challenges." *The White House, President Barack Obama*, 23 November. www.whitehouse.gov/blog/2011/11/23/games-grand-challenges.

Steinman, Joshua. 2016. "Imagine the Starling: Peak Fighter, the Swarm, and the Future of Air Combat." *War on the Rocks*, 17 February. http://warontherocks.com/2016/02/imagine-the-starling-peak-fighter-the-swarm-and-the-future-of-air-combat/.

Stephenson, Neal. 1999. *Cryptonomicon*. New York: Avon Books.

Stoner, James Arthur Finch. 1961. *A Comparison of Individual and Group Decisions Including Risk*. Unpublished master's thesis, Massachusetts Institute of Technology.

Stop Terror. 2017. *Home*. https://stopterror.in.ua/.

Stroud, Michael J., and Susan Krauss Whitbourne. 2015. "Casual Video Games as Training Tools for Attentional Processes in Everyday Life." *Cyberpsychology, Behavior, and Social Networking* 18 (11): 654–60.

Sulea, Camelia, Ahmad Soomro, Chelsie Boyd, and Brenda K. Wiederhold. 2014. "Pain Management in Virtual Reality: A Comprehensive Research Chart." *Cyberpsychology, Behavior, and Social Networking* 17 (6): 402–13.

Sunstein, Cass. 2007. *Republic.com 2.0*. Princeton, NJ: Princeton University Press.

Taleb, Nassim Nicholas. 2007. *The Black Swan: The Impact of the Highly Improbable*. London and New York: Penguin Books.

Taleb, Nassim Nicholas. 2013. "The Fourth Quadrant: A Map of the Limits of Statistics." In *Thinking: The New Science of Decision-Making, Problem-Solving, and Prediction*, edited by John Brockman, 225–51. New York: Harper Perennial.

Taleb, Nassim Nicholas. 2015. "The 'Long Peace' is a Statistical Illusion." http://www.fooledbyrandomness.com/pinker.pdf.

Thaler, Richard H., and Cass R. Sunstein. 2008. *Nudge: Improving Decisions about Health, Wealth, and Happiness*. New York: Penguin Books.

The Economist. 2016. "Goggling at Britain: An Unlikely Television Hit Offers Togetherness in a Fragmenting Country." *The Economist*, 12 March. www.economist.com/node/21694562/print.

Thompson, Clive. 2014. "A Sad Fact of Life: It's Actually Smart to be Mean Online." *Wired*, 11 July. www.wired.com/2014/11/be-mean-online/.

Tilly, Charles, ed. 1975. *The Formation of National States in Western Europe*. Princeton, NJ: Princeton University Press.

Timmer, John. 2016. "NP-Complete Problem Solved with Biological Motors." *Ars Technica*, 25 February. http://arstechnica.com/science/2016/02/np-complete-problem-solved-with-biological-motors/.

Tinder, Glenn. 1964. *The Crisis of Political Imagination*. New York: Charles Scribner's Sons.

Toffler, Alvin, and Heidi Toffler. 1993. *War and Anti-War: Survival at the Dawn of the Twenty-First Century*. Boston: Little, Brown and Company.

Trimpop, Rüdiger M. 1994. *The Psychology of Risk Taking Behavior*. Amsterdam: North-Holland Publishing Company.

Tucker, Patrick. 2016. "How Putin Weaponized Wikileaks to Influence the Election of an American President." *Defence One*, 24 July. www.defenseone.com/technology/2016/07/how-putin-weaponized-wikileaks-influence-election-american-president/130163/.

United Nations. 2016. *Convention on the Prohibition of the Use, Stockpiling, Production and Transfer of Anti-Personnel Mines and on Their Destruction: Procedural History*. http://legal.un.org/avl/ha/cpusptam/cpusptam.html.

United States, Department of the Air Force. 2015. *AF Agency for Modeling and Simulation*. http://www.afams.af.mil/.

United States, Department of the Army. 2015. *America's Army Background*. Redstone Arsenal, Huntsville, Alabama: AMRDEC Software Engineering Directorate. http://www.americasarmy.com/press.

United States, Department of Homeland Security. 2014. *Open Government Plan 3.0*. http://www.dhs.gov/node/12110.

United States, White House. 2009. *Memorandum on Transparency and Open Government*. 21 January. https://obamawhitehouse.archives.gov/the-press-office/2015/11/16/memorandum-transparency-and-open-government.

United States, White House. 2016. *The United States Digital Service*. https://www.usds.gov/.

Vaccari, Cristian, Augusto Valeriani, Pablo Barberá, Rich Bonneau, John T. Jost, Jonathan Nagler, and Joshua A. Tucker. 2015. "Political Expression and Action on Social Media: Exploring the Relationship between Lower- and Higher-Threshold Political Activities among Twitter Users in Italy." *Journal of Computer-Mediated Communication* 20 (2): 221–39.

Van Creveld, Martin. 2013. *Wargames: From Gladiators to Gigabytes*. Cambridge, UK: Cambridge University Press.

Vanderschuren, Louk J. M. J. 2010. "How the Brain Makes Play Fun." *American Journal of Play* 2 (3): 315–37.

Van der Velde, Frank W., Christa Hooykaas, and Joop van der Pligt. 1992. "Risk Perception and Behavior: Pessimism, Realism, and Optimism About AIDS-Related Health Behaviors." *Psychology and Health* 6 (1-2): 23–38.

Vidmar, B., and T. C. Burdeny. 1971. "Effects of Group Size and Item Type in the 'Group Shift' Effect." *Canadian Journal of Behavioural Science* 3: 393–407.

Vissers, Sara, and Dietlind Stolle. 2014. "Spill-Over Effects Between Facebook and On/Offline Political Participation? Evidence from a Two-Wave Panel Study." *Journal of Information Technology & Politics* 11 (3): 259–75.

Von Ahn, Luis. 2006. "Games with a Purpose." *Computer* 39 (6): 92–94.

Von Clausewitz, Carl. (1832) 1976. *On War*. Translated by Micheal Howard and Peter Paret. Princeton, NJ: Princeton University Press.

Wakefield, Jane. 2016. "Microsoft Chatbot Is Taught to Swear on Twitter." *BBC News*, 24 March. www.bbc.com/news/technology-35890188.

Wallach, Michael A., Nathen Kogan, and Daryl J. Bem. 1962. "Group Influence on Individual Risk-Taking." *Journal of Abnormal Social Psychology* 65 (2): 75–86.

Wallach, Michael A., Nathen Kogan, and Daryl J. Bem. 1964. "Diffusion of Responsibility and Level of Risk-Taking in Groups." *Journal of Abnormal Social Psychology* 68 (3): 263–74.

Walsh, Lucas, and Julien Barbara. 2006. "Speed, International Security, and 'New War' Coverage in Cyberspace." *Journal of Computer-Mediated Communication* 12 (1): 189–208.

Walt, Stephen M. 1991. "The Renaissance of Security Studies." *International Studies Quarterly* 35 (2): 211–39.

Walt, Stephen M. 2014. "The Big Counterterrorism Counterfactual." *FP*, 10 November. http://foreignpolicy.com/2014/11/10/the-big-counterterrorism-counterfactual/.

Walton, Mark. 2016. "Microsoft Is Using Minecraft to Train AI and Wants You to Help Out." *Ars Technica*, 14 March. http://arstechnica.com/gaming/2016/03/microsoft-minecraft-aix-artificial-intelligence/.

Wang, Jun, Eric Pohlmeyer, Barbara Hanna, Yu-Gang Jiang, Paul Sajda, and Shih-Fu Chang. 2009. "Brain State Decoding for Rapid Image Retrieval." *Proceedings of the 17th ACM International Conference on Multimedia*, 945–954. MM'09, Beijing, China. 19–24 October. http://dl.acm.org/citation.cfm?id=1631272.1631463.

Wang, Ye Diana, and Henry H. Emurian. 2005. "An Overview of Online Trust: Concepts, Elements, and Implications." *Computers in Human Behavior* 21 (1): 105–25.

Watson, Peter. 1978. *War on the Mind: The Military Uses and Abuses of Psychology*. London: Hutchinson.

Weber, Max. (1922) 2013. *Economy and Society*. Edited by Guenther Roth and Claus Wittich. Berkeley and Los Angeles: University of California Press.

Weinstein, Neil D., Judith E. Lyon, Alexander J. Rothman, and Cara L. Cuite. 2000. "Preoccupation and Affect as Predictors of Protective Action Following Natural Disaster." *British Journal of Health Psychology* 5 (4): 351–63.

Weiss, Michael. 2016. "The Baltic Elves Taking on Pro-Russian Trolls." *The Daily Beast*, 21 March. www.thedailybeast.com/articles/2016/03/20/the-baltic-elves-taking-on-pro-russian-trolls.html.

Werbach, Kevin. 2014. *Gamification*. Online course material. www.coursera.org/course/gamification.

Willmott, Hugh C. 1986. "Unconscious Sources of Motivation in the Theory of the Subject: An Exploration and Critique of Giddens' Dualistic Models of Action and Personality." *Journal for the Theory of Social Behaviour* 16 (1): 105–21.

Wojtczak, Markus, and Michèle Morner. 2015. "Bringing the Citizen Back In: Motivational Aspects of Knowledge Sharing through Web 2.0 Technologies in Public Administration." *eJournal of eDemocracy and Open Government* 7 (2): 29–44.

Wojtkowiak, Joanna, and Bastiaan T. Rutjens. 2011. "The Postself and Terror Management Theory: Reflecting on after Death Identity Buffers Existential Threat." *International Journal for the Psychology of Religion* 21 (2): 137–44.

Wolfers, Arnold. 1962. *Discord and Collaboration: Essays on International Politics.* Baltimore: The Johns Hopkins Press.

Work, Bob, and Paul Selva. 2015. "Revitalizing Wargaming Is Necessary to Be Prepared for Future Wars." *War on the Rocks*, 8 December. http://warontherocks.com/2015/12/revitalizing-wargaming-is-necessary-to-be-prepared-for-future-wars/.

World Economic Forum. 2016. *The Future of Jobs: Employment, Skills and Workforce Strategy for the Fourth Industrial Revolution.* Cologne and Geneva: World Economic Forum. www3.weforum.org/docs/Media/WEF_Future_of_Jobs_embargoed.pdf.

World Wide Web Foundation. 2015. *Open Data Barometer, Second Edition (January 2015).* http://opendatabarometer.org/2ndEdition/.

Yee, Nick. 2014. *The Proteus Paradox: How Online Games and Virtual Worlds Change Us—And How They Don't.* London: Yale University Press.

Yee, Nick, Jeremy N. Bailenson, and Nicolas Ducheneaut. 2009. "The Proteus Effect: Implications of Transformed Digital Self-Representation on Online and Offline Behavior." *Communication Research* 36 (2): 285–312.

Yeh, Puong Fei. 2007. "Using Prediction Markets to Enhance US Intelligence Capabilities: A 'Standard & Poors 500 Index' for Intelligence." *Studies in Intelligence* 50 (4). https://www.cia.gov/library/center-for-the-study-of-intelligence/csi-publications/csi-studies/studies/vol50no4/using-prediction-markets-to-enhance-us-intelligence-capabilities.html.

Zand, D. E. 1972. "Trust and Managerial Problem Solving." *Administrative Science Quarterly* 17: 229–39.

Zimmerman, Marc A. 1990. "Toward a Theory of Learned Hopefulness: A Structural Model Analysis of Participation and Empowerment." *Journal of Research in Personality* 24 (1): 71–86.

Zirker, Daniel, Constantine P. Danopoulos, and Alan Simpson. 2008. "The Military as a Distinct Ethnic or Quasi-Ethnic Identity in Developing Countries." *Armed Forces & Society* 34 (2): 314–37.

Zooniverse. 2016. *About Us, All Publications.* www.zooniverse.org/about/publications.

Zuckerman, Marvin. 1979. *Sensation Seeking: Beyond the Optimum Level of Arousal.* Hillsdale, NJ: Lawrence Erlbaum Associates.

Zweibelson, Ben. 2015. "Let Me Tell You about the Birds and the Bees: Swarm Theory and Military Decision-Making." *Canadian Military Journal* 15 (3): 29–36. www.journal.forces.gc.ca/vol15/no3/page29-eng.asp.

Index

About the Author

Jesse Paul Lehrke is a research fellow at the German Research Institute for Public Administration in Speyer, Germany. He received his BA in International Studies from the University of Washington, Seattle (2003); his MSc in Development Studies from the London School of Economics (2004); and his PhD in International Relations from the University of Kent in Brussels (2010). His research and teaching activities cover the fields of security studies (especially counterterrorism), conflict analysis, military sociology, and contentious politics and political violence. His previous research has been published in international journals such as *Armed Forces & Society*, *Studies in Conflict & Terrorism*, *European Security*, and *Security Studies*. Other publications include the monograph *The Transition to National Armies in the Former Soviet Republics, 1988–2005* (2013) and the collected volume *Public Administration and the Modern State: Assessing Trends and Impact* (2014), for which he served as a co-editor and contributor. He has contributed policy-relevant research to, inter alia, The Project on National Security Reform (USA), the Center for Applied Policy Research (Germany), *Euro-Atlantic Quarterly* (Slovakia), and IHS Jane's (UK). From 1996 to 1999 he was an active-duty enlisted soldier in the US Army and subsequently served in the Washington State Army National Guard until 2003.

www.ingramcontent.com/pod-product-compliance
Ingram Content Group UK Ltd.
Pitfield, Milton Keynes, MK11 3LW, UK
UKHW012037150926
475560UK00001B/53

9 781538 105283